France Since 1930

France
Since
1930

Edited with an Introduction by
John E. Talbott

A NEW YORK TIMES BOOK

 *Quadrangle Books*
A NEW YORK TIMES COMPANY

Library of Congress Catalog Card Number: 77-130395
International Standard Book Number: cloth 0-8129-0254-8
                                    paper 0-8129-6196-X

The publishers are grateful to the contributors herein for
permission to reprint their articles.

Contents

3. The Fourth Republic

4. The Fifth Republic

France Since 1930

Introduction

AS RECENTLY as the mid-1950's many observers were writing of France as the new sick man of Europe. Over the preceding quarter-century, in the face of economic instability, political turmoil, and an unending succession of wars, pessimism about France's future had become an easily acquired habit. Yet a half-dozen years after the establishment of the Fifth Republic (1958), the gloomy prognostications of the fifties had virtually disappeared from the press. In the early 1960's some journalists claimed to see a "new French Revolution" at work, equal in magnitude, the phrase was meant to suggest, to the cataclysm which ended the Old Regime. If these observers had some regrets about the passing of an older France, an optimistic mood nonetheless pervaded their writing. Today no one regards France as a sick man. Whether the French have embarked on a new course, whether the changes now taking place amount to a "revolution," remain controversial questions. At any rate, recovery did not take place overnight; many of the forces whose cumulative impact some now regard as revolutionary were already at work in the darkest days of the recent past.

The following articles discuss aspects of the French experience from 1930 to our own day. These years have been as turbulent as any in the history of France since the era of the Great Revolution. But turbulence alone is probably not sufficient excuse to regard the period from 1930 to the present as an historical unit. What gives these years an underlying unity, and at the same time accounts for at least some of their turbulence, is the breakdown of an old order and the emergence of a new. To be sure, any scheme of historical periodization is always debatable. Some writers have argued that a strong and stable France never recovered from the disastrous effects of the First World War, and that the years 1914–1918 constitute the most important watershed in the history of modern France. Others have claimed that the Second World War marked such a traumatic break in the continuity of the French experience that the history of contemporary France should in fact begin in 1945.

Yet a strong case can be made that the Third Republic weathered the terrible storms of the First World War intact. The political, economic, and social system—the "old order"—which the Third Republic represented, began to crumble only with the onslaught of the depression, in the thirties. Once the wreckage of the Second World War was cleared away, the most perplexing issues France confronted were those inherited from the pre-war era. Thus the obsession of the Gaullists with the weakness of the authority of the executive, for example, cannot be understood without some knowledge of the historical experience of the thirties, which marked General Charles de Gaulle as deeply as the war years did. Finally, talk of the emergence of a "new" order of politics, society, and economics makes little sense unless one has a grasp of what the old order was like. By 1945 that order had already been substantially altered; in the early 1930's it was still pretty much intact.

In 1930 France was still predominantly a nation of small farms, small industries, and small businesses. More people made their living from the land than in any other Western European nation—in 1930 about 35 per cent of the active French population were farmers. Most were smallholders, many of whom raised only enough to support their families. Still, in good years, so abundant was agricultural production that France could not only feed its own people but export a surplus as well. But what some Frenchmen considered a healthy "balance" between industry and agriculture, others regarded as economic backwardness. The pace of industrialization in France had been slower than that of any other major industrial power. Some historians have placed the blame for this on material handicaps—on France's scarcity of coal deposits, for example. Others have argued that the psychological attitudes of the French businessman—his sense of the firm as a precious family inheritance and his consequent reluctance to undertake risks, his suspicion of outsiders with capital to invest, his acceptance of social values which disdained business activity—have had more to do with economic retardation than a lack of important material resources. Still others have cast doubts on both the psycho-sociological and the material-structural explanations for French economic backwardness; some have maintained that, except for the interwar period, the French economy has not performed as badly as some critics have suggested. In any case, just as the small peasant dominated French agriculture, so the small firm dominated French industry. In 1930, 80 per cent of French firms employed fewer than twenty workers; and only a handful employed more than five hundred. Retail trade was similarly dominated by small, family-run shops.

In this land of the little man, the schizophrenic ideology of France's Radical party exemplified the little man's outlook: in favor of equality but hankering after property and individual achievement; against social injustice but convinced that one's own bootstraps afforded the only legitimate means of social ascent; patriotic but suspicious of the government; generous in principle but made uneasy by the poor and at the same time envious of the wealthy.

The Radical party had dominated the French parliament since the turn of the century, and under the Third Republic, parliament reigned supreme. Mainly because of historical accident, parliament had acquired at the expense of the executive more power than the founders of the Third Republic had meant for it to have. No government lasted very long in such circumstances. But the political instability of the Third Republic is easy to exaggerate. In the first place, under the Third Republic a stability of ministers compensated for ministerial instability. Year after year, the same deputies kept popping up in one ministry after another, often in the same posts, thus making the development and execution of policy less subject to twists and turns than the waltz of ministries made it seem. The instability of political authority was also counterbalanced—too strongly counterbalanced, many people thought—by the highly centralized administration, whose high civil servants assured continuity in the conduct of the state's business even as the political ministers came and went.

The political machinery of the Third Republic worked very well at keeping things from getting done, which many Frenchmen considered one of the virtues of the system. The peasantry and the middle classes who dominated the Third Republic did not want the government to do a great deal, apart from maintaining order and passing a limited amount of legislation on behalf of themselves. This is not to say that social issues were ignored. Few who held positions of responsibility opposed the use of state power to alleviate the worst abuses of industrialism. But most believed that narrow limits should be set to government intervention in the economy on behalf of industrial and agricultural workers. The working class itself was too poorly organized and too underrepresented in the National Assembly to make its weight felt. Concessions came grudgingly, and France lagged behind Germany and Great Britain in passing social legislation.

To be sure, the Third Republic had shortcomings aplenty. The political system functioned well only so long as no one called upon it to do anything; social problems were in the main glossed over and economic backwardness held to be a virtue; the working class was kept at arm's length from the rest of society; the birthrate, on the decline since the middle of the nineteenth century, and the lowest of any country in Western Europe, suggested that Frenchmen had no great confidence in the future of their own society. Nevertheless, had the Third Republic been as brittle a structure as some of its critics have maintained, it is hard to see how it could have withstood the strains of the First World War. But in fact the Third Republic emerged intact, having summoned from Frenchmen the utmost in blood and treasure. In the absence of further severe trials, the system might have adjusted itself to the demands of the twentieth century. But just as recovery from the material costs of the war appeared to have been accomplished, the old order fell victim to a series of blows. The first of these was the Great Depression, to which the troubles of the 1930's were all in some way related.

Shielded by its relative economic self-sufficiency, France escaped the depression for a time. By 1932, however, the French found themselves deep in the economic doldrums. Industrial production plummeted, and scraped along for years at a level fully 20 per cent below that of 1929. Unemployment soared. While in the United States the power and the moral authority of the presidency lay ready to hand as weapons against the crisis, in France no such instrument existed. The French parliament seemed to hope for the discovery of a miracle cure. Governments succeeded each other at an accelerating rate; large sectors of an increasingly restive and worried electorate began to suspect that their representatives had chosen to deal with the crisis by turning their backs on it. Anti-parliamentary feeling ran high.

In the winter of 1933–1934 revelations began to be made about the financial manipulations of Serge Stavisky, a big-time con man who got along, it was rumored, with a little help from his friends in high places in the government and the administration, and especially in the Radical party. Right-wing leagues seized upon the Stavisky Affair to mount a demonstration against parliament which degenerated into a bloody riot. The riot, which drastically affected the politics of the 1930's, remains a controversial episode. What were the rioters' intentions? What was the nature of the organizations that took part? In the view of some, the rioters meant only to demonstrate their contempt for parliament—at the most to force the resignation of the despised Radical government (an aim which they accomplished). Others contend that the leaders of the demonstration aimed to bring down the Third Republic itself. To support this claim they point to the well-organized character of the demonstrations and to the prominent role played in them by the anti-republican leagues. But it is a long way from a well-organized demonstration to a *coup d'état*. If the leaders had a *coup* in mind, their behavior was singularly lackadaisical; among other things, they apparently made no effort to sound out the armed forces or even to secure control of strategic points in the capital.

Some historians have argued that the major participating organizations in the riot represented yet another outburst of an anti-parliamentary, nationalist, and Catholic traditionalism deeply rooted in French history. Colonel François de la Rocque and his troops, they suggest, represented a kind of boy-scout movement for grownups. Others have detected something more sinister: a manifestation of a home-grown variety of fascism. The rioters, they contend, were toughs of the radical right, whose leaders aimed to replace the Third Republic with a Hitlerian regime. Elements of both traditionalist groups and of self-styled fascist organizations took part in the Stavisky riot (to complicate matters further, so did members of the Communist party), but it would be hard to say which gave the predominant tone to the affair. Whether France narrowly averted a fascist revolution in the early 1930's remains an open and, in the end, probably unanswerable question.

At any rate, the parties of the Left believed they had barely escaped a fascist revolution. The Stavisky riot provoked counter-demonstrations against the threat of fascism and a series of arduous negotiations which ended in the formation of the Popular Front. As recently as the end of 1932, insurmountable differences had appeared to stand in the way of a coalition of Radicals, Socialists, and Communists, the three main parties of the Left. But in January 1933 the Nazis came to power in Germany. The Stavisky riots overnight transformed fascism into a domestic threat. Meanwhile, the Soviet Union subordinated hostility to the capitalist states of the West to the need for a common struggle against fascism. The change in Soviet foreign policy removed the most serious obstacle to the unity of the Left, and the French Communist party, faithful to its duty to defend "socialism in one country," abandoned its intransigent hostility to the bourgeois Third Republic and wrapped itself in the French tricolor.

The program of the Popular Front incorporated long-standing demands for reform, but the coalition itself rested on a shaky foundation. Each of the major partners had joined the Front for reasons which did not altogether square with those of its allies. The Communists were mainly interested in promoting the foreign-policy aims of the Soviet Union; the Radicals wanted to stay afloat on a leftward-running tide; only the Socialists unequivocally embraced the whole program.

Nevertheless, the Popular Front's electoral victory in May 1936 generated enormous enthusiasm and gave rise to immense hopes. Léon Blum became the first Socialist prime minister in French history, and in the mythology of the French Left the early months of 1936 took their place alongside the early months of 1848, when revolution swept Europe, as a "Springtime of the People."

The major accomplishments of the Popular Front came early. A wave of largely spontaneous strikes swept across France on the eve of Blum's assumption of office. Blum, however, managed to turn a serious embarrassment into a tool for reform. Management, angered but frightened by the workers' occupation of the factories, was brought to accede to a series of measures known as the Matignon Agreements, which granted wage increases and recognized the principle of collective bargaining and the right of workers to a paid vacation. Parliament then limited the work week to forty hours. The paid vacation in itself accomplished a small social revolution, for it meant that leisure was no longer to be exclusively the prerogative of the well-to-do. Blum later remembered the summer of 1936, when for the first time working-class families headed for the beaches and the mountains, as one of the proudest times of his life.

But the Matignon Agreements also symbolized the predicament of the Popular Front. As social reform, the forty-hour week, for example, met a long-standing demand. But the reduction in the work week also hampered efforts to increase industrial production, a prerequisite of economic recovery.

Financial stability was another prerequisite of recovery. During the election campaign the Popular Front had unwisely pledged not to devalue the franc, which was still pegged to gold at too high a price. But French goods continued to be overpriced in the world market; holders of overvalued francs continued to unload them in favor of sounder currencies; and capital continued to flee the country. In October 1936 the Blum government finally devalued the franc, but the right psychological movement for such a measure had passed.

In 1937 production continued to bump along at a level far below that of the late 1920's. In February, in the face of the government's continued economic and financial difficulties, Blum called a "pause" to social reform; in June he sought from parliament the authority to stem the flow of capital by the device of decree-laws issued by the government. The Radical-dominated Senate refused him powers granted other prime ministers in the recent past, and Blum resigned. With the fall of his government the Popular Front experiment died, and dead along with it were most of the hopes to which it had given birth.

Control of the government returned to the moderates and those members of the Radical party's conservative wing who had been in power before 1936. The *élan* having gone out of the Popular Front, the fears it had inspired among conservatives subsided somewhat, but the ideological passion aroused by the strife of the previous years lingered on. In such conditions perhaps a policy of national union against the depression or against fascism was impossible. The program of the Popular Front gave way to a policy of drift. In any event, from the mid-1930's on, foreign policy increasingly diverted the attention of the government from domestic concerns, until at last it had little time or energy for anything else. In the end the Third Republic did not give way to internal weaknesses but to the blast of war.

In 1930 France was the strongest military power on the continent. Since 1918 the main preoccupation of French foreign policy had been security from renewed German aggression. To accomplish this aim, France counted on both traditional bilateral military-defense treaties, notably with Poland and the new states of Rumania, Yugoslavia, and Czechoslovakia—the so-called "Little Entente"—and on the new concept of collective security, based on multi-lateral commitments of the membership of the League of Nations. Aristide Briand, the architect of this policy, was one of the most accomplished masters of diplomatic sleight of hand, if not the greatest diplomat, ever to occupy the Foreign Ministry. To the French Left, which regarded the League of Nations as the best hope for the maintenance of peace, Briand's policy seemed to be based squarely on a rapprochement with Germany and a reliance on collective security. To the Right, Briand's treaties appeared to have woven a web of militarily enforceable restraints around the German frontiers.

As the 1930's wore on, both the "liberal" and "conservative" aspects of this policy fell into disuse. France played its last strong hand in 1934, the year after Hitler came to power, when Louis Barthou, a veteran politician of the Right, sought to round up a grand alliance of the European powers against Germany. But an assassin's bullet put an end to Barthou and to his scheme in October of the same year. Some of Barthou's successors refused to believe that Hitler meant what he said; they convinced themselves that he was a reasonable man with reasonable demands. If some of these demands were met, they believed, surely he would stop making trouble. But each time a concession was made, Hitler raised the ante on his next move. Other French policy-makers, notably Pierre Laval, believed Mussolini might be used against Hitler. But courting one dictator did not discourage the ambitions of another. Foot-dragging in negotiations undertaken with the Soviet Union in 1935 only heightened Soviet suspicions of Western aims.

In March 1936 the military occupation of the Rhineland destroyed the bases on which French foreign policy had rested since the end of the First World War. Despite some sentiment within the French Cabinet for an immediate military riposte, the army command advised against such a move; the government, reluctant to act without the assistance of England, in the end did nothing. Hitler's gamble paid off. The German frontier was closed to invasion and the French alliance system lay in ruins, for France's eastern allies could no longer believe France would come to their aid and so moved into the Nazi orbit.

In a democracy the conduct of a coherent foreign policy requires a substantial national consensus on the government's aims. Ideological divisions within France made this task increasingly difficult. When the Spanish Civil War broke out in the summer of 1936, shortly after the Popular Front assumed office, important sectors of the Right sided with General Franco's rebellion, which received aid from Italy and Germany, while the Left supported the legal republican government. At the outset, the Blum government agreed to ship arms to Spain's loyalist forces; but under criticism from allies, domestic opponents, and from within the cabinet itself, it quickly retreated to a position of nonintervention. The decision against intervention may have sealed the fate of the Spanish Republic, as some historians have argued, but it is questionable whether French involvement in the Spanish Civil War would have discouraged Hitler, as Blum's critics have contended, for the German dictator's designs on Eastern Europe were clear. Indeed, the commitment of the French army in Spain might have played right into his hands.

Having absorbed Austria in the spring of 1938, with scarcely a murmur from the Western powers, Hitler began to turn the screws on Czechoslovakia. The Nazis backed a German separatist movement whose demands, if recognized, meant the dismemberment of the country. Despite formal obligations to assist the Czechs if they were attacked, the French government subordinated itself to the lead of England, whose prime minister, Neville Chamberlain, had publicly declared his government's lack of interest in what happened in Eastern Europe. Chamberlain and Edouard Daladier, the French premier, met Hitler in Munich in September 1938; with Mussolini looking on, they gave him pretty much what he wanted: the cession of territory which foreshadowed the end of Czechoslovakia as a viable state.

Daladier realized what had been done, but he received a hero's welcome when he returned from Munich, for the agreement meant that war had been averted. Five months later the German army occupied Czechoslovakia. Western resistance to German expansionism now stiffened. The British government hastened to guarantee Poland, the next victim on Hitler's list, from attack; France reluctantly went along. But domestic opinion on French foreign policy remained deeply divided. Marcel Déat, a renegade Socialist, declared himself unwilling to die for Danzig—a sentiment large numbers of his countrymen probably shared.

In the summer of 1939 the French and British governments sought an alliance with the Soviet Union. But Stalin could hardly have been impressed by Western steadfastness in the face of German expansionism thus far, and he chose to come to terms with Hitler instead. The stupefying news of a Nazi-Soviet nonaggression pact was made public in late August 1939. If the Western powers were to honor their declarations on Poland, war with Germany now seemed inescapable. Still, Georges Bonnet, the French foreign minister, found himself able to inquire whether Poland would be willing to commit suicide as a national entity in order to avoid war.

The German army invaded Poland on September 1. Two days later, on September 3, France and Great Britain declared war on Germany.

Why did the nearly unassailable military and diplomatic position of the France of 1930 deteriorate so rapidly and so badly? In their memoirs some leading French policy-makers made themselves out to be the victims of their fainthearted British allies, but such self-serving arguments are clearly suspect. At the time many journalists remarked on the hold an almost instinctive pacifism exercised over the French people. In their view, Frenchmen were ready to go to almost any lengths to avoid a repetition of the horrors of the First World War. Some historians have emphasized the ideological divisions that cut deeply into France's sense of national unity, especially the Right's propensity to see in Hitler an ally against "bolshevism" at home and abroad. Others have blamed the failures of the thirties on a lack of political leadership. The most able members of a generation had been killed in the First World War; among the older men there was no one of the stature of a Clemenceau, who might have rallied the nation against the most discouraging odds. Still others have suggested that France was overwhelmed by circumstances not even such giants as Clemençeau could have overcome. They argue that the Third Republic simply faced too many problems, in too short a time, with too few material and psychological resources.

After a winter of silence along the Western front—the so-called "phony war"—the German army smashed into Belgium and the Low Countries on May 10, 1940, and crossed into France on May 12. Within a week, French defenses were almost completely disorganized; communications broke down; refugees clogged the roads. The ensuing weeks were a long nightmare of chaos and disaster. On June 10 the government fled from Paris to Bordeaux. A week later Paul Reynaud, the premier, resigned when the majority of his cabinet voted to ask the Germans what their conditions for an armistice might be. Even to ask such a question was to admit defeat. Marshal Philippe Pétain, the old war hero who had been brought into the government to fire resistance to the Germans, replaced Reynaud and became instead a front man for the defeatists. On June 22, barely six weeks after the German invasion had begun, French representatives signed an armistice at Compiègne, in the same railroad car where the victorious Marshal Foch had received the Germans two decades before. As the historian Gordon Wright has put it, "Never before in modern history had France been so prostrate, so stunned and broken in spirit. Defeat the French had known, in 1814, 1815, 1871. But this was far more than defeat: it was utter humiliation, almost too deep for any Frenchman to comprehend."

The war years constitute one of the most bizarre and tangled episodes in modern French history. The question of what attitude should be taken toward the invader—should one resist? should one instead sit the war out?—opened new divisions among Frenchmen. Decisions made in wartime followed their makers into the peace, establishing the careers of some men and ruining the lives of others. The era of the German Occupation remains a period which continues to trouble the consciences of many Frenchmen.

After the armistice the government moved to the resort town of Vichy. On July 10 the parliament of the Third Republic, with only eighty dissenting votes, vested full powers in Marshal Pétain, who declared himself Head of the French State and dispensed with the need to consult any representative bodies on the governance of France. Defeat had discredited the politicians, but Pétain, though a leading defeatist himself, had managed to preserve intact the legendary reputation for leadership he had acquired in the previous war. In the summer of 1940 he probably had the support of the overwhelming majority of a demoralized and bewildered people. On June 18 a former protégé of Pétain, one Brigadier General Charles de Gaulle, declared over the BBC that the war had not ended and called upon all French military personnel who wished to continue the struggle against Germany to join him in London. Very few Frenchmen heard the appeal; at the outset, even fewer joined de Gaulle. Shortly thereafter the Vichy government condemned him to death on charges of desertion. De Gaulle, however, refused to accord the government of Pétain a shred of legitimacy.

Despite their unremitting hostility, the men of the Resistance and the men of Vichy shared in common a determination to turn their backs on the political system of the Third Republic and to build a new France.

Vichy, a town where people were used to living out of suitcases, provided the perfect setting for the transient factions which made up Pétain's regime. The state administration, like the discreet and efficient management of Vichy's resort hotels, provided the one element of stability amidst the constant coming and going of the guests: patriots and idealists who believed it their duty to come to the aid of an eternal France in its hour of need; politicians who were ready to play any tune in exchange for a seat on the bandwagon; the authoritarian reactionaries in Pétain's immediate entourage, whose corporatist program, grandly referred to as the National Revolution, never got far beyond the phrase-making stage; outright collaborationists of several varieties—pre-war Fascists and recent converts, ideologues of Right and Left, most of whom were contemptuous of the Pétainists and their boy-scout schemes and preferred Paris, where the real power sat, to Vichy; well-meaning technocrats, who had nothing much to begrudge the Third Republic but its inefficiency; hired guns and social misfits whose membership in the Vichy police enabled them to draw the cloak of legality around the settling of old scores.

But the single most important actor on this crowded stage was Pierre Laval, who didn't believe in much of anything except his own considerable ability. Laval, who thought the Third Republic had slighted and thwarted him when he had been prime minister in the thirties, had pulled the wires which dropped full power into the hands of Pétain. He seemed to have thought of Hitler as just another politician, and as vice-premier of the Vichy government he sought to win a place for France as faithful second in Hitler's New Order.

In December 1940 Laval fell victim to the perpetual intrigue that surrounded Pétain and was dismissed from office. His successor, Admiral François Darlan, brought to office the intense Anglophobia of the French Navy and a tireless zeal for seeking favors from the Nazis in return for favors done. Despite Darlan's fourteen months in office, nothing much came of these efforts. In the spring of 1942, after the United States had entered the war, the more cautious elements of the Vichy regime began to fear that Darlan had stuck his neck out too far, and Laval was returned to office. The permanence of the German mastery of Europe now seemed in doubt, and Laval began to play a muted tune of his own by seeking to evade the steadily rising exactions of the Nazis whenever the opportunity presented itself. But Laval's policy did the Vichy regime little credit. It is true, for example, that he saved many French Jews from the extermination camps of the Nazis. But he did so at the price of handing over to them non-French Jews found on French territory.

Pétain's defenders have maintained that he was engaged in a double game. The Marshal, they claim, regarded the Resistance as the sword of France; he saw himself as the shield, cooperating with the Germans in order to protect an occupied France against the fate of Poland, but all the while working in secret with the Allies. But no evidence has been brought forward to support this thesis. Certainly the independence of Vichy was the sheerest illusion. If France escaped "polonization," it was not because of the efforts of Pétain and Laval, but because the Germans believed it was not to their advantage to subject France to the rule of a gauleiter. Pétain fully deserved the reputation he had established in the First World War. But when the Second War broke out he was eighty-four years old, and little remained of the brilliant military commander but a stubborn craftiness and an overweening vanity. "Old age," Charles de Gaulle wrote in his *Memoirs,* "is a shipwreck." He was writing of his former patron, and in the case of Pétain, at least, there seems little reason to dispute this judgment.

As the France of Vichy flickered on in the shadow of the conqueror, the France of the Resistance grew in strength. Drawn together by the common aim of hurling the Germans out of France, the men of the Resistance came from the most diverse backgrounds. Many had been bitter antagonists in peacetime; once the war ended, they resumed their quarrels. De Gaulle's headquarters in London had serious disagreements with the Resistance in France. Factional struggles raged within each camp.

Charles de Gaulle's political career was filled with dramatic moments, but none was finer than its beginning on June 18, 1940, when he spoke for a France which refused to accept defeat. Few French leaders have aroused such bitter hatred and such fervent admiration, and opinion on de Gaulle's career and his achievements is likely to remain divided for some time to come. As he himself once wrote, "It is not easy to write about General de Gaulle." Aloof, authoritarian, very hard to get on with, de Gaulle intentionally wrapped himself in mystery. Yet Stalin, who was a shrewd judge of men, is said to have remarked that de Gaulle was really quite simple. It is true that the Gaullism of de Gaulle rested on a few unshakable principles—above all on the insistence that France must play a role of the first importance in world affairs; that to execute this role France must be independent of the will of any other power; and, finally, that France is the sole judge of its own interests. But de Gaulle's interpretation of these principles was characterized in practice by a high degree of pragmatism and tactical flexibility. Gaullism was an historical doctrine, and what it meant depended on how de Gaulle interpreted the demands of the moment. Stridently imperialist and anti-communist in the late forties, for example, de Gaulle had become by the mid-sixties a friend of both the Third World and the Soviet Union.

As a member of de Gaulle's inner circle in London has written, wartime Gaullism above all meant resistance to the Nazis. All other considerations were to be subordinated to the aim of routing the invader from French soil. De Gaulle's refusal to speculate about the postwar era gave rise to Allied mistrust of the London-based Resistance, especially among American leaders, some of whom suspected de Gaulle of plotting to establish a fascist dictatorship of his own. Indeed, relations between the United States and the London Resistance were troubled from the beginning and went from bad to worse. American suspicions of de Gaulle were heartily reciprocated. The French leader could not bring himself to swallow America's recognition of the Vichy regime; he believed the United States and England had designs on the French Empire. Intense personal antagonism between Franklin D. Roosevelt and de Gaulle sharpened disagreements over policy; legitimate grievances piled up on both sides. On the whole, the American wartime relationship with France was neither a very successful nor a very happy episode.

De Gaulle feared the end of the war might simply mean that a friendly occupier would replace the hostile one. If the British and the Americans were to liberate France, he believed, they might also insist on governing France, at least until the nation had recovered from the effects of the war. In order to forestall this possibility, de Gaulle insisted that Frenchmen must participate in their own liberation—not as part of another nation's army but as an independent military force. The instrument of this policy was the Free French forces, which grew from the little band of men initially gathered in London and in the Empire into the divisions which participated in the Italian campaign and the landings of 1944. In de Gaulle's view, the military capability of the Free French mattered much less than their usefulness as a political and diplomatic weapon—a constant and visible reminder of the independence of France.

In France itself, tiny bands of resisters began springing up after the first shock of defeat had passed. The Communist party, anxious to overcome the blackened reputation which support of the Nazi-Soviet Pact had given it, later claimed to have been the first group to have taken up arms against the invader. Individual Communists may have done so, but there is little evidence that, as a party, the Communists contributed much to the Resistance before Germany attacked the Soviet Union in June 1941. Nevertheless, the party was well prepared to undertake a clandestine struggle, and once in the field the Communists compiled a heroic record.

Active members of the underground remained a tiny proportion of the population, for to join the Resistance was an easy commitment to avoid and a very difficult one to undertake. At the outset the disparate movements of the Resistance operated independently of each other, printing clandestine tracts, gathering intelligence, and committing acts of sabotage against German military installations and personnel. In 1942 Jean Moulin, de Gaulle's personal representative, parachuted into France in order to unify the movements under a national leadership. The Gestapo caught up with Moulin and tortured him to death in Lyons, but not before his work had been done. Under his successor, Georges Bidault, the National Council of the Resistance laid down a sweeping program for the reform of postwar France, and the scattered guerrilla bands of the Resistance were unified as the *Forces Françaises de l'Intérieur* (FFI).

In early 1943, soon after the allied landings in North Africa, de Gaulle moved his headquarters from London to Algiers, in order to operate from French territory. Admiral Darlan had turned up in North Africa, making himself available as negotiator of a cease-fire between the Vichy and Allied forces. But the deal with Darlan also involved recognition of him as the chief French authority in North Africa. The Admiral's murder, at the end of 1942, released the Americans from their commitment to this odious expedient. Still mistrustful of de Gaulle, the Allies tried to impose their own chosen leader, General Henri Giraud, upon the anti-Vichy forces. But de Gaulle pushed the politically inept Giraud aside in the space of a few months and established himself as undisputed leader of the Free French. Late in 1943 the British accorded de Gaulle full powers to re-establish the legitimate government of France once liberation had been achieved, but the Americans, still suspicious of his intentions, held off *de jure* recognition until the fall of 1944.

If the British considered de Gaulle the rightful organizer of postwar France, they did not bother to inform him of the Allied invasion of Normandy on June 6, 1944, until troops had begun to land. This deliberate oversight nearly caused an open breach between Winston Churchill and de Gaulle. Nevertheless, de Gaulle had won the major battle he had been waging since 1940: the Allied invasion forces turned over the governance of the newly liberated areas of France to Gaullist representatives. As the Germans retreated before the Allied advance, Gaullist and Communist agents raced each other into the vacuum of power created by the Nazi departure, and a struggle for control ensued until the Communist party leadership, calculating that it might come to power by legal means once the war had ended, gave way to the Gaullists. The liberation of Paris was mainly a French affair, triggered by a rising of the populace and the advance of the troops of General Jean Leclerc. On August 26, 1944, de Gaulle marched down the Champs Elysées to the wild acclaim of a people who would not have recognized his name four years before.

Skeptics have questioned whether either the Resistance or the

Free French merited the sacrifices made for them. Neither, they contend, altered the outcome of the war or shortened it by so much as a day. It is hard to dispute this judgment. But without the Resistance, and in the absence of de Gaulle, the French memories of the war would have been limited to the humiliation of the defeat and the government of Vichy, badly compromised by its dealings with the Germans. The military contribution of the Resistance may have been negligible. Its contribution to the self-regard of the French people was incalculably great.

At the moment of liberation, the burdens of history seemed to have dropped away and the future to be filled with promise. With the Germans gone, Vichy discredited, and the old politicians lying low, the heroes of the Resistance were ready to remake French democracy. So exalted a mood was impossible to sustain. As the giddiness induced by newly recovered freedoms subsided, a kind of emotional and psychological gap opened up between the Resisters, who had risked their lives for a republic *pure et dure,* and the majority of the French people, who didn't feel up to new sacrifices. The war, as Sir Denis Brogan points out, had not resolved the old problems; the burdens of history had to be taken up again.

The provisional government of General de Gaulle faced an enormous task simply repairing war damage, but this was done with considerable dispatch. The Resisters, however, considered the restoration of the productive capacity of pre-war France only a prelude to the remaking of the economy and society. First of all, they aimed to extend the principles of political democracy to economic and social life. Public control of key sectors of the economy had been a long-standing aim of the Left, and in 1946 the provisional government moved swiftly to nationalize coal mines, the electricity and gas industries, transportation facilities, and certain banks and insurance companies.

The outstanding accomplishment of this period, however, and one of the most far-reaching undertakings in the history of postwar France, was the adoption of a system of economic planning. Under the leadership of Jean Monnet, the first plan, drawn up to cover a five-year period, established guidelines for investment in the re-equipment and modernization of industry. The economic and financial staff of the plan, a lean and efficient organization by the usual bureaucratic standards, drew on the advice of representatives of government, industry, and labor. The plan had no legal coercive authority; it could only make recommendations. Still, the Monnet Plan converted some of the most skeptical defenders of the free market into believers in planning. Industrial production reached pre-war levels by 1951; shortly thereafter France crossed the threshold of a growth rate not experienced for a century.

Postwar French politics provided a less happy story. In a referendum of October 1945, voters overwhelmingly rejected the idea of a return to the Third Republic; the same month they elected a constituent assembly charged with preparing a new constitution for France. Leading pre-war politicians of the right and center had been discredited by their association with Vichy. The parties of the Left, whom voters identified with the Resistance, dominated the constituent assembly. The Communists won the most seats, followed closely by the Socialists. But the major surprise of the election was the success of the new Christian Democratic party, the *Mouvement républicain populaire* (MRP), whose liberal Catholicism represented an old but hitherto distinctly minor force in French politics.

Charles de Gaulle became head of a government composed of Communists, Socialists, and Popular Republicans, an arrangement known as "Tripartism" that became increasingly unworkable once the chill of the Cold War set in. Everyone in the constituent assembly agreed on the desirability of a republican form of government, but serious disagreement existed on how power should be distributed within the republican system. The assembly had two distinct alternatives before it. De Gaulle wanted a presidential regime in which the naming of ministers and the initiative in policy-making rested in the hands of the chief executive. The Left favored a parliamentary regime purified of the old abuses. When de Gaulle saw that he had little chance of getting his way, he seized upon the first pretext he could find to resign, convinced that his views would eventually prevail. Perhaps he expected to be recalled immediately; perhaps he saw that French democracy was in for difficult times, and withdrew from politics in order to hold himself ready for the crisis which would return him to power. Whatever his expectations, he remained out of power for the next dozen years.

With de Gaulle out of the way, the constituent assembly chose a parliamentary regime. But the three main parties disagreed on how parliament should be organized. The Communists wanted an all-powerful, one-house legislature. Citing the precedent of the Revolutionary Convention, they claimed that such an assembly would be more responsive to the demands of the people than a two-house parliament. The Socialists reluctantly went along. But the majority of the electorate, fearful that a Communist-dominated unicameral legislature would open the way to a Communist seizure of power, rejected a constitutional draft that embodied this scheme.

Voters then returned a new constituent assembly in which the MRP emerged as the largest party. The only solution open to this new and more conservative assembly seemed to be a return to something on the order of the Third Republic. Various stabilizing devices were installed in the new constitutional draft in the hope of avoiding the governmental gyrations of the Third Republic. In an almost total absence of enthusiasm the voters, who had now been called to the polls four times in less than a year, approved this draft and the Fourth Republic was born.

As Jacques Fauvet's article, "Tragic Circus—France's Parliament," shows, long-standing habits prevailed against the gadgets built into the constitution. By 1947 Frenchmen discovered they had wound up with a regime much like the Third Republic after all, and the aversion of their representatives to the old system soon seemed about as ingenuous as Br'er Rabbit's distaste for the briar patch.

Governmental instability seemed to have passed from the Third Republic to the Fourth like some hereditary affliction. The revolving-door governments in the Palais Bourbon seemed remote from the concerns of ordinary Frenchmen, struggling to make ends meet against a runaway inflation. But if parliament seemed a "tragic circus," the appearance of government instability could be as misleading as it had been under the Third Republic. The regime was strong enough to meet a serious challenge from the extreme Left, in the form of the potentially insurrectionary strikes of the winter of 1947, and wily enough to head off a challenge from the extreme Right, in the form of General de Gaulle's *Rassemblement du peuple français*. By 1952 the government of Antoine Pinay had mastered inflation (or had been lucky enough to come to power when the trend had run its course), and the economy was once again beginning to show the vigor it sustained without let-up for more than a decade. Like its predecessor, the Fourth Republic did not collapse from internal weaknesses; it was to be a casualty of another war.

The Second World War, by loosening the grip of the major European powers on the lands they ruled in Asia and Africa, opened the way for the anti-colonialist revolutions that have dominated the history of our own times. Some of the Frenchmen who had served in the Empire during the war had sensed that the reassertion of the old system of direct rule in the face of nationalist demands for autonomy might provoke troubles with which France was not prepared to deal. This view was reflected in the constitution of the Fourth Republic, which provided for the reorganization of the Empire into a "Federal Union" whose members were to be largely autonomous. But the pace of events outran this scheme.

In September 1945, as the short-lived Japanese domination of Southeast Asia came to an end, Ho Chi Minh proclaimed the independence of Vietnam. France wavered between two sharply different reactions to this challenge to the reassertion of its rule in Indochina. General Leclerc, the French military commander on the scene, favored a negotiated accord, to the point of pronouncing the word "independence," if necessary, prior to a French re-occupation of Vietnam. But Leclerc was the subordinate of the High Commissioner, Admiral Thierry d'Argenlieu, a monk turned sailor and one of the more bizarre figures to have rallied to General de Gaulle. D'Argenlieu favored the military reoccupation of Vietnam first, with talks to come later, if at all. Paris appeared to want to avoid a head-on clash with the forces of Ho Chi Minh, but it was unable to control d'Argenlieu's actions. In the end the government chose to attempt to put down the revolution instead of seeking a negotiated settlement which might have left France with influence in Indochina and avoided the tragedy which ensued.

The army, short of equipment and personnel, found itself engaged in a war it had not been trained to fight. The aims of French policy in Indochina were never clearly defined. Each government seemed less eager to prosecute the war than to unload it on its successor. As the fighting dragged on, some high official would occasionally declare that he could see light at the end of the tunnel. Then came the defeat at Dien Bien Phu, in May 1954, and it became apparent overnight that France had lost not only a battle but the war.

Four years earlier Pierre Mendès-France, leader of the reformist wing of the Radical party, had warned parliament that the country had to be told the truth about the painful choices before it in Indochina. After Dien Bien Phu, when there were no longer any choices to be made, Mendès-France was called upon to extricate France from the war. He not only negotiated an armistice in Indochina; he also took important steps toward granting independence to the North African colonies of Tunisia and Morocco.

Mendès-France and the young reformers gathered around him intended the settlement of the Indochina war to be the prelude to sweeping economic and social reform at home. But the bitter struggle over the European Defense Community distracted their attention. The EDC, a plan for the formation of a multi-national army, divided the center parties internally and squeezed adherents of the plan between the Gaullist Right, which charged that such a force would divest France of its sovereignty and put Europe under American domination, and the Communist Left, which regarded a European army as a threat to the security of the Soviet Union. Mendès-France managed to shelve the EDC, but in January 1955 he was driven from office before his reform program had made much advance. Aside from de Gaulle, Mendès-France was probably the most able political leader to have emerged in France since the end of World War I, but he was not popular in parliament, and his government lasted only seven months.

If most Frenchmen were glad to be rid of the war in Southeast Asia, the Indochina settlement did not make everyone happy. The extreme Right, nostalgic for the grandeur of Empire, complained of a sellout. The army resented having been made to swallow one more defeat, and this proved to be much more dangerous than the noisy posturing of the Right. Many career officers had scarcely set foot in France for more than fifteen years, and they had long since begun to feel intellectually and emotionally isolated from their countrymen. Some of the army's best units had been sacrificed in Indochina; these losses seemed pointless, and the abandonment of the Vietnamese who had fought alongside the French seemed dishonorable. At home, nobody appeared to care. Officers who had discovered the writings of Mao Tse-tung in Vietnamese prison camps began to think they had found a magic formula which the French army could employ in a future encounter with guerrillas . . . and against the moral rot at home.

Their opportunity came sooner than anyone expected. In the early morning of November 1, 1954, terrorist activity signalled the beginning of a revolt against French rule in Algeria and of a war that dragged on for nearly eight years. Mendès-France had negotiated the beginning of an end to French rule in Morocco and Tunisia. But Algeria was not just another French colony. More than a million settlers of European origin lived there. Many of them had ancestors who had come to Algeria a century before, and most were determined to stay. The Nobel prizewinner Albert Camus, born and reared in Algiers, remarked that if it came to choosing between justice and his mother, he would choose his mother. Therein the tragedy lay.

At the outset of the rebellion, most metropolitan Frenchmen believed Algeria was French, as their schoolbooks had taught them, but they were not prepared to go to any lengths to maintain French rule. In the elections of January 1956, the platform of the victorious leftist coalition called for a negotiated settlement of the war. But the diehard, or "ultra," faction of French settlers in Algeria fiercely opposed any negotiation with the rebels, and the government of Guy Mollet, the Socialist premier, gave in to the pressure of the ultras and their sympathizers in France. Conscripts were sent to join the professional army in the hunt for guerrilla bands; soon France had committed more than 400,000 troops to Algeria. The ultras in Algiers replied to terrorist tactics with terrorism of their own. Army officers convinced themselves that torture was a justifiable weapon to use in such a war. As city and countryside both deteriorated into a state of general insecurity, the army accumulated more and more power until it had become the real ruler of Algeria. To concentrate so much authority over civilian affairs in the hands of army officers who had lost all respect for the regime was asking for trouble. For a time, what went on in Algiers became more important politically than what happened in Paris.

For a medium-sized city, Algiers had more than its share of plotters: competing factions of ultra settlers, some of whom toyed with fascist ideas and all of whom were determined to keep Algeria French; Gaullists who saw in the Algerian affair a means of bringing de Gaulle back to power; army officers bent on avoiding another humiliating defeat and who belonged to both the Gaullist and ultra camps.

The government of Felix Gaillard fell on April 15, 1958, opening a parliamentary crisis which gave the plotters a chance to act. Rumors circulated that a new government would seek to negotiate a settlement with the rebels. In early May the military high command in Algiers threatened in scarcely veiled terms to disobey any government that opened negotiations. On May 13 ultra leaders, with the connivance of key regimental commanders in Algiers, seized government buildings and set up a "Committee of Public Safety" to take over civil powers from the legal government. The Gaullist plotters managed to elbow the ultra and army leaders aside and to use the Algiers Committee as a public platform from which to appeal for the return of de Gaulle. The Gaullists apparently acted without the knowledge of de Gaulle, but once the wheels had been set in motion he was kept informed of developments.

While rumors flew that paratroopers were about to descend on Paris (plans for such a move were indeed afoot), de Gaulle let it be known that he would accept the responsibility of government, but only if it were legally invested. The moderates and some elements of the Left swung round behind de Gaulle when they began to fear they might have a civil war on their hands if they did not. Many of the army leaders and ultras were bitterly anti-Gaullist, but they persuaded themselves that only de Gaulle could keep Algeria French. The General did not yet disabuse them of this notion. On June 1, 1958, by a vote of 329 to 224, he became the last prime minister of the Fourth Republic. Three weeks earlier, he probably would not have received a hundred votes.

De Gaulle must have savored the ironies of the situation in which he now found himself: an aging army officer, hero of a previous war, called upon as a savior in a time of national crisis, and voted full powers by a parliament once dominated by a coalition of the Left. Pétain had played the same role in 1940.

The settlers had appealed to de Gaulle because they believed he would keep Algeria French. Most of them had no political aims beyond this. But de Gaulle considered France's inability to resolve a long colonial war merely a symptom of fundamental domestic weaknesses, especially of the feebleness of the state. He did not mean to allow the Algerian tail to go on wagging the metropolitan dog. In any event, no solution to the Algerian question could be found until the crisis of governmental authority had been surmounted in France.

The constitution of the Fifth Republic, drafted in the summer of 1958, was an attempt to codify de Gaulle's views on the problem of governing France. The theme he had most often sounded since 1946 had been the need to endow France with a strong executive authority. Unlike the constitution of the Fourth Republic, which ended as an attempt to correct the flaws in the political system of the Third, the constitution of the Fifth Republic sought to turn republican institutions in a new direction.

The constitution provided for a president and a parliament, just as earlier constitutions had done, but this time the balance of power was clearly tilted in favor of the president, who now had the authority to choose his own ministers. Most important, the president chose the prime minister. Thus the making of a government rested completely with the head of state; the prime minister no longer received his mandate to govern from parliament. The respective responsibilities of the president and the prime minister within the two-headed executive were not very clearly defined, and this was a possible source of conflict. Under the first two presidents of the Fifth Republic, however, serious conflicts have not arisen. Thus far the president has laid down the main lines of policy and the prime minister has been an executor, carrying on the day-to-day business of government.

The Algerian War dragged on nearly as long after de Gaulle came to power as it had lasted under the Fourth Republic. The General had always regarded secretiveness and surprise as weapons no less important in diplomacy than in warfare. He managed to retain considerable room for maneuver in the Algerian affair by keeping everyone guessing about his intentions. But he revealed the drift of his Algerian policy in a speech of September 1959, when he announced that the French could choose among three options: integration of the Muslim population into France (the ultra solution); complete independence (a solution, de Gaulle charged, which would lead a war-torn and underdeveloped country to disaster); and a form of cooperative association between Algeria and France which would leave Algeria virtually autonomous (the solution which de Gaulle himself favored).

Despite this speech, de Gaulle's Algerian policy followed a tortuous path—now appearing to twist in the direction of a "French Algeria," in order to appease dissident and still powerful elements in the army, now veering toward a negotiated settlement. Some of de Gaulle's critics have charged that all this twisting and turning unnecessarily prolonged the war, that he could have arrived at a negotiated settlement much sooner had he bent all his efforts in this direction. But his defenders have maintained that such a straightforward course was out of the question until de Gaulle had surmounted the threat to his regime from the diehards —the very groups that had brought him to power.

As the war dragged on, it raised deeply troubling moral and political issues which came to dominate French public life. The attempt to crush the rebellion militarily, and the methods employed by the Army—especially the use of torture—caused opponents of the war to fear that the Algerian experience was rotting away the moral fiber of the nation. The student Left and leading French intellectuals mounted demonstrations and published exposés and petitions against the war; the government countered with police batons and the seizure of anti-war literature. In the meantime, ultra settlers and diehard army officers rightly sensed that the ground was giving way beneath their feet, and they sought to repeat their success of May 13, 1958—the imposition of the will of Algiers on Paris—and this time to dislodge de Gaulle from power. But these efforts failed miserably. The attempted *putsch* of April 1961, a ludicrous flop, ended the army's threat to the regime. In desperation the diehards went underground, and in the OAS, or Secret Army Organization, embarked on a campaign of vengeance and terror which the government mercilessly put down. At the same time, de Gaulle had maneuvered steadily toward a negotiated settlement with the FLN, as the Algerian liberation front was called. In March 1962 the Evian accords brought a cease-fire, and on the following July 1 Algeria became independent.

Some deputies grumbled about de Gaulle's machiavellian methods, but parliament did not seek to intervene in his handling of the Algerian problem. The president feared that once a settlement had been reached, however, the deputies would seek to reassert the power they had enjoyed under the Third and Fourth Republics. The Algerian crisis had already transformed the office of the presidency from the arbitrator of the constitution of 1958 into an advocate of his own policies, similar in this respect to the American presidency. De Gaulle wished further to strengthen the executive by having the president elected by the direct vote of all the people. But among the deputies such an idea aroused historical memories of enemies of republican government. De Gaulle bided his time until an attempt on his life provided him with a dramatic opportunity to raise the question of his "succession" and to call for a referendum approving the election of the president by universal suffrage. This move, and the dubious constitutional procedures by means of which de Gaulle sought to get his way, raised a storm of opposition, but the president prevailed.

In 1962 France was at peace after twenty-three years of war. Many people doubt whether anyone but de Gaulle could have mastered the Algerian crisis. If they are correct, the demise of the Fourth Republic is perhaps a cheap price to have paid. Still, the Gaullists have been inclined to exaggerate the weaknesses of the regime they succeeded (and for whose downfall they themselves bear some of the blame), and to claim more credit for improvements in the well-being of Frenchmen than they deserve. Whatever their claims, the economic prosperity of the 1960's was a legacy of the unlamented Fourth Republic. The evolution of economy and society under the Fifth Republic has been pretty much a continuation of earlier trends.

After all the years of stagnation, rapid economic growth was news; change was what got reported in the newspapers. But in the late 1960's one could still find old people in France who believed the earth is flat and who had never traveled more than a few miles from the village in which they were born. Of course they might live down the road from teen-agers who dressed in the latest left-bank fashions. As John Ardagh has remarked, contrasts between the old and the new were sharper in France than in almost any other Western nation.

A static France dwelled in the shadow of the dynamic France which got most of the attention in the press. The Northeast, from just south of Paris to the Belgian frontier, constituted less than one-fifth of French territory and contained something over a third of its population, but it possessed more than half the productive capacity of the nation. France south of the Loire, especially toward the southwest, remained an area of poor and inefficient farms, and in that respect bore some resemblance to southern Italy. In addition to the persistence of geographical contrasts between poverty and progress, a sharply uneven distribution of wealth persisted among social classes. In 1971, for example, some postal workers in Paris had to make do on less than $200 a month; and some old-age pensions remained pitifully small. The venerable French custom of tax-dodging continued to make it hard for the state to tap existing sources of wealth for public purposes.

Like their American contemporaries, Frenchmen spent a great deal on individual consumption and scrimped on social investment. Thus the boom economy of the fifties and early sixties had not been an entirely unmixed blessing. The automobile, symbol of the consumer society, threatened to devour Paris. The telephone was a public scandal. A housing shortage put a strain on pocketbooks, marriages, and in-laws. Mass transportation facilities in the Paris region were inadequate, and hospitals were crammed with more patients than they had been designed to care for. It is true that the government was struggling to surmount these problems; some imaginative solutions had been laid down on paper. But the telephone system, for example, had suffered from decades of neglect;

French technicians have nearly all they can do to keep over-strained facilities from deteriorating still further. But the decay of an aging economic infrastructure is a problem common to all advanced industrial societies. It would be hard to contend that the Fifth Republic's efforts to combat the decay have been markedly less energetic than those of any other industrial power.

In the early 1960's the opposition did not make much headway in pinning the blame for the diffuse aggravations of day-to-day existence on the Gaullists. The end of the Algerian War left a kind of vacuum in French political life. The atrophy of parliament, the government's stinginess with radio and television time on the state-controlled networks, the divisions of the Left, and de Gaulle's lofty disdain for his opponents made it hard to find a vulnerable spot at which to strike at the regime. Beyond the "political class"— the professional politicians, party activists, and politically engaged intellectuals—most people were content to leave things up to de Gaulle, whose own main concerns, defense and foreign policy, were remote from those of the citizenry at large. This mood of public indifference to politics was widely commented on in the press, and dozens of theories were contrived to explain it. Nonetheless, slippages in the popularity of the president and of his regime began to appear: de Gaulle himself was unexpectedly forced into a runoff ballot in his campaign for re-election to the presidency in 1965; and the Gaullists were reduced to the slimmest of majorities in the parliamentary elections of 1967.

Still, as the tenth anniversary of the founding of the Fifth Republic approached, published assessments of the regime's first decade were on the whole favorable. Then France suddenly plunged into a grave social and political crisis, and for a few days the Fifth Republic appeared to be on the verge of collapse. Less than a revolution, more than a series of riots, what happened in France in the spring of 1968 is simply referred to as "the events of May." The events came as a surprise to the most seasoned and well-informed observers. As if to make up for being caught unaware, students of French society flooded bookstores with accounts of why everything had happened and what everything meant almost before the tear gas had settled. Historians of the events of May already have a mountain of information to mine. But some of the literature is more a manifestation of the crisis than an explanation of it; the whole story of what was a very complicated episode is still far from known. But at least an outline of the crisis can be sketched in here.

In a year that witnessed violent outbreaks of student discontent from Tokyo through Berkeley and New York to Berlin, perhaps it is not surprising that Paris had its own student rising. French university students had plenty of grievances. The demographic tidal wave had washed over the universities, leaving them overcrowded, understaffed, and underequipped. Enrollments increased tenfold in the thirty years between 1938 and 1968; in the five years between 1962 and 1967 alone, they more than doubled. The students charged that, aside from the problems sheer numbers created, the curriculum, modes of instruction, and the examination system were antiquated, insensitive, and unresponsive to their needs.

These educational grievances were articulated in a highly politicized milieu. On the Left, leadership of student activism had passed from the Communist party to Maoist and Trotskyite splinter groups, whose tactical adroitness and lack of scruples compensated for their small numbers. Educational grievances and radical political activism came together at the University of Nanterre, a new and cheerless campus located in an industrial slum on the outskirts of Paris. The activists provoked confrontations with the authorities over everything from dormitory regulations to the war in Vietnam, but for a year prior to 1968 run-ins between students and the police had been confined to Nanterre.

On May 3 the trouble spread to Paris. University officials called in police to clear the courtyard of the Sorbonne of demonstrators who had gathered to protest disciplinary proceedings against student leaders. The students left without incident, but the police then proceeded to herd them into police vans in order to undertake a "routine identity check." This proved a serious blunder. Latecomers believed their comrades had been arrested; scuffling broke out between themselves and the police. Exchanges of rocks and tear gas soon engulfed the Latin Quarter. The Sorbonne was closed down. On successive nights police and students engaged in running battles. The behavior of the police, who took to roughing up nearly everyone they encountered in the neighborhood, initially rallied public sympathy to the side of the students. A week after the incident at the Sorbonne, barricades sprang up in the streets, calling to mind the Parisian revolutions of the nineteenth century—only this time radio reporters on the scene carried the battle to the entire nation.

The crisis, limited thus far to an especially serious form of student rioting, suddenly deepened and broadened over the weekend of May 10-12. Prime Minister Georges Pompidou returned from a state visit to Afghanistan prepared to reopen the Sorbonne, in the hope that such a gesture would put an end to disorder. Pompidou's critics claim that this conciliatory move transformed the student riots into a nationwide social crisis. Had the government employed the army against the students, they contend, further trouble would have been averted. Instead the workers, thinking they too might have something to gain from seizing the government by the throat, went on strike. Pompidou's defenders claim the conciliatory gesture avoided the possibility of bloodshed and won the government time to recover its poise, a policy which paid off in the elections of June.

At any rate, a movement that began as a wildcat strike spread quickly, as disciplined trade-union members joined in. Throughout the country, workers occupied their factories. The historical precedent everyone thought of this time was the summer of 1936. But the strikes of 1968 were more widespread than those of 1936. Eventually, between 6.5 and 7 million Frenchmen (not 9 to 10 million, as reported at the time) walked off their jobs. The French economy was brought to a virtual standstill. The workers' movement was potentially a much greater threat to the government than the agitation of the students. But the strikes lacked the revolutionary *élan* of those of 1936. Despite the effort of student activists to forge an alliance with the workers, the majority of strikers remained aloof, sensitive to generational and cultural differences, suspicious of the students' motives and endurance, and alarmed by the rhetoric of some of the student leaders.

De Gaulle himself, imperturbable in crisis after crisis, now seemed to have lost his grip. Having flown off in the midst of the events on a state visit to Rumania, he suddenly returned, appeared on television, and said something vague about a referendum. But the medium that had served him so well in the past turned against him; viewers saw not the commanding presence of earlier times, but a tired old man. Some of the worst rioting followed the speech.

On May 25 Pompidou managed to bring the government, employers, and trade-union leaders together for an agreement which accorded substantial wage increases and improvements in certain welfare benefits. The government hoped acceptance of this accord would lead to a return to work that would leave the students isolated. But rank-and-file union members rejected it. The strikes continued; student rioting worsened; and the parliamentary opposition began to talk openly of a successor to de Gaulle.

An industrial society brought to a standstill made a disquieting spectacle. To be sure, there was something greatly appealing in the lyricism of the wall posters and slogans plastered up and scrawled everywhere in the Latin Quarter; the calls for putting "imagination in power" seemed to insist that revolution could wear a gentle face. But the suddenness and unexpectedness of the crisis, the breakdown of order, the ineptitude of a government which had always prided itself on its toughness and efficiency, also provoked widespread fear and uneasiness.

On May 29 de Gaulle suddenly disappeared. Rumors circulated that he had packed his bags and gone off to his country house to write the remaining volumes of his memoirs: this time, many thought, he was finished. In reality he had flown to Baden-Baden to confer with General Jacques Massu, commander of French forces in West Germany, apparently in order to assure himself of the loyalty of the army. Exactly what they talked about remains unknown, but de Gaulle returned to Paris and on May 30 made a tough new speech in which he cast aside his earlier proposal for a referendum, dissolved the national assembly, and scheduled new elections. He seemed to have recovered the old magic. The dissolution of the assembly pulled the rug out from under the Opposition leaders, the strikers began to return to work, and by mid-June the student activists had isolated themselves from a society by now grown weary of disorder.

The Right turned out to be the chief beneficiary of the specter of revolution. In the election campaign the Gaullists followed the

General's lead in heaping blame for the events on the Communists. Some observers have contended that, at the height of the crisis, the Communists flirted with the idea of bringing down the regime; others have argued that the party, dismayed and frightened by the undisciplined behavior of the student leftists, remained the General's staunchest ally throughout the events. Clearly, the Communists were not the driving force behind the events of May. Whether or not the voters swallowed the government's line, they returned a huge Gaullist majority to the assembly. For the first time in French history a single party controlled parliament. Yet Pompidou, who had emerged as the most resourceful and steady-nerved member of the government, and who managed the successful election campaign, was dismissed from his post as prime minister. He and de Gaulle had clashed over how the crisis should be met; gratitude for services rendered had never been one of the General's virtues.

The causes of the Great Revolution of 1789 continue to provoke controversy as the two hundredth anniversary of its outbreak nears; discussion of the causes of the events of May has scarcely begun. Some Frenchmen subscribed to a variety of conspiracy theories. Was the CIA, everyone's favorite scapegoat, behind the events of May? Or were old-line Stalinists, the Chinese, the East German secret service? Not a shred of evidence has been brought forward against any of these alleged culprits, but conspiracy theories often need no other support than faith alone, and the willingness to see a plot in the events of May at least suggests that the French have not abandoned a cherished tradition. Some aging leftists saw the events as a spontaneous outburst against a society corrupted by American-style consumerism, and as such a revenge of the spirit against materialism. Many students were probably motivated by such feelings, but the workers were in the main after solid economic gains, which they presumably sought in order to enjoy more of the benefits of the consumer society. Perhaps revenges of the spirit are more likely to seize the privileged than groups wresting free of the pinch of want for the first time in their lives. Still another explanation has seen in the events of May the adumbration of a new form of class conflict. In place of the old conflict between the possessors of capital and labor, this new struggle internally divides the educated middle class, pitting the managers, who now possess most of the power of decision, against the technicians, who seek a share of that power. This is an intriguing theory, and perhaps it does afford a glimpse of conflict in an emerging society, but there is little evidence that would permit one to regard it as the driving force behind the events of May. A leading dissenter from the enthusiasm that overtook many of the observers of the crisis was the conservative sociologist Raymond Aron, who dismissed the events as a kind of "psychodrama," a release of pent-up energies and emotions for which French society, prosperous and at peace, afforded no other outlet.

If the causes of the events are likely to provoke controversy for a long time to come, the events themselves are still so near at hand that discussion of all but their most immediate consequences can hardly be other than speculatory. The crisis had severe short-term effects on the French economy and finances. The concessions that workers extracted from their employers gave another jolt to the inflationary spiral; speculation against the franc and the fear of unrest drained away the enormous gold reserves de Gaulle had piled up and eventually forced a devaluation of the currency. The events also left the authorities in an extremely jumpy mood, ready to call in vanloads of police at the first sign of trouble in the streets, behavior which merely maintained the yawning breach between themselves, a large segment of the press, and especially the young. The most positive immediate consequence of the events was the passage in September 1968 of the Faure Law, which promised, if carried into effect, to make sweeping changes in the structure of the French university system, where the trouble had all started.

De Gaulle's reassertion of his old powers of leadership was a fleeting triumph. It is doubtful whether he quite recovered from the events of May, either in his own eyes or the nation's. The French have had a weakness for saviors in military uniform. But they have also consistently shown a healthy lack of gratitude for being saved. As the man of June 18, 1940, de Gaulle had saved his country from dishonor; as the man of May 13, 1958, he may have saved his country from civil war. He had extricated France, as probably no one else could have done, from a futile colonial war. But the heroic mood that sustained de Gaulle for a lifetime could sustain a whole people only in the most exceptional moments. The presidential campaign of 1965 had already betrayed the French people's disenchantment with their distant hero. Indeed, perhaps the distance from mundane concerns that he had long ago identified as one of the precepts of leadership was in the end too distant, too detached.

In April 1969 de Gaulle chose to stake his presidency on a referendum on a relatively unimportant set of reforms. A majority voted against the reforms; de Gaulle immediately resigned. He returned to his country home and set to work on his unfinished memoirs. Perhaps he consoled himself with the thought that his own low opinion of the French people had once again been confirmed. His real love affair had always been with France. On November 9, 1970, de Gaulle died, two days before the anniversary of the armistice ending the First World War, when his own career had begun, and two weeks before his eightieth birthday.

Georges Pompidou, who for a time appeared to be the great victim of the events of May, turned out to be the great victor instead. Pompidou had spent his entire public career in the shadow of de Gaulle, but it was he, and not the General, who rallied a shaken government in the crisis of 1968. As an editorialist for *Le Monde* wrote at the time: "One has the impression that the government, and at moments even the state, no longer exist, just a solitary man who is courageously striving against the storm." Despite his dismissal as prime minister, Pompidou maintained his identification with Gaullism; this, along with the reputation he had established during the events of May, made him the leading candidate for the succession to de Gaulle. In June 1969 he was elected president of the Republic.

The new president is not simply the executor of the Gaullist political testament. Indeed, it may be doubted whether such a testament would be capable of fulfillment. The Gaullist style of leadership is not something that can be imitated or institutionalized. De Gaulle regarded himself as the unifier of the French nation, above the strife of parties; he was no one's man but his own. He held himself as aloof from the conservative bourgeoisie from whom he derived much of his electoral support as he did from the Communist party. He never showed much interest in the Gaullist parliamentary organization unless he needed its aid.

It is unlikely that parliament will remain as supine under his successors as it did under de Gaulle. The ten years of his lonely mastery of French public life may eventually seem to be a kind of parenthesis in the continuity of French political history. Pompidou, on the other hand, can be placed within a long political tradition. He is a representative of the outlook known as Orleanism, the down-to-earth but not unenlightened conservatism of the haute bourgeoisie, attached to parliamentary government, favorable to business interests, willing to concede social reform if not to agitate for it. He can count among his spiritual ancestors another professor, François Guizot, minister of the constitutional monarchy of Louis Philippe, and another self-made man, Adolphe Thiers, who characteristically served both monarchy and republic. Under Pompidou, defense and foreign policy no longer have that primacy over domestic affairs that characterized the rule of de Gaulle; social and economic issues occupy a considerable share of his attention. Or, as someone recently put it, Pompidou has substituted *bonheur* for *grandeur* at the top of the priorities of the government.

As Keith Botsford remarks, "Pompidou is ambiguous; the system is ambiguous; France is ambiguous." The French have a long tradition of confounding observers both foreign and domestic; anyone tempted to make predictions about even the immediate future has the experience of 1968 to remind him how risky such undertakings can be. Just as France seemed to have escaped the turmoil that has characterized much of the last forty years, it fell once again into a severe domestic crisis, and some people thought the French were up to their old game. Still, France has changed enormously since 1930. Do these changes amount to a revolution?

The recent French past is as ambiguous as the present of which Botsford writes. The France of the 1970's operates under essentially the same administrative and legal system as the France of the 1930's. The similarities between the political systems of the Third and Fifth Republics are as striking as the differences. The elites which dominate the economy, the society, and the political system in the France of today are drawn from the same social strata as they were in 1930. But a vigorous economy has supplanted the stagnant economy of the thirties. Despite the experience of 1968, the political instability of the Third and Fourth Republics has given way to stability and a consequent strengthening of the executive power.

In the 1930's France remained the second-ranking imperial power in the world. The loss of Empire was an agonizing experience, but only a small minority of Frenchmen now regret the retreat of *La Grande Nation* to its European hexagon. Decolonization has not had the dire economic consequences some observers predicted; the abandonment of the imperial role has redounded to the benefit of French prestige abroad and has allowed economic and foreign-policy-makers to give their main attention to the potentialities of an economically and perhaps one day even politically united Europe. But perhaps the most significant changes which France has undergone in the last forty years have been those which have taken place at the grassroots level, whose subtleties elude the thick-fingered vocabulary of historians and social scientists. Perhaps it is well to remember that for the people experiencing them, the processes characterized by such flat and unemotional words as urbanization and modernization can mean bewilderment, anxiety, and loss as well as an improvement in material well-being and an expansion of cultural horizons.

But the last word can be left to Aléxis de Tocqueville, a great historian of his own times and a man who wrote of his compatriots about as well as anyone ever has:

"When I examine that nation in itself, I can not help thinking it is more extraordinary than any of the events of its history. Did there ever appear on the earth another nation so fertile in contrasts, so extreme in its acts—more under the domination of feeling, less ruled by principle; always better or worse than was anticipated—now below the level of humanity, now far above; a people so unchangeable in its leading features that it may be recognized by portraits drawn two or three thousand years ago, and yet so fickle in its daily opinions and tastes that it becomes at last a mystery to itself, and is as much astonished as strangers at the sight of what it has done; naturally fond of home and routine, yet, once driven forth and forced to adopt new customs, ready to carry principles to any lengths and to dare any thing; indocile by disposition, but better pleased with the arbitrary and even violent rule of a sovereign than with a free and regular government under its chief citizens; now fixed in hostility to subjection of any kind, now so passionately wedded to servitude that nations made to serve cannot vie with it; led by a thread so long as no word of resistance is spoken, wholly ungovernable when the standard of revolt has been raised—thus always deceiving its masters, who fear it too much or too little; never so free that it cannot be subjugated, or so kept down that it cannot break the yoke; qualified for every pursuit, but excelling in nothing but war; more prone to worship chance, force, success, éclat, noise than real glory; endowed with more heroism than virtue, more genius than common sense; better adapted for the conception of grand designs than the accomplishment of great enterprises; the most brilliant and the most dangerous nation of Europe, and the one that is surest to inspire admiration, hatred, terror or pity, but never indifference?"

Part 1

THE THIRD REPUBLIC

A Key to the Political Maze in France

by André Maurois

GREAT BRITAIN, the United States and France all live under a so-called "Parliamentary and democratic" régime. But in reality their institutions are so different that the citizens of any one of them have the greatest difficulty in understanding what is going on in the other two. Thus, during the recent French crisis, my American friends asked me innumerable questions: "How can a government that has a majority of sixty one day have ten the next, with the Deputies unchanged?" "How can the Senate upset the government, and what happens when the Senate and the Chamber cannot agree?" "In England, when one party is in power, it remains in power for the duration of the Legislature and, if the voting reveals an unexpected rift in the party, Parliament is dissolved by the Prime Minister. Is this impossible in France, and can you explain the constant changes which seem to us to be going on in a world of Alice in Wonderland?" It is difficult, but I will try.

I

It would be a mistake to blame France's Constitution of 1875 for her political fluctuations. This Constitution does not prohibit the formation of large parties which would come into power in turn, as in England the Whigs and Tories, the Conservatives and Liberals, and as in the United States the Democrats and the Republicans have done for so long. It recognizes and provides for dissolutions of Parliament.

President Doumergue, if he wished, could propose tomorrow in the Senate that the present Chamber of Deputies should be dissolved. In point of fact no President of the French Republic has availed himself of this right since 1877. Then Marshal MacMahon did dissolve the Chamber; but he did so maladroitly, at an inopportune moment, and the country replied with a slap in the face by sending him back the same majority.

Ever since this untoward incident the idea of dissolution, which should seem legal and natural, has been associated in the French mind with the idea of a coup d'état, a spectre which has haunted French Republicans ever since the 18 Brumaire and the 2 Décembre. This unfortunate memory of MacMahon has been a prime historical source of instability for the last forty years; it stopped a wheel in the Parliamentary machine that ought to be far from useless.

Let us consider the feelings of the average French Deputy and of the average British M. P. toward the Ministry in power, supposing them to be equally endowed with ambition and patriotism. What hopes are there for the British Parliamentarian who votes against his party and helps to upset the Cabinet? None to speak of. He places himself outside his party, and this renders his re-election difficult, if not impossible. He will have no chance of taking the place of one of the Ministers, because the Cabinet almost certainly will have recourse to a dissolution. Finally, this dissolution will entail on him the expenses of an election sooner than would otherwise have been the case. Even if he should become a Minister, without a dissolution, he will be required in accordance with the excellent British practice to offer himself again for election. Therefore the personal interests of the British parliamentarian lie on the side of stability. In England no premium is put upon the upsetting of Ministries.

In France there is such a premium, and the personal interests of the Deputy lie on the side of instability. What has he to fear if he helps to upset the Ministry? Will he be obliged to incur again the risks of an election? Certainly not, because, as we have seen, the tradition opposed to dissolution has become fixed. Will he be excluded from his party? Possibly, but there are so many parties in the French Chamber that he will easily find another.

Will he, on the other hand, take the place of some member of the Ministry that has been upset? It must be admitted that he has a chance of doing so. The head of the government, when forming his Ministry, frequently takes note of help given him by such or such a Deputy through an adroit manoeuvre against the preceding Cabinet. He prefers to have with him rather than against him a man known to be dangerous. Whence arises a temptation to even the most upright French Parliamentarian. Our practice has put a premium upon the upsetting of Ministries.

II

The temptation would be less strong if there were great organized parties contending for power. Such parties would maintain discipline within their ranks. Even in opposition they would be led by groups of men ready to form a Cabinet after a successful election. At the time of the last election in England there was no question at all as to who would be called by the King if the Labor party came to power; it was known that it would be J. Ramsay MacDonald, just as it was known that it would be Mr. Baldwin in the event of a Conservative victory. There may be conflicts within one of the parties in respect to the leadership (and such conflicts are frequent), but in Parliament a certain loyalty is traditional.

In France it is very difficult for great parties to come into existence. In the Chamber there are Communists, United Socialists, Socialist Republicans, Socialist Radicals, a Radical Left, a Social and Radical Left, Republicans of the Left, National Republicans, a Democratic Republican Union, Independents of the Left, Independents, and some Deputies so independent that they do not wish even to form a section of the group of Independents. Why this multiplicity of parties?

Every race has its qualities and its defects, and must be governed with due regard for both. In governing the French it must not be forgotten that they are individualists and have always been so. Caesar remarked that the Gauls submitted with difficulty to the authority of a single chief. France showed herself capable of discipline in the World War, and again under Poincaré, at the moment of the great effort to save the franc. She would always be so in situations of danger. But in tranquil times she likes to criticize her leaders. Since the last two Napoleonic experiences, especially, a large number of Frenchmen have felt an almost instinctive dread of every man who rises too swiftly and too high above the level of the rest. A popularity of a transcendent kind in the country would be, I believe, a handicap in Parliament for any French statesman.

This profound equalitarianism, as we call it in France, and this out and out individualism, stand in the way of anything like blind loyalty toward the leaders of a great party. In a Parliamentary group, apart from a few dumb, simple-minded and submissive individuals, every Deputy of any talent thinks that he ought to become at least an Under-Secretary of State, and that he will obtain such a post. If he is in disagreement with the senior members of his group, or even if, apart from any disagreement in regard to political dogmas, he is conscious that he has ahead of him in the group too many brilliant and self-assertive personages, he is tempted to form a new group of his own.

In this way from time to time we see various smaller groups formed and, hanging on to them, seceders from groups of similar bent.

Our Parliamentary game favors such secessions. Because no great party is numerous enough to take office by itself, every Ministry has to depend on a coalition of groups. In order to obtain the support of these groups it must welcome their representative leaders. Thus a man who has been an obscure member of the Radical party and who has never been a Minister, may become a Minister if he is head of a little group—a "social, anti-clerical Left," shall we say—founded by himself with a score of friends and very important to a government if it is to have a majority.

Let it not be said that such ambitions are to be condemned. They exist in every country. Spinoza has shown in his "Tractatus Politicus" that men's passions are always more or less the same and that the good institutions are those which turn to account human defects in such a way as to lead a nation wisely, just as a trainer of animals turns to account their appetites and their fears when putting them through their paces. The British Parliamentarian is as human as the French Parliamentarian. Like the latter he is at once mean and generous, ambitious and jealous, admirable and detestable. But the rules of the game are different.

III

This is not the only reason why the existence of great parties that alternate in office has not been possible hitherto in France. Great parties correspond to definite divisions in a nation. In the United States the two great parties had their origin in a conflict of interest between North and South. In England the cleavage between Whigs and Tories separated the rebellious nobles and often the Nonconformists from the partisans of the King and of the Established Church. When that dividing line disappeared it was replaced by the one between Conservatives and Liberals. Today the division between Conservatives and Laborites is very clearly defined. In France the lines of separation are much more numerous.

Before the Revolution the French were cut into two divisions more definitely than other nations. The privileged landowners who paid no taxes and who were absent from their estates, were separated more profoundly from the peasantry than was the English squire, who was himself often half a peasant and who, moreover, was subject to taxes like his tenant-farmers. The Church was a source of vexation to the French populace—although the populace were orthodox believers—because of its privileges and its alliance with the nobility; the Church and the Château were coupled together and the peasants had no love for either. Then came the Revolution, enlarging still further this abyss between France's "two nations."

The hatred, long felt on the one hand, was opposed, on the other, by a natural feeling of resentment. We must not forget that there exists in Paris a small cemetery—the most aristocratic of any in the city, because the oldest French families have themselves buried in it alongside their ancestors who were guillotined and thrown into the common ditch. The dividing line, between Revolution and Counter-Revolution, is tending gradually to become less accentuated, but it has been and still remains an important feature of the French political landscape. Only a few months ago the leader of the Radical party, speaking in the Chamber of Deputies, used the words: "Blancs contre Bleus." Such historic memories have their danger.

Now it must be noted that the dividing line between Revolution and Counter-Revolution, does not accord precisely with the dividing line between wealth and poverty. A rich peasant will not be in the same political party as his lord of the manor.

Some "petit bourgeois," economical, quiet, and a hundred times more conservative than many English Conservatives, will vote for the Radical candidate because he has an invincible distrust of the curé—a sentiment which seems astonishing when we think of the poverty and harmlessness and goodness of most of the French curés, but which is based on ancestral traditions. It is these traditions that lend a grave political aspect to all debates upon laws bearing upon French schools and French education, debates which in other countries would have nothing to do with questions of party.

In addition to these great dividing lines, there are countless others of a less pronounced nature. There are divisions between the North and the South, between the industrial regions and the agricultural regions, between agriculturists and wine-growers. Even among the Socialists there are Internationalists and Nationalists, and among the Radicals there are out-and-out Radicals and Opportunist Radicals. In addition, we must take into account the little groups and coteries that gather around an individual leader because he serves their purposes. All this makes clear why it is almost impossible to form two great political blocs in France, with an alternation in power that would assure stability in politics.

IV

"Good!" the American or Englishman will say to me. "But when out of this multiplicity of groups a political bloc has been formed numerous enough to accept office and to support a Ministry, why does this bloc not remain homogeneous, at least for the duration of a Parliament? How is it that a Chamber elected on a certain program will vote the Opposition into power? For that is what we have twice seen in the course of the last few years. The Chamber elected in 1924, the Chamber of the Cartel, the Chamber of the Left, finishes its fourth year under a man whom it began by getting rid of—Poincaré. The Chamber of 1928, the Chamber of the National Republicans, the Chamber of the Centre, runs its course in such a fashion as to render possible a Radical Ministry, if only for a day. Why and by what mechanism?"

It is not difficult to understand. In France, because the parties are not very well defined, there is not always strict discipline in the groups. The discipline is always much better in opposition than in power. It has been somewhat better preserved in the course of the present Parliament. Certain groups have expelled Deputies who have not respected decisions taken collectively. But a Deputy who has been expelled from one group can always join an allied one. Toward the centre of the Chamber there are certain groups which we call "charnières" (hinges) half of whose members vote for the Ministry and half against. At need, a Deputy who leaves a group will find refuge among the Independents. Therefore a party in opposition, like a party in power, can always try to wear out the bloc confronting it.

There are numerous methods for achieving this. The government is able to dispose of posts, decorations, favors. The Opposition can make use of promises and turn to account disappointed hopes. Above all, the Opposition has on its side, first, the fatigue inspired by every reign that is too long (the old story of Aristides), and, second, the natural difficulties that attend all action. A man in power is continually making mistakes. Give him enough rope, said Disraeli, and he will hang himself. That is what always happens. And when the Opposition sees the government tottering it is able, by raising a question which will disquiet the electors, to place the Deputies on the government side in the dilemma of having to choose between their re-election and their loyalty. It is not always their loyalty that wins the day.

The equilibrium of a Chamber of Deputies is a thing so unstable that the turn taken in a single sitting may change the whole political situation. A distinguished parliamentarian has declared that a speech has often affected his opinion, but never his vote. That was witty, but it is misleading. An adroit or maladroit speech may affect fifty votes. A French Chamber is extremely responsive to eloquence. It is not made of cast-iron parties upon which no orator can hope to make an impression. It is made up of individuals who are honest, but who are susceptible, and who are carried away by eloquent speeches.

I have seen Briand win over a hostile Chamber. I have seen Briand and Franklin-Bouillon win the applause of the entire Chamber within an interval of ten minutes for absolutely contradictory propositions. It was a subtle speech by Chautemps which, for a brief moment last year, gave the present Chamber the illusion that after all it was perhaps on the Radical side. It was a tactful silence on the part of Tardieu which afterward proved to it that it was not. For a clever tactician no struggle upon such a field of battle is ever quite hopeless.

In conclusion, it should be pointed out that this instability is less dangerous than it would seem. Its disadvantages are, of course, manifest. A head of the government is so occupied defending himself against relentless enemies in ambush that he cannot free his mind for serious matters. In particular it is regrettable that truces cannot be concluded at times of important international negotiations. But as a matter of fact, continuity of policy exists in France to a greater degree than foreigners imagine.

There are countries in which the surface seems to be united and in which division is really profound. In France the surface is broken up but the depths are homogeneous to a remarkable degree.

Just because the dividing lines are innumerable, there is little real difference among the programs of the different governments. Certain men are classed as being of the Left, others as being of the Right. If one did not know their political record, it would be difficult to understand why. The foreign policy of the country has for some years past been so consistent that M. Briand has been able to conduct it in all the Ministries, whether of the Right or of the Left.

Moreover, the task of the President of the French Republic is to secure a relative continuity by the choice of the men whom he calls to office. In appearance the President of France has no power. In fact, he has more power than the King of England, and he is always able quietly to correct the instability of our parliamentary institutions. For the votes of the French Chamber are like the oracles of the Sibyl: they can always be interpreted in more than one way.

The French View of the World

by P. J. Philip

PARIS

WHOEVER ASPIRES to be considered a good militant of the French Radical and Radical Socialist party must wear a soft black felt hat. It is not a party uniform, for if one is a Radical Socialist one is very much of an individualist and will have nothing to do with uniformity in shirts or even in hats.

But in a soft black felt hat there is a great capacity for nice distinction. Its form is democratic, which is essential. Its sobriety of tone marks it as moderate and dignified. Being of soft felt, it can easily have individuality imparted to it, and, when it is worn for a considerable length of time, its individuality may become very marked. Finally, a soft black felt hat conveys just the right note of superior intellectuality. It can even be made to indicate a wide, generous culture which condescends to mix with less fortunate people.

Probably its choice as the party emblem just happened as natural things do. It was so essentially the right head-wear for a party whose leaders affect individual liberty, social equality and are slightly professional in their habit.

From the *New York Times Magazine*, December 11, 1932, copyright © 1932, 1960 by The New York Times Company.

There are, of course, no regulations as to its shape or the width of the brim. (Only Socialists, like Léon Blum, wear wide, stiff brims. They are more doctrinaire than our individualist Radicals.) Premier Herriot, after several choices, has seemed to select as his particular fancy something in the round pork-pie order. M. Chautemps's hat is heavier in form and substance, and, it may be his pale face that does it, rather funereal in aspect. M. Daladier gives his somehow an artistic touch. François Albert defiantly wears a large size—being a very small man. In a group one may easily pick him out by his hat without seeing him. Léon Meyor, Mayor of Havre, likes a high crown. Albert Milhaud, the General Secretary of the party, and several others affect little round hats which are as individual to Radicalism as tight black trousers to a Spanish dancer.

As soon as any young man obtains any administrative post in the party his first action is to select his particular type of hat—so long as it is black and soft. There are a few exceptions. M. Jammy Schmidt is one. He persists in wearing a black derby perched high above his long aquiline nose, but even his derby manages to have a Radical look and resembles in no way those that London city men wear for business. And there is Caillaux. But Caillaux never did conform. He alone in the party wears an eyeglass and he has been known to wear white spats. He persists even now in his seventieth year in sporting gray hats and brown hats and even green hats.

It isn't that Caillaux is not a good Radical Socialist. Many times, and to his cost, he has proved himself far more courageous in his radicalism than any of his followers or his successors. Perhaps that he does not wear a soft black felt hat is his final admission that he just cannot belong. He is not, except doctrinally, "one of us." There has remained through all his political adventures and misadventures a great deal of the aristocratic bourgeois in the gentleman who was baptized with the gentle-sounding names Marie Joseph Augustus Napoleon Caillaux.

This idiosyncrasy of the soft black felt hat apart, there is much in the Radical Socialist party in France which is comparable to the Democratic party in the United States. Perhaps it may prove fortunate for the world that there should be coincidence in their terms of office. For whatever successive governments France may have in the next four years—and a change may happen any day

—the Radical party, as the strongest single party in the Chamber and in the Senate, must remain the pivot of all governmental combinations.

It may be without real significance, but at least it is interesting as a point of similarity with the Democratic party, that the stronghold of the Radicals in France is the South. Toulouse is their Atlanta. There they have their most influential newspaper and there they recently held their Twenty-ninth Annual National Congress.

One would not wish to push the comparison too far, but it may be noted in passing that the South of France is less industrialized, more agrarian, than the North. The sun is hotter in the Summer time. The Winters are not hard. There is more leisure and ease of life. There is also an aptness for oratory among the people which finds natural outlet in political discussion in the corner café. When one has spoken eloquently, one seems to have done something if the sun is warm. And one is somebody when one belongs to a great organization of the eloquent who believe in liberty of debate and enjoy the discussion of great principles.

Also, it must in truth and justice be added, the "Midi" offers few chances to a young man who knows himself to have great ideas and a fine talent for expressing himself. He must go to Paris, at least occasionally, if he is to find scope. And what better road is there than the political road, along which so many Southern young men have traveled to comfortable jobs, including on more than one occasion the Presidency of the republic?

Politics in France's democratic party is always a shrewd mixture of high principle and mutual help. There are no Frenchmen so clannish in many ways as the Radicals; among them is a strong tradition of Freemasonry. Without reflecting on any—for all of us are human—there is a good strong touch of Tammany in France's Radical Socialist party.

There is another characteristic of the South which cannot be overlooked. Life being easier than in the bleak North, there is naturally a greater warmth of heart, a greater liberalism among its people. They believe very sincerely, very eloquently, in the principles which they profess and, if in action they sometimes do not quite live up to those principles—well, life is like that with all of us.

Though, as in all political parties in all countries, there are sections from all classes of society, it may be said of the French Radicals that, while their numerical strength lies in the South, they are essentially a middle-class party representing the middle classes from all over France. For nearly thirty years—with the exception of a few disastrous periods—they have been the predominant party in the country. In the words of one of their founders, Ledru-Rollin, they were formed "to bring into reality in the lives of men and of peoples the triple symbol of liberty, equality and fraternity."

It was a fine, high-sounding phrase, typical of both party and national rhetoric. In reality it amounted to saying that the middle class, which had never had a real chance at government, wanted that chance and was determined to get it. Though the origins of the party date back to the "bourgeois" revolution of 1848 and the "patriot" government of 1871 and Gambetta (these were radicalism's frock-coat days), the modern Radical and Radical Socialist party really began in 1904. Even then it was a party of combat, almost of civil war.

Until the end of last century, despite her many revolutions, control of the government in France had somehow always managed to slip back into the hands of the aristocracy and the very wealthy. It was the Dreyfus case, above all, which contributed to the organization of this middle-class party which adopted the name of Radical and Radical Socialist to mark its tendency rather than its creed. For, in trying to frame an opinion of just what the Radical and Radical Socialist party of Edouard Herriot is, the reader should disassociate from his mind the ideas which are conveyed in American speech by such a title.

It is one of the foibles of the Frenchman that he likes to think he is advanced and to label himself that way. Poincaré was always pleading that he was a man of the Left. There are only two groups in the Chamber which do not lay claim in their titles to Democracy or radicalism and there are three which profess some form of socialism. That does not in the least prevent any of them from being just as conservative as any Connecticut Republican who votes as his grandfather did.

Just how middle class the party is can be shown by its composition. Of its leaders, Herriot, Daladier, Milhaud, Nogaro and François Albert are or have been professors; Chautemps, Caillaux, Margaine and Julian Durand all began their careers in the upper branches of the civil service. Albert Sarraut is a newspaper owner. Many, like those two young intellectuals, Pierre Cot and Gaston Bergery, are lawyers. The party members are the shopkeepers, the State employes, the farmers, the doctors, the schoolmasters and all the lesser bourgeoisie of France, with, of course, recruits from the upper middle class and the workers. Many of them are Mayors in country towns.

By its very composition, therefore, it is conservative in the strict sense of the word. The heritage of liberalism to which it always pays tribute comes from the tradition of 1793 and 1848, from the revolt of the middle classes against the throne and the aristocracy which abused their power. These dates are still invoked—they were invoked the other day by Herriot.

But, though the modern Radical Socialist likes to think that he is of the race of the Revolutionaries, it would be more accurate to say he is the conserver of what the Revolutionaries won for his class, and he intends to hold on to his inheritance against all new challengers. For the rest his liberalism—more marked in some leaders than in others—might very easily be construed as a stout determination not to permit church interference with liberty of conscience, a warm desire to increase education and opportunity for the deserving, and a great anxiety to prevent the State, in the shape of the tax collector, from prying too deeply into his private affairs.

With the church he fought his battle twenty years ago and won. But since then, having established the laic principle, he has shown himself very lenient toward the activities of Rome. There is not any longer the old hatred of the clergy among the Radicals that there was when Gambetta declared: "Le clericalisme, voilà l'ennemi" and when Papa Combes separated the church from the State and the monasteries were closed.

For education the Radicals have undoubtedly done more than any other political party in France, though there is still a very great deal to be done in widening and improving general education. While opportunity is given to the clever boy, the State education in the primary schools is not carried to a sufficient age. There still lurks in many minds a suspicion that too much education is not good for the proletariat.

The great strength in doctrine and weakness in execution of the Radical party is its attitude toward public finance. It believes in a balanced budget, in economy, in the reduction of military expenditure, in the increase of education and social service and in the just distribution of the burden of taxation. But somehow it never seems to get the answers right in actual practice.

Therein, no doubt, it does not differ from any other democratic government in any other country. Every Parliament nowadays has its deficit, its tendency toward economy in the wrong place, its unfair taxation, its overinflated departments and its demagogic tendencies. Only somehow it seems that in France for many reasons these difficulties are more inherent and less exceptional than in other places.

Unfriendly people allege that it is because the French do not pay their taxes. That allegation is founded on an entirely wrong conception of what happens. The case should be put this way. If a Frenchman did pay all the taxes that the State demands of him he would have nothing left to live on and leave to pay his death duties. Therefore he dodges. Ways of dodging are indeed in many cases provided for him by the law. For the law-makers' argument is that the law can never take account of every circumstance and a little compensatory dodging is therefore only wise if the machine is to work smoothly.

Caillaux discovered years ago how ingrained is this habit of the French mind. There was enormous clamor against his "fiscal inquisition" in 1906 and the Finance Minister had to abandon his dream of a tidy taxation system. That fact does not prevent the party from solemnly demanding on every possible occasion the repression of fraud. Indeed, no resolution is ever more heartily applauded in a party congress than that calling for fiscal equality and the strict enforcement of the law. Where the catch is, is that most of those who applaud believe that they are the victims of an unfair system and that the strict enforcement of the law would in their case be a terrible injustice.

There is another aspect of the French Parliament's method of dealing with finance which, though it does not concern the Radicals only, is worth attention as typical. There is always much bother about balancing the budget and much discussion about appropriations and revenue, but there is no real control of expenditure. The figures are mostly hypothetical, and in a country which has two or three budgets of hypothetical figures it is only natural that the income-tax payer who never can know how his money is really spent should return a somewhat hypothetical figure.

In international affairs the Radical's doctrine is for cooperation. But representing as he does the commercial classes, his attitude is best summed up in his own phrase, "Donnant donnant," which may be interpreted, "Nothing for nothing."

Added to that the Radical has the French passion for juridic right, and so when one comes to a concrete case like that of the interallied debts he is always to be expected to show himself a firm creditor and at least a very argumentative debtor.

In all the departments of political life the Radical program is always more or less a compromise between doctrine and expediency. The Radical believes in fairly free trade except where the vital interests of "the nation," which includes his party, are concerned. Thus he can be counted on to protect the farmer up to the point where the price of bread does not cause active loss of support among the bread consumers. He can be expected to be active one day in attacking the problem of the cost of living and to be passive the next day when there is a recovery of basic prices on the Bourse.

With regard to disarmament and peace his reactions follow much the same rule. There is always an underlying contradiction between his doctrine and its application. Then, too, his doctrine is often complicated by logic and by his love of formulae. The "Liberty, Equality, Fraternity" of the Revolution has become: "Arbitration, Security, Disarmament" in this generation. The invention of these trilogies and their constant use by orators and in the press has many serious disadvantages. They express and so satisfy the aspirations and take little account of the possibility of practical fulfillment.

But there is no doubt whatever that in his heart every French Radical and nearly every Frenchman is sincerely attached to peace. He wants it for himself and for his children. He believes almost that he invented the idea and has a monopoly in this desire. He will claim passionately that France is not only a pacific country but the pacific country above all others. He always talks about Germany as if Germany had always been and would always be the great perturber of world peace. He never admits, if he ever remembers, that France has given the world far more scares than Germany ever did, and that Napoleon still looms bigger in the memory of the rest of humanity than Kaiser William II of Germany.

This forgetfulness is perhaps more on the surface than real. For the intelligent Radical of France's Third Republic seems somehow just at present to be devoting a good deal of his attention to tying up not only other people's war-like tendencies but his own also. That logic which dogs him all his life and is so difficult of comprehension to pragmatic Anglo-Saxons has led his professorial mind to the invention of a complete pyramid of pacts, covenants and conventions, whereby not only all others but he himself will be restricted and confined.

Perhaps it is because he recognizes that underneath his doctrine and his idealism, behind his democracy and his internationalism, there still is in him and his kind a strong instinct to battle. But he is a declining race. He is realist enough to take that into account. The day is past in history when France was the most numerously populated country in the world and the most inventive. War has cost her dearly under the Bourbons, under the Napoleons, and even under President Poincaré of the Third Republic. Her whole effort should be and must be toward preservation.

But the middle-class Radical is not sure that the other parties in France will accept that conception of France's rôle. He is not quite sure that in certain events, under certain provocation, he himself would accept it. When he talks of "security" he has in mind not only security from attack but also at times security from temptation to war.

Meanwhile, as it seeks to show the world the road to security and disarmament, which, with its national clearness and courage of mind, it knows to be the true road, France's Radical government with the whole Radical party behind it can be counted on to be prudent about abandoning the old system. There is not a single

Radical who will not continue to vote every penny necessary and possible for the upkeep of the army and navy and the air force at its full strength so long as the other peoples of Europe have not agreed to come into his mutual protection system.

As a party they stretch up to very high ideals. There are very few among them who will not individually admit that the case of Germany has been mishandled in and ever since the Treaty of Versailles. They will tell you that the Polish Corridor is a crime against reason. They will admit that the reparations claims of past days were folly. They will argue for good-will toward Germany more eloquently than any American. But they are a middle-class party, still rather unsure of themselves in the art of government, still rather terrified by the memory of war, and always hampered by the fact that, as in all democracies, their pace must be regulated by that of their slowest members.

And so, while as liberal humanitarians they reach toward their ideals—"Liberty, Equality, Fraternity"; "Arbitration, Security, Disarmament"—as Frenchmen they like keeping their feet firmly planted on solid ground.

France Feels the
Sweep of New Tides

by Harold Callender

PARIS

FOR A long time to come the politics of France will be governed by
memories of the recent Paris revolt, when normally law-abiding
young men longed for nothing so much as for an opportunity to
unhorse the Gardes Mobiles and throw them into the Seine; when
many threw marbles under the feet of the troops' mounts so that
they might slip and throw their riders; when men proceeded de-
liberately and methodically to smash with hammers the glass en-
closing traffic lights in the rue de Rivoli; when mobs tried to force
their way into the Chamber of Deputies and the Elysée Palace
(where the President lives) and were driven back by volleys of
bullets and drawn sabers; when many thousands of Parisians of
the most respectable classes—"the decent people" of the capital,
as they have often since been called—engaged in a revolutionary
demonstration against the French Parliament which turned into the
most violent uprising that Paris had witnessed since the Commune
of 1871.

If this spectacle haunts the minds of French politicians for years,
there will be good reason for it. For when due allowance has been

made for the prankish destructiveness of youth and the careful organization which preceded the demonstration, the fact remains that it represented an odd mixture of aggressive reaction, of real indignation at the scandals in public life, of economic discontent, of disillusionment with democracy as practiced: a combination of forces such as in other countries—though not yet in an experienced democracy like France—has threatened or overthrown parliamentary régimes.

While in France, particularly in the provinces, there are deeply rooted republican traditions and a profound distrust of "strong men" with dictatorial ambitions, the counter-revolution (if it may be called that) has considerable support in the upper middle class, especially in Paris. And it is prepared to make strong appeal to other classes, and to youth of all classes, by utilizing the world-wide unrest and confusion which economic disorganization has accentuated in all countries and under all types of government.

The republic in France has always drawn its principal strength from an inherited fear of reaction. To the peasant, the worker and the small business man the republic was a defense against the rich, the church, the aristocracy and all who might dream of reclaiming the privileges which the Revolution abolished. Years before the present crisis one was surprised by the challenging vehemence with which the Frenchman said, "I am a republican!" For were not nearly all Frenchmen republicans and was not the republic safe enough?

Not at all. Its supporters regarded the republic as being constantly in danger from some new Napoleon or Boulanger. The preservation of French liberties, they thought, demanded unremitting vigilance. The Third Republic, even after sixty years, still kept a watchful eye upon the enemies within.

The republic now has a new enemy. It has long managed to hold its own, even during four years of war and its tragic aftermath, against the remnants of the feudal aristocracy, the royalists, the reactionaries and the militarists. But now a new doctrine has appeared which, oddly allied to some extent with the old anti-republicanism, has cast a strange spell upon many of the younger generation of both "Right" and "Left" antecedents.

One refers, of course, to the doctrine of "authoritarian" government, of economic planning by capable technicians; the alluring conception of a society organized on economic rather than on political lines; the dream of a community where the traditional dogmas will have lost all meaning and where statesmen will be preoccupied not in restricting the clergy's privileges or safeguarding laical schools or upholding vague ideologies derived from eighteenth-century philosophers but in constructing a new type of State in harmony with the unprecedented requirements of a mechanized and troublesomely productive age.

These are the ideas and aspirations which have captivated many of the youth in France, at least many of the university youth, from whom future leaders will largely come. These young men look with something like contempt upon the pre-war politicians who have led France in the accustomed paths. They have no more use for the traditional terminology of politics, or the multifarious divisions and subdivisions of political groups in Parliament, or the pleasant abstractions which so long have been the stock in trade of party leaders than they have for the refined dialectics of medieval scholastics.

They are not yet at all clear as to what they want. They are not united under a leader or agreed upon a program. They may be moved by impulse more than by knowledge. But they represent perhaps the most remarkable and novel element, if as yet a somewhat fluid one, in the field of French political thought.

Without them it would be much the same old contest between "Right" and "Left," Conservative and Radical, Republican and clerical, capitalist and Socialist. But if these younger men are driven by economic events to push their way, perhaps prematurely, into the places that normally would be filled by the men who lie under white crosses in Northern France—men who would now be 35 to 55 years of age—the course of French politics may be radically changed. The middle generation is short of talent, many of its best having fallen in battle; there remain the old men with (as the youth would say) mostly old ideas, and the very young with startlingly new ideas.

Not that these ideas and longings were consciously championed by many of the mob which fought the police and howled at the Deputies. That mob was inspired by reactionaries of the old school, by Royalists, by Fascists and by people who genuinely believed that to give the deputies a fright would be a salutary measure. The mob represented, among other things, a revival of the rebellious, "frondeur," Boulangist spirit of Paris; and in consequence of its success Paris, which made the nineteenth-century revolutions, but since Boulanger's adventure in 1889 has had little influence upon French politics, may again take the lead, or at least play a more active role.

But the Parisian uprising was nothing if not anti-parliamentarian, and in this, at any rate, it coincided with the inclination of those, chiefly among the youth, who despair of the present political methods and machinery and seek something less cumbersome and better disciplined. Some rose against the present Chamber because it was dominated by the Left, others because they wanted a king or a dictator; but these diverse groups were at one in disliking the present Parliament, if not parliamentary government as such. Both their unity in opposition and their complete lack of unity as to program were revealed in the recent revolt.

In a recent procession in honor of one of those killed by Gardes Mobiles in the Place de la Concorde marched several thousand persons representing the following groups: The Action Française, the militant Royalist organization, which seeks to place the Duke of Guise upon the throne of France: the Jeunesses Patriotes (Patriotic Youth) in dark blue uniforms, an equally militant league of youth of the Extreme Right, which proclaims the need of a "national revolution" and maintains its "shock troops" on Fascist lines; the Solidarité Française, looking even more Fascist with their light blue shirts and their salutes; a group of Municipal Councilors of Paris, fifteen of whom had issued a vehement proclamation which helped to incite the city against the late Radical government, and the war veterans of the Croix de Feu and some members of the Union Nationale des Anciens Combattants.

Here, in formal array, was the organized advance guard of anti-parliamentarism as manifested in the recent demonstrations. The first three groups have decidedly Fascist characteristics, though the first places primary emphasis upon restoration of the monarchy. The youthful members of all three remind one of the militant and mystical young Nazis in German universities. The Municipal Councilors typify Parisian resistance to provincial radicalism and to what the "Right" generally regarded as an attempt by a radical government to increase its power and crush its enemies.

The veterans' organizations are more difficult to classify. They represent no avowed doctrine and profess to be republican, non-partisan and interested solely in good government, order and national defense; but the Croix de Feu, a recent organization of frontline soldiers, conducted an active campaign against the government and joined with Royalist and Fascist groups in an anti-parliamentary demonstration. A government which had the confidence of the Chamber was overthrown by a crowd in the streets of Paris, thanks largely to the Croix de Feu.

The commander of the Croix de Feu, Colonel de la Rocque, objects to comparisons between his organization and the Nazis, saying, "We are not romanticists," and pointing to the fact that his men wear no uniforms. But the comradery of the trenches, which the Croix de Feu represents, is not unlike that developed by the Nazis, though it perhaps resembles more closely that of the German Stahlhelm, composed, like the Croix de Feu, of war veterans. The Stahlhelm, too, stood for order, discipline and national defense; it, too, was made up of men of many classes; but it was frankly monarchist and military and closely allied to the Nationalist party.

The Croix de Feu are regarded by the "Left" as virtual Fascists, as tools of a conservative reaction. It will hardly be possible for them to remain aloof from the party and class conflict, in which they have, indeed, already taken sides, whether they intend to do so or not. In Germany the veterans' organizations were frankly political, one group being Socialist, one group Nationalist and some such split may come sooner or later in France. There is a marked tendency for many of the intellectual youth to ally themselves with the Croix de Feu; but others look upon the Croix members, whose ages range from 35 to 50 or more, as middle-aged and therefore hopeless.

In the Jeunesses Patriotes, in the Action Française, and perhaps in the Croix de Feu, are Fascist possibilities; but these groups are not united, are not led by a single dominant leader, and have not gained anything like the support among the youth which the Nazis had in, say, 1931. They would be resisted by the Radicals, the Socialists and the Communists and would be stronger in Paris than in the more sternly republican provinces.

While there are certain striking resemblances between the anti-parliamentarian movements in France and those that brought down the German republic, there are equally noteworthy differences. Both gained many followers among the youth, who were unemployed and without hope, and among the ex-soldiers. Both were supported by conservative middle-class interests and were regarded as enemies of labor and socialism. Both proclaimed, in almost identical terms, a "national awakening" and a cleansing of public life.

But while the German Nazi movement was directed against a republic that was new and weak, the French anti-parliamentarians and Fascists attack a republic that is sixty-three years old and has become firmly established. While the Nazis, though backed by industrialists, appealed chiefly to the lower middle-class masses who had hardly any property and hence cheered denunciations of bankers and promises of "national socialism," the French movement represents primarily the upper middle or propertied class and so makes no pretensions to economic radicalism, such as the Nazis made (before they came into power). The French movement shows no signs of anti-Semitism—though it may be expected to enjoy the support of the same classes that condemned Dreyfus—and it lacks the military spirit and form of the Nazi movement.

Most important of all perhaps, the French movement, far from having the marked anti-intellectual bias of the Nazis, is one in which intellectuals are leading. French fascism, if it becomes more than an aspiration, is not likely to be a revolt against intelligence.

The division among its enemies and critics will help the republic to resist the new attacks, though they are no longer the familiar onslaughts of a purely reactionary or clerical "Right." Moreover, the attacks come primarily from Paris, whose republicanism has long been tinged with Boulangist leanings and cosmopolitan skepticism. The real strength of the republic has been in the provinces, which are predominantly moderate and radical, even when they vote Socialist, while Paris tends to the Extreme "Right" and the Extreme "Left." It was the largest party in France, the Radicals, whose government was overthrown by the mob in Paris.

The provinces are habitually suspicious of Paris, which, as Professor Seignobos observes, is out of touch with the French masses. Most of the French political leaders come from the provinces. The Deputy from the provinces attending parliamentary sessions in Paris usually is a visitor living in a hotel. He must take care, says André Siegfried, not to become a Parisian, lest he be regarded by his constituents as a backslider from the republican faith. It should be noted that the recently developed anti-parliamentary movement is first and foremost a Parisian phenomenon.

But if the republic is to survive in substantially its present form, it may have to become far more efficient and more capable of meeting economic difficulties. It will have to meet the challenge of the "decent people" who have lost confidence in its officials and in its judiciary and resent the power of the trade unions of State employes, who even enjoy the right to strike. It will have to meet the attacks of the foes of liberal capitalism who want a planned economy and a strong central power. It will have to learn to act more decisively and to attain a higher standard of honesty among its representatives. It will have to become more attractive to the youth.

On the side of the existing régime is the stubborn republicanism of the provinces, a heritage of the past. Working against it are the trend of economic events and the contagious example of "authoritarian" political doctrines in the other major Continental countries —and also, strange as it may seem, the influence of the New Deal in the United States, whose President is widely regarded in Europe as a kind of benevolent but courageous dictator. Many times has the writer heard Frenchmen condemn their own Parliament while pointing with admiration to Mr. Roosevelt and wishing that France had a similar leader.

In Germany fascism, breaking from the reactionaries and monarchists who sought simply a return to the semi-feudal past, aligned itself with the more modern reactionaries who sought to crush the trade unions and federalism so as to establish a powerful State which they could control. In France the anti-parliamentary movement, and what incipient Fascists there are, have not decided how reactionary, in the old or the new style, they are going to be. The "authoritarian" movement has not yet crystallized and can hardly hope to do so until it finds a commanding leader. France has had her Bonapartes and her Boulangers and, on the whole,, is not keen on repeating the experiment.

France is one of only three great free nations left in the world. If she should eventually adopt a dictatorship or go Fascist, she would be the first country with long experience of democracy to do so.

Puzzled France: Which Way?

by André Maurois

PARIS

TO UNDERSTAND what has happened in France one must recall the traditional political alignment and how it had been transformed before the recent national election.

During the years following the war three great political groups were clearly discernible in France—leaving aside the finer shades of division. On the Right was a moderate group embracing many middle-class electors, a large number of peasants, especially in the West and East, and Catholic wage-earners. In the center were the Radicals, the most numerous group, representing the smaller business and professional people (the petits bourgeois), government employes and a part of the peasants of the central and southern provinces. On the Left were the Socialists supported by most of the workers, certain State employes (particularly school teachers) and intellectuals.

The Radical party held the balance of power. It was allied by sympathy with the Socialists, though in practice it often found itself at odds with them. André Siegfried defined the Radical party by saying that its heart was on the Left but its pocket impelled it to the Right. That party, composed of people with small savings, feared some of the financial measures the Socialists might adopt. But above all, being a patriotic party—the heir, as it often proclaimed, of the Jacobins of Valmy—it could not govern with the sole support of the Socialists, who refused to vote credits for national defense.

Consequently from 1919 to 1932 the Radical party was torn between its sympathies with the Left and the necessities of government. Sometimes it leaned toward the Right and France had a Poincaré or a Laval Ministry; sometimes it joined the Left in trying a Cartel (Left coalition) Cabinet in conjunction with the Socialists. This swing of the pendulum did not represent in France, as it does in England, a movement of the mass of voters in one direction or the other; it was merely the shifting of a parliamentary group in alternative coalitions.

As for the Communists, although they won a large number of votes in elections in those years, they obtained few seats in the Chamber. The reason was that in France an election consists of two ballotings, a week apart, and the outcome depends upon the alliances made between the first and second ballots. The Communists were on bad terms with the other Left parties. They were regarded by the Socialists as dangerous rivals and by the bourgeois and patriotic Radicals as international revolutionaries. In 1932 proportional representation would have given forty-five seats to the Communists, but they won only twelve.

If the Communists had remained enemies of the Socialists, if the moderates had remained on good terms with the Radicals, if the French voters had been fairly well satisfied with the government of the country, we probably should have witnessed this year the traditional comedy. That is, the voters would have given a small majority to the coalition of Radicals and Socialists, a Left government would have faced financial difficulties, and about 1938 the Left coalition would have foundered and been succeeded by a moderate government.

But new circumstances, combined with the errors of the moderates in their relations with the Radicals, altered the entire situation. The most important novelty was the transformation of the Communist party into a governing party. This was due to foreign causes. Soviet Russia, feeling itself menaced by Nazi Germany, had decided that the best defense lay in an alliance with the French Republic.

Two necessities were imposed by that alliance: *First,* that France should be strong, and therefore that the French Communists should support military expenditures: *second,* that France should have a government sincerely favoring the Russian alliance, and hence that the French Communists in the 1936 elections should seek the aid of the other Left parties and in turn should support the Radicals and Socialists.

This explains why the Communists, for the first time, were moved to ally themselves with the Radicals. But why should the Radicals have accepted such an alliance? Here is where the mistakes of the moderates played their part.

On the occasion of the Stavisky financial scandal the moderates made, or permitted, a campaign of extreme violence against the Radical leaders. That campaign had three results. It drove the Radicals toward the extreme Left; it convinced a part of the middle-class youth of the need to oppose the existing régime and, after the disturbances of Feb. 6, 1934, encouraged the formation of leagues like the Croix de Feu; and it provoked, as a reaction against the leagues and from fear of fascism, the formation of the electoral coalition of Communists, Socialists and Radicals called the People's Front. It was this People's Front which united behind a single candidate in each constituency at the second ballot in the recent election.

Any one acquainted with the political map of France could have predicted the victory of such a coalition and foreseen that it would give the Communists a much greater number of seats. But the victory of the People's Front exceeded the expectations of the experts. The coalition desired by the party leaders likewise coincided with the will of the mass of voters, who favored the extreme Left of this Left coalition—that is, the Communists and Socialists —at the expense of the Radicals.

Why did middle-class citizens, peasants and State employes vote for a change of leadership? Electoral strategy does not suffice to explain the sudden swing to the Left of so many voters. Let us then seek the reasons for it.

The most important reason was the extreme discontent among almost all classes caused by the policy of deflation. One need not discuss whether that policy was wise or not. It was necessary if the franc was to be defended. But it had painful consequences for everybody.

A series of decrees reduced the salaries of State employes, which naturally irritated that powerful class. The small shopkeepers suffered from the depression and from the absence of foreign tourists. Privately paid wages and salaries followed government payrolls in their descent to lower levels. Unemployment, though less acute than in the United States or in England, nevertheless caused much suffering.

The public had long waited patiently for the government to "do something." First the people were told that all the trouble came from politics and that a reform of the Constitution would remove the evils from which France suffered. During the administration of M. Doumergue, who assumed power after the 1934 riots, such a reform had been planned, but it was never carried through. Later the country was assured that deflation would bring back prosperity. Deflation was applied at the cost of great suffering, but the crisis continued. The least revolutionary of the middle class then began to wonder whether a change of government was not necessary.

These small, middle-class people had long been alienated from the Left parties by the question of national defense and by the religious question. But the Communists, 1936 model, spoke of the army with enthusiasm and of religion with sympathy. The influence of the Vatican, moreover, inclined the church toward social reforms.

To the small landowners who would have been frightened away by a too Socialistic or Communistic program, the candidates of the People's Front said: "It's not your wealth which is in question. Nobody thinks of touching your property, your land or your capital. Small and moderate fortunes will not be disturbed. It is only the great ones that are in danger. It is the 200 families who among them own nearly all the great business enterprises in France. They are the ones—the only ones—we are after."

Every effective propaganda campaign is founded upon a myth. "The 200 families" served as the myth of the 1936 French elections. It had among the masses a success not difficult to understand, for it offered a simple and naive explanation of all the country's troubles. It suggested easy remedies, and since it held a threat for only an infinitesimal minority, it provoked little opposition. It explains to a great extent why so many small property owners, middle-class Radicals, were willing on the second ballot to vote Communist or Socialist.

In domestic affairs the program of the Socialist and even of the Communist leaders is, at least for the moment, not at all revolutionary. It could hardly be revolutionary, for many of the new supporters of the Left parties do not wish a Left program. The Russian Communists, who seek the aid of France, have no desire to see France weakened by dissension. Above all, the most ardent wish of the masses is for economic recovery, which cannot take place in an atmosphere of apprehension and conflict. It must be added that the Right opposition has no more intention than the Left of carrying the struggle outside the parliamentary sphere.

"To assure the recovery of economic life"—that is the phrase now reiterated in newspaper articles and interviews by Léon Blum, the Socialist leader who is to become Premier. He desires, it appears, to undertake an experiment resembling that which President Roosevelt made in the United States and M. van Zeeland in Belgium.

But in those countries the point of departure, the fillip given to the national economy, was monetary devaluation. That would be difficult for the parties which have placed the defense of the franc at the head of their program. Some suggest that M. Blum would prefer to try a method somewhat analogous to that of Dr. Schacht; that is, of controlled exchanges and a semi-closed economy. Yet the export of gold, which since the elections has attained large proportions, might force him to devalue the currency.

In their election platforms the victorious parties promised to impose a levy on capital and to use the proceeds for public works designed to reduce unemployment. The specialists have no great confidence in the yield of such a tax. It would be difficult to collect because many forms of capital are such that they cannot be reached; it would reduce the yield of the income tax in subsequent years; it would hamper rather than help the restoration of normal economic activity. The Communists, nevertheless, have announced that they will propose such a measure as soon as the new Chamber meets.

The new government, on the other hand, will certainly attempt to nationalize the munitions industry. In so doing it will antagonize only certain private interests, for the bulk of the country is not hostile but rather favorable to this plan. Other monopolies will also be tackled.

There has been a suggestion to nationalize all insurance, but that apparently is not intended. Rather is it nationalization of the petroleum trade which is discussed. As importation is concentrated in a few hands, it would be relatively simple to take over the industry, and the intervention of the State could be justified to a certain extent by the importance of oil for national defense. Finally, the Bank of France certainly will be transformed and subjected to more drastic control by the State.

This immediate program is no more revolutionary than was that of the British Labor party, and it is quite possible that the Socialist and Radical parties in France will tend toward a kind of reform socialism after the fashion of the Laborites. That is, just now, the desire of several of their leaders. But one must take account of the inevitable resistance which always exasperates those who are resisted.

When the battle begins, will the majority behind the government remain faithful? Will the opposition have the wisdom to adhere to parliamentary methods, without having recourse to its great influence over owners of small savings accounts or bonds? Above all, will the Senate vote for State monopolies and new taxes?

If the Senate resists, we can expect a struggle like that against the House of Lords in England at the time of Lloyd George's budget in 1910. But the French Senate is elective while the Lords are hereditary, and until now it has not been unpopular. The Senate would defend itself, perhaps with the tacit support of the Radicals in the Chamber. The question is: Where, in the last analysis, is the real power in France? The Socialist victory, which is indisputable and undisputed, does not insure an easy path for the government, especially if the Communists refuse to share the responsibilities of power.

In foreign affairs the victory of the Left signifies first of all fidelity to the League of Nations and to the principle of collective security—precisely what Great Britain would have welcomed so eagerly a few months ago. But France and Britain seem fated to play at cross purposes, to wish different things at a given time or the same things at different times.

At this moment, when public opinion in France has by its vote sought to give a new lease of life to the League, the British Government contemplates a reform of the covenant so drastic that the League would not survive it. The French Socialist government will certainly ask the British to regard last year's difficulties as a misunderstanding and to give the League a few months more. But will they agree?

Regarding Germany, M. Blum says he desires to reopen negotiations for European disarmament, if that is still possible. He would call the Disarmament Conference into session again and ask Germany to participate. If she refused, a disarmament convention would be drawn up without her, and it would then be presented by the European States jointly to the German Government. That government has always said it favored such a project, and in these circumstances, M. Blum believes, the issue would have to be faced by Germany.

In foreign as in domestic affairs the new government's path will be strewn with difficulties. The three parties which compose its majority in the Chamber are not entirely in accord. The Communists wish above all a close agreement with Moscow; the Socialists favor a frankly pro-League policy; and it is no secret that M. Daladier, the Radical leader, used to urge a direct understanding with Germany and to support the Four-Power pact. There is no reason to assume that he has altered his opinions.

Will new leaders solve the old problems? In politics problems are never solved; or, rather, hardly are they solved before new obstacles appear. In France the great evil since the war has been the weakening of the power of the State. Governments of both the Right and the Left have complained of it and suffered from it.

If the Cabinet now assuming power re-establishes the authority of the State and governs with a realistic appreciation of the national interest, many Frenchmen who are neither Socialists nor Radicals will rejoice. If it falls into demagogy and takes orders from irresponsible party congresses, it will fail and quickly lose all prestige. Leaders and doctrines may change; they have just changed in France; but the principles of government are immutable. Votes do not transform men.

In What Direction?
A Puzzled France Wonders

by P. J. Philip

PARIS

WHATEVER THE outcome of the present political struggle in France
may be, it is accepted here as almost certain that this country will
not "go Fascist" or "go Communist," as these terms are understood and practiced in Italy, Germany and Russia. France will
remain French. If a name must be given to the system which is
most likely to evolve that name is "collectivist."

Everybody agrees that changes are coming. Events have been
developing swiftly in France. Differences of opinion resulting from
the Munich agreement and of the decree laws which led to the
attempt to stage the recent general strike are growing. The signing
on Tuesday of the "good-neighbor" pact between Germany and
France is not likely to lessen the conflict over the social and
economic policies of the nation and over the duties of the State
and the rights of its citizens.

On top of the factional quarrels which are going on in France
there has come the acute perception that economically this country
is fast slipping from the rank it used to hold. The national income
has shrunk to a greatly diminished number of billions of very

From the *New York Times Magazine*, December 11, 1938, copyright ©
1938, 1966 by The New York Times Company.

greatly diminished francs. There has been little or no construction, little or no development in recent years. Housing has been neglected; even existing properties have been allowed to fall into decay from lack of the will or the money to keep them painted and repaired. Industries have fallen back because of the lack of the will or money to install new modern machinery. In shipping France has dropped back from third place to seventh. The commercial balance of the country continues to be unfavorable by hundreds of millions of francs a month.

Meanwhile, expenditure not only for armaments but for social service of all kinds has continued to pile up unendingly. M. Daladier recently gave the figures: National income, 250 billion francs; government expenditure, 137 billions; normal government revenue, 85 billions.

How to change these conditions and to achieve stability is the problem the country is facing amid great confusion of counsel. What is fundamentally at stake is the conception of the relations of the State and the citizenry which has established itself firmly in the French mind throughout a good many generations and especially in the last twenty years.

To understand the situation, or rather the conception the French have of the State and its duties, one must go back to the 19th of Fructidor, 1798, when Genenral Jourdan got the Council of Five Hundred to pass a little law making all men between 20 and 25 years old "defenseurs conscrits"—compelling them to take arms for the defense of their country. It is that little law—perpetuated throughout every regime ever since—which has made France different from other "democracies," however much the French may seek to conceal or to justify the difference.

That was the law which began the gradual conversion of France into a collectivist State. In return for military service the citizenry began to demand more and more from the government until even those governments and parties which were the declared opponents of socialism were compelled to join the procession, so that now the State seems to control and direct everything from the election of an academician and a schoolmaster to the railroads, the highways, the telegraphs and telephones, the manufacture of Sèvres pottery, the opera and some theatres, museums and art galleries. Add to this list huge forests, the manufacture of matches and tobacco, the refinement of oil, the Bank of France, potash mines in Alsace, coal mines in Flanders, steamship companies and mineral springs like those of Vichy.

There is scarcely anything in which the State does not take a hand and that, in the opinion of those opposed to such laws as the forty-hour week, is the source of the present difficulty. State intervention, it is argued, has killed private initiative; it has killed the desire of the capitalist to risk his capital in enterprise.

State intervention, too, runs the argument, has killed the desire of the workman to work and save. He has derived from his experience as a soldier—and of course the demands of the war veterans are cited in this connection—the feeling that the State owes him his livelihood. He obtained from the Blum government the forty-hour week and paid vacations. In themselves these improvements in the workers' lot in many industries are conceded to have been legitimate and beneficial. But it is contended that they spread the conception that the individual could "take things easy" and the State would provide.

If France were a sufficiently populated country with peaceful neighbors the task would be easier. But the awkward fact is that out of the profits and earnings of a Malthusian citizenry must be drawn, in addition to all that is needed for the upkeep and smooth running of the State, twenty-five billion francs a year for armaments, and that excluding the normal cost of the army, the fleet and the air force. If capital will not work and labor will not work, the necessary wealth cannot be produced and quite humanly they will not consent to work so long as the State would provide.

Neither capital nor labor is willing yet, it would seem, to admit that the State cannot go on providing. Capital wants labor to pull the country up by working longer hours. Labor, led by M. Blum, gives the old answer, "Tax the rich." It is rarely argued by the French capitalist that his indolence in attending to his business set an example to the workers or by the workers that there are very few "rich" left in France who can be so extensively and repeatedly taxed as to bring any real solution.

Out of this triangular struggle among the State, labor and capital there has evolved a political as well as an economic situation which to many observers has every appearance of becoming extremely dangerous. For there is no issue except a change of temper and attitude, and it is regarded doubtful whether that change can be accomplished without a change of regime.

Even in the country one now finds people—people who a few years, even a few months, ago felt and said that the republic was solidly built and would never need to be changed—who begin to say that the republic is "used up," that some firmer form of government is becoming necessary. In part the change of opinion is attributed to the disillusion caused by the Munich settlement. The mass of people are saying for the first time that France, the country which twice invaded the Weimar Republic to compel respect for treaties, had not sufficient confidence in herself and in what she wanted to invade Hitler's Third Reich.

Although the traditional collectivist spirit engendered by conscription sent 1,800,000 men to the frontier without question, there were people who professed to see only the form and not the substance of unity in the ranks. It was said that too much talking, the vanity of party leaders, their demagogy, their lip-service to strange doctrines, had sapped that spirit of national purpose which in the old days followed a leader, whether he was right or wrong, for the honor of France and the republic.

The great demand in France today is for a leader and discipline. During the mobilization in September both the regular army officers and the reservists were amazed to find that the men who were so troublesome as workmen and employes were so tractable and willing as soldiers. Once the soldier had donned his képi he seemed to forget that he had been a Radical, a Socialist, a Communist, a Doriotist or a member of de la Rocque's French Social party. He became a real collectivist and not merely a dependent on the collectivity. He seemed to be happier than he had been as a civilian faced with the problem of having to make up his voter's mind as to the rival merits of Reynaud's doctrine of recovery by individual action and the doctrines by the scores of different parties which the egoism of the French has created.

As to what will happen no one can prophesy. But if some different system of government from that which has controlled France for the past three generations has to be set up, one thing appears certain at this juncture—it will confine itself to the direction of the economic and military life of the country and not, as other dictatorships have done, interfere in the spiritual and free intellectual life of the people.

Part 2

THE SECOND WORLD WAR

The Titanic Struggle
Inside France

by Pertinax [André Geraud]

PIERRE LAVAL has just taken up the reins of command at Vichy. In choosing his colleagues he has been somewhat groping; but in his program he shows neither hesitancy nor doubt. Laval's political exile lasted sixteen months. The better part of this time he spent in Paris, under German protection, in endless conversations with Otto Abetz, representative of the Reich in occupied France, and Abetz's masters. He knows what he wants. And it is only too likely that he is in perfect agreement with the occupying power as to the way, the place, the time, the rhythm of the French contribution which will bring German victory—and he longs for it. But how can he carry out his promise against the will of the French people?

Today, all witnesses agree on the intensity of popular feeling against the Germans which rages in France under seeming resignation or even apathy. In vast numbers Frenchmen understand that they can never again become free and independent except by a victory of England, the United States and Russia. The majority of them also believe that the entrance of the United States into the struggle spells German defeat. And let us not forget that lasting horror branded on men's hearts by the mass killing of hostages, that burning indignation which occasionally bursts through in some violent gesture—in Paul Colette's pistol-shot. Is that comparable in essence to the knife thrusts of Charlotte Corday?

Even before America's declaration of war Laval had many times privately admitted that his compatriots detest the Nazi conqueror. But those who have had access to him say that the fact neither gives him pause nor bothers him. All the longings and hopes of his countrymen, he says, will not alter the inevitable reality. They will have to bow to Germany's triumph.

Laval has always scorned public opinion. No Minister is worth his salt, he thinks, who does not know how to mold that opinion as he thinks the interests of the country require. And in the present instance his task is all the easier, he boasts, because it is hitched to Hitler's star. Is his optimism justified? We are indeed forced to grant Laval a certain number of trump cards.

First, in a country without representative bodies, without a free press, without right of assembly or joint action, but honeycombed with police—in such a country public opinion takes shape only in private conversations, private letters, etc. Men are separated one from another. Each broods in his own little corner. A public opinion thus shaped must remain flighty, uncertain, vague. The politician who is in charge of the Ministry of Information (be it noted that Laval regards this post as equal in importance to that of Foreign Affairs or the Interior) easily persuades himself that he can do with opinion as he wills.

Second, particularly in unoccupied France, Marshal Pétain's personal prestige has kept up well among the "conservative classes," long living in fear of "popular fronts." In doubtful matters they will follow him without understanding what he is doing. They will allow him a generous drawing account. They will accept the assertions of the old soldier as against the English and American radio and even against their own judgment. Here is a great help to Laval in an hour of need.

But, third, there is something more. One result of collaboration with Germany has been the creation of vested interests. For at least eighteen months many industrialists, against personal preference, have had to work for the Germans in order not to be dispossessed of their machinery, of their family property, in order to live and give their employes a means of livelihood. They have become used to this collaboration, which is remote, scarcely felt, minor, tenuous. If its scope were little by little to widen, they would offer no resistance.

Alongside these collaborationists—timid, holding back, even a little shamefaced—there are the rich and the greedy who have staked their all on the Nazi cause and now feel too deeply involved to withdraw. For instance, a famous French family has had brilliant business dealings with the Germans—dealings which have restored that family's fortunes. Several million "occupation marks" were received in exchange for bottles of champagne. From that moment the wine itself became an unanswerable argument for collaboration. And, of course, there is Renault, the classic pro-Nazi industrialist, and his Cabinet Minister son-in-law, Lehideux. Such people will be collaborationists to the bitter end.

In the fourth place, we must always remember the million or so civil servants who depend upon the government for their salaries or their pensions and who are therefore at its mercy. And the reprisals, the persecutions, large and small, which are possible by reason of the 1,500,000 war prisoners held in German hands, by reason of France's being split up into separate administrative compartments, by reason of the fact that most daily necessities are obtainable only through favor.

Such are Laval's major weapons. But what about the basic question—his method of procedure?

The French counter-revolutionaries (by whom I mean that party which ever since 1815 has untiringly sought to destroy the 1789 "Rights of Man" and their social and political consequences) have always maintained that the greatest upheavals in a state are the work of resolute and violent minorities, and that the broad mass of people can be won over by them. Hence these men have held that the essential thing is to have within reach at the crucial moments and in the crucial positions men of daring who are brutal and unscrupulous.

At the beginning of this century in his "Enquête sur la Monarchie" (Inquiry into Monarchy) Charles Maurras said that sooner or later the Republic would lead France to military defeat. In order that France might not perish it would then be needful, he said, to overthrow the Republic. Force the will of the nation by means of small groups skillfully led: that is the system.

Laval and Maurras came together in that counter-revolutionary movement which sprang from bourgeois fear and terror of socialism and communism, and for which military defeat opened the road to power. All alone, through adroit manipulation of a few men, Laval succeeded in effecting the abdication of Parliament on July 10, 1940—in accomplishing the "National Revolution." He is confident that in external affairs he can now repeat what he succeeded in doing internally. It is merely a matter of horse-trading and flair, and boldness. The whole thing is to know when to grasp the fleeting opportunity.

Hence while major groups of Frenchmen—I should say the majority—can easily be prevented from following their feelings, impulses and desires, relatively small factions, both civil and military, will be able to achieve results entirely out of proportion to their number, affecting the destiny of their own country and also of the rest of the world—provided always that a well-chosen leader guides their efforts and that they themselves are carefully selected beforehand.

This idea requires some elaboration, for it is the crux of the whole business. What can a man like Laval expect from the armed forces toward the fulfillment of his schemes? It is clear enough that since June, 1940, in those instances that we are able to judge, the acts of a few men, or even of one man, have most often determined the attitude of the whole.

Thus what took place at Mers-el-Kebir resulted from a decision taken by the commander in chief of the French squadron, Admiral Gensoul. He could easily have concluded that there was no need for him to consult his superiors at Vichy—since all telegraphic and telephone messages were under German surveillance—before answering Admiral Sir James Somerville's ultimatum. But Gensoul did ask Vichy's advice and had to fight. Three days later, however, Vice Admiral Godefroy at Alexandria acted in very different fashion. Against Vichy's orders he came to an agreement with the English by which his squadron was neutralized. In both cases officers and men obeyed the admirals, in spite of the fact that their decisions were totally opposite.

These episodes, however, took place almost two years ago. Since then Vichy has gone over its civil and military servants with a fine-tooth comb, and in all posts of major importance we now find out-and-out collaborationists.

Such are the evidences of the past. From Laval's point of view they are encouraging. All the general officers judged capable of independent action are at present tucked away in second-rate berths. And what steps some of the officers took to make their conversion to nazism showy! A few of them went so far as to have their official files falsified, even to have documents manufactured, in order to prove their sympathies for the Axis. Note also that generals now holding important posts were released from German prison camps, that the thousands of French sailors captured at Dunkerque and Cherbourg were sent back to their ports—officers and seamen.

But the reverse of the coin shows a number of things that should offer Laval food for thought. In all naval establishments, among the mechanics, the stokers, the "black gangs," Communist propaganda has always thrived. Today it works to the same end as French patriotism.

Would Laval find as great a stumbling block in the army if, carrying Pétain with him, he tried to hurl French regiments against English or American Commandos in Brittany or Normandy? I have no recent information, but everything seems to indicate that the spirit of the troops is not different from that of the surrounding populations.

One must distinguish strictly between French units stationed in Syria, for instance, well within control of their military superiors, and units in garrison at home, immediately dwelling in an atmosphere not friendly to the officer class. The Vichy régime does not yet seem to have succeeded in building up a professional army cut off from the rest of the nation, and everything indicates that it will not succeed in doing so.

And if it is hard to imagine French soldiers going out to fight the English, the idea of a battle between French and Americans under Laval's orders is nothing less than fantastic. For the first time in history would Frenchmen fire upon Americans in order to prevent them from loosing the bonds of France? The only men who would hurl themselves into such a combat would be the "legionnaires" of the inner set, that is, the imperial guard of the régime, men recruited among the most fanatical elements of the counter-revolution, the men who, on the day when Anglo-American victory looms, would have the task of protecting Pétain, Laval & Co. from French vengeance.

Now we come to the puzzling side of the new Cabinet set-up. What is the true relation betwen Darlan, commander of the military forces, and Laval? In comparison to Laval, Darlan is a mere amateur in politics. His personality must be explained in terms of vanity and opportunism. His hatred of everything English is only a case in point. Darlan's position, to the extent that he opposes Laval and that Laval has the support of the Nazis, is equivocal. To keep his fleet whole and afloat, to avoid its dismantlement, which the Germans can require under the terms of the armistice, Darlan had to enlist the personal good-will of the conqueror. How could he afford any resistance to Laval—the protégé of Hitler— without laying his ships open to reprisal?

But from a broader point of view, and looking more deeply into things, the French people's reaction to Laval's criminal undertakings will not be determined by this or that part of the army or navy, by any general or admiral. Whatever Laval and his henchmen in the Ministry of Information may think, there is always a powerful and uncrushable popular feeling, even in the suffering and oppressed nations, among which the phrase "public opinion" no longer has much meaning. And for Laval, such a feeling is perhaps more to be feared, for it has the spontaneity and persistence of nature itself.

The killing of German soldiers, the execution of hostages, the sickening prostration of the multitude—from such things emerge political impossibilities which Laval himself, however much he has been won to the German cause, can never fathom. No matter what his heart's desire, Laval would not dare, on the day the news goes out that the Germans have massacred a thousand Frenchmen, to order French soldiers to kill English. And if—something not at all beyond the range of possibility—Frenchmen, determined to strike at "collaboration," started to raise their arms not against German soldiers wandering the streets by night but against the men of

Vichy, the "head of the government" would lose much of his
boldness.

Laval, as ridden with superstitions as any Calabrian or Sicilian,
believes that because Colette missed his aim he has paid his debt
to the evil destiny threatening dictators, that now he is quits and
that he will be spared a sudden death. But his opinion in this
matter can easily suffer a sudden change.

Again Liberty, Equality, Fraternity

by D. W. Brogan

LONDON

ALL DISCUSSION of the future of France should begin by reaffirmation of the basic fact that even before all France was formally occupied, France as a territory, as a tradition, as a national group, was occupied—completely occupied in Paris and Dijon, imperfectly occupied in Lyons and Marseille. France was the greatest, the most famous, the richest prize of the Herrenvolk. For their own reasons the Germans permitted some liberty of action to the government of Vichy. But the brutal fact remained, incapable of denial, hard even to camouflage: when the Germans wanted to take over Vichy they could do it in a day. And when their hands were free, when the victory they counted on was at last secured, all French assets would be at the disposal of the victor who could have no more to fear than at worst a desperate and hopeless "point of honor" resistance in the French Empire.

Under the open or disguised yoke France has changed. But the direction of the change can only be inferred, can only be estimated, in most general terms. The years 1940, 1941 and 1942 probably have been the most important in the history of France since the

From the *New York Times Magazine,* February 14, 1943, copyright © 1943, 1971 by The New York Times Company.

Revolution. The "revolutions" that followed the Revolution were minor adjustments of political forms. They were not unimportant, but they did nothing to alter the social, cultural, religious and political settlement of the Revolution and the first Napoleon. No fundamental changes cutting down into the quick of the national life were made; they were hardly even attempted.

France in 1939 as in 1919 was a country deeply divided, but tolerating divisions. In 1939, it is true, the violence of the divisions was more openly expressed than in 1919. No government in the previous twenty years had been powerful enough to suppress for more than brief periods the extreme parties on the Left and on the Right. Old-fashioned Republicans asserted that the Republic was strong enough to disregard the froth; to ignore Doriot and Daudet, Thorez and Taittinger. Below, the still waters of republican loyalty ran deep, especially in the provinces neglected by Paris correspondents and foreign critics.

The confidence of old-fashioned leaders in the electoral fidelity of the provinces was justified enough. Fascism and communism alike seemed much less formidable in the Corrèze or the Cantal than they did in Billancourt or Passy. But the political immobility of the provinces was proof of a deeper immobility. In a world in flux the necessity of adaptation was stoutly denied by the normal leaders of the French countryside. And they were the political rulers of France.

It was not a peculiarly French fault to refuse to see that the old order was going to be changed if it did not change itself. But the error had immediate and disastrous fruits in France—defeat, surrender, loss of national independence.

After the disasters of 1870 Daumier drew a picture of a peasant, who had voted in the plebiscite of that year for Napoleon III, contemplating the ruins of his house, burned by the Germans, and saying, "I did not vote for that." The French peasant, the French townsman in 1940 had the same natural revulsion. He had not voted for the third and even more terrible invasion.

In the disaster of June, 1940, all but the strongest minds were torn from their anchorage. And the granting to Pétain of full powers by the Parliament of the Republic was certainly the expression of the public will or, at any rate, of the public despair. Had other leaders than the Marshal been in power, had other centers of public trust survived, a policy of resistance in the empire might have carried the day. France, like all the other occupied countries from Norway to Greece, might have pinned her hopes on a British victory which would ultimately deliver Europe from the monster. But the slow dissipation of the political authority of the French State was now complete and there was no national figure to set against the Marshal, no obvious alternative policy to set against that "honorable peace" between soldiers which the Marshal hoped would be possible.

The Vichy regime was faced with a task of immense difficulty; indeed, of insuperable difficulty. That it was difficult was admitted; more, it was stressed; that it was insuperable was naturally concealed. On the one hand, there was the material problem of restoring French life, profoundly disorganized by the invasion; on the other, there was the moral and political problem of creating a new State form. Indeed, only a more vigorous State organization could possibly cope with the problems presented by the collapse of 1940.

This was the primary justification of the "Vichy Revolution" for entrusting all powers to one man. France needed revolution—profound reorganization. For the moment the vested interests of the old political order were powerless. The French people had not voted for that.

The solution of the material problem was only impossible because of the German occupation and the continuance of the war. But that only illustrates the basic miscalculation of the founders of the Vichy regime. For the war could only end quickly by a German victory over England—after which the destiny of France would be decided by non-French hands; or the war would go on and Vichy would be more involved in the necessities of German strategy, political and economic as well as military. It was a total war and it was a naive mistake to think defeated France could make it a limited war—as far as she was concerned. Germany and England, the two main belligerents in 1940, learned that lesson which Russia and the United States learned later. And France was not even the sorcerer's apprentice but the prisoner of the sorcerer's apprentice.

The solution of the political problem was impossible for even deeper reasons. In the collapse of the parliamentary system the men of Vichy turned, as was natural, to the existing bureaucracy, to the existing hierarchies (the political alone excepted). The political personnel was discredited and, in any case, the victor could not permit the reconstruction of a democratic regime, discredited or not.

So Vichy had to be "reactionary." It had to turn (even if we abstract from the account) the natural prejudices of the marshal and his closest associates to the "notables," to the upper class economically, politically and socially. And that meant that it had to turn to the sections of French society which for a century past have lost every political battle they have waged as soon as they have antagonized the "people," the mass of Frenchmen and Frenchwomen in town and country, the workers, peasants, petits bourgeois or such proletarians as France possesses.

It was a wise British Ambassador who declared, after long experience of France, that he had only to listen to what his fellowmembers in smart Paris clubs said and bet on the other side. They are never right. Ideas, doctrines, recipes for political cookery that have come from the Right, from Maistre to Maurras, have been mere obstructions. They have not been effective programs.

In default of the odious energy that the Paris-Nazified demagogues possessed, and possess, the men of Vichy, the more honest, patriotic and intelligent of them (and there were many in Vichy entitled to one of these epithets, if not many who deserved all of them) could, but for one handicap, have tapped that great reservoir of national feeling from which Hitler, Mussolini, Stalin and Churchill have drawn the strongest ingredients of their power. Vichy could have stressed that "All is not lost; the unconquerable will."

But the whole policy of the armistice, or the refusal to carry on resistance in Africa, in so far as it had other basis than the conviction that England must soon surrender too, was based on the conviction that France could not afford more heroism or heroics; the Gambettas, Dantons and Clemenceaus were outmoded. In any case it was evident that the Germans would not permit any defiant policy, any cultivation of "the study of revenge, immortal hate."

So Vichy was reduced to mere expedients or bogus gestures of energy. Its edicts were often well designed, often dealt with real weaknesses, real evils. But even when the proposed remedies were not (like the restoration of the old provinces) mere antiquarianism or window-dressing, the material and the moral means of carrying them out was lacking.

For Vichy had to be silent on the basic fact of French life. In the last war Clemenceau hammered on the theme "Les Allemands sont à Noyon." Pétain, Darlan and their collaborators had to keep silence on the fact that this time the Germans were at Strasbourg, Little Paris, Nantes, even though such outrages as the expulsion of loyal Alsatians or the murder of the Nantes hostages were events crying out at least for comment.

Because France was the greatest prize of the German war, the wealth of the country was not available for an economic restoration. Because France was all conquered and two-thirds occupied the moral power of a national insurrection could not be used—and Vichy had no other resources to draw on. The professional loyalty of army officers or of the navy, the discipline of civil servants, the claque provided by an enslaved press and radio were no substitute for a real movement of national resurgence that could only be directed against Germany.

In vain Darlan, Maurras, Cardinal Baudrillart and lesser scribes and pharisees tried to make the English and the Jews and the Russians serve as target for the hatred, self-criticism and bitter pride of the French people. Within a few months of the establishment of the new regime it was manifest that, with the facts so undeniable, you cannot deceive all the people all the time. Not that way lay the resurrection of France in a Europe that had seen the heroism of Greece and was soon to see in the blunting of the German sword on Russia's armor a light from the East.

As each month passed, as the prudential calculations of the armistice policy seemed more and more doubtful wisdom, the Germans accelerated the speed of French evolution. Inside France they were no longer "correct." Despite Vichy-inspired attacks on the British blockade, the French people knew why cold, hunger and disease gripped the pleasant land of France. As the Germans were forced to greater and greater efforts, they were forced to squeeze from France more and more ruthlessly the last resources, human and material.

French reaction provoked reprisals. There is now blood between the occupying army and the French people—and between the French people and the political allies, present and recent, of the Germans.

It is no wonder then that there is evidence of a revival of faith in the republic—not in the parliamentary machinery of the old regime but in the ideals of liberty, equality and fraternity which the old order so imperfectly embodied, but which, unlike the drab Etat Français, it did not deny. There is even a turn to the more dignified and respectable of the old political leaders, most of them now in prison. In so far as Pétain's system was accepted in 1940, it was not accepted for this enslavement of France to Germany.

And if Germany had a choice of winning or alienating France in 1940, she has none now. She must plunder and oppress. The consequence is not merely that resistance is stimulated but that the social revolution is carried on. Inflation is completing what the earlier inflation began, the ruin of the rentier—and how much of the stability and conservatism of France was due to the rentier! Bankruptcy seems inevitable.

Then, the Germany policy has accentuated the division between the industrial North and the rural South. It is the occupied North that has been most openly "Gaullist." In liberated France the old political predominance of the South will not have its old institutional basis. And France badly needs a reconstruction that will enable her to acquire that industrial power without which she cannot be a powerful nation again. So much will have to be done to rebuild from the foundations and even to alter some of the traditional ground plan that a new French revolution will be imposed by the nature of things. Another year of German exploitation and few in France will have much to lose but their chains.

It is a fact on which moralizing is unnecessary that the French directing classes and the officially recognized "élites" have been more deeply compromised by collaboration than any other groups. For it is the function of leaders to lead. Whatever the wisdom of their policies since 1940, the old élites have inevitably dissipated the only effective emotional asset they had to set against the dominant French revolutionary tradition, the asset of being par excellence the custodians of the national interests and the national honor. Ruling classes are pitilessly judged. And what can these rulers say to a passionate reviving French national spirit? What can they say to a Europe whose enslavement for two years they observed—at best—in silence?

Once liberated from the German bonds the purging of France from the taint of Vichy's compliance will seem to be, and will be, a necessary national act of purification. No free France in a free Europe will be possible on any other terms. For at times the only alternative to indicting a nation is to indict its rulers. The French people by their acts have indicted theirs.

In a Europe tainted with fascism, with racism, with inequality, France could be at best a feeble plagiarist, a servile imitator. France must be a trusted friend to her neighbors who have, like her, endured and resisted German tyranny. Those elements in French society that with varying degrees of guilt shared in policy of nonresistance to the enemy will be excluded from the construction of a new France which has been made more easy as well as absolutely necessary by the German tide.

That some of the men so excluded were guilty of no more than human weakness is true; that others may by later services redeem their past errors and even crimes also is true.

But historical necessity is under no obligation to be just. Inevitably, elements in France, mainly the working classes of the industrial and occupied North who have been the backbone of resistance to the Germans, and the men outside France who have made it true that some representatives of France have never been absent from the battle will provide the initial leaders in this remaking of France.

Whether they will remain leaders no man can say or even guess. But it is not a guess to say that Vichy cannot be salvaged and given new life in Africa—or in a liberated France. No man or group of men, no power or group of powers can force the marriage of a free France with a counter-revolution that is now in its last agony. They can but increase the chances of a civil war that can have only one possible issue.

Inside France:
The Conquered Stir

by André Philip

FOR MORE THAN two years France has been under the Nazi heel. During that period the Germans have been in control of the press and radio and maintained a strict censorship on all outgoing mail. There is, as a result, an almost complete blackout of information on developments inside France, particularly on the evolution of public opinion in that country.

Having only recently escaped from France to England I am able to provide something of an insider's view of what the people are thinking in my country today, how their spirits have gradually changed from deep despair to faith in ultimate Allied victory.

In the beginning morale was terrible. The Vichy people—and this is their unforgivable sin—not only yielded to German military force but also accepted defeat and capitulation. They gave to it moral acknowledgment. Immediately after the armistice Marshal Pétain spoke of the defeat as necessary punishment for our sins. Newspapers, among them infamous Gringoire, declared openly that France was guilty of having taken the initiative in a war against poor, innocent Hitler. They declared that responsibility both for the war and the defeat rested on the shoulders of the working class,

From the *New York Times Magazine,* November 1, 1942, copyright © 1942, 1970 by The New York Times Company.

on the spirit of democracy of the great writers, the intellectuals and the spiritual leaders of our country.

All this produced a moral vacuum. France was knocked down and remained so for many months before beginning to recover. The military defeat, which, as we know today, was the result of the incompetence of our military leadership and the skillful work of a fifth column, came at the time as a complete shock to every one of us. The nation was scattered on the roads of the country. Administrative and industrial leaders had fled before the enemy and the people were left without guidance, without the élite to whom they used to look for leadership.

Add to this the personal prestige of Marshal Pétain, hero of Verdun, among many soldiers of the First World War, and the general feeling of chaos, and you will understand that the majority of the people simply thought in this fashion: "All this is too complicated. We don't understand anything any more. Let us have confidence in the great-grandfather who has taken charge of his children." (By the way, it is typical of France that the only type of dictator she would accept was the great-grandfather.)

"Let us believe that he is really for resistance, that he is lying to the Germans, double-crossing them in order to gain time to fight again if some day a miracle makes that possible."

Already at that time the first organization of resistance had been formed in Paris in the occupied zone and it gradually spread to what Parisians called with contempt "the Nono Zone." Its members came from different social groups, among which the most important were the working class (trade unions and Socialist groups), intellectuals and religious bodies.

The working class first: Here you find the greatest support of the resistance movement. With the treachery of René Belin, who became Pétain's Minister of Labor and dissolved the Federation of Labor, a hard blow was struck at the labor movement. The Trade Union Council, however, although strictly forbidden by a new law, remained strong and became the nucleus of our first group. Unity was realized between Socialists and Christian trade unions and it was they who began publication of our papers and organized massed demonstrations.

It is quite a symbol that just when the official Nationalists, who before were always inflamed against Germany, asking for her partition into small States, suddenly turned collaborationists the so-called Internationalist workers became on the other hand a bulwark of resistance; but it is quite logical. Men who believe only in force abuse it when they get it, become slaves when they are weak. Those who believe in justice give it to others when they are strong and fight stubbornly to get it when they are defeated.

Beside the working class you find the French intellectuals: On the whole they have behaved well. I do not speak, of course, of members of the French Academy living in the corrupted circles of high society without contact with the people, but of the really great French writers and also of the whole university body. French professors have carried on their lectures with independence and courage, refusing to obey the orders of Vichy and, I may state from personal experience, that until recently it was quite possible for a professor to mention in his lecture anything he desired without any one's reporting it to the Vichy administration.

As to religious groups: If official leaders of the church have been very cautious and noncommital, the rank and file, particularly laymen and humble clergymen, have been quite outspoken against Nazi rule and the autocratic methods of Vichy. I have heard from many pulpits striking condemnation of anti-Semitism and totalitarianism.

This merging in resistance groups of Socialists and trade unionists with liberals and Christian intellectuals who formerly were so opposed to one another is of utmost importance for the future reconstruction of our country, and it is in the presence of the religious element which has given our group one of its most important characteristics.

When we began work most of us did not believe in the possibility of victory. We admired General de Gaulle as a great spiritual leader but thought of him as a Bayard who fought to the end without hope rather than accept surrender. We did resist because nothing else was possible if we wanted to be faithful to the eternal values of our civilization. We believed that freedom and liberty are the supreme reality, that nothing is greater than respect for human dignity and individual responsibility—that it was better to die than to deny this.

We believed that ten tons of material reality do not make an ounce of verity; that possession of 5,000 tanks is not enough to change a lie into the truth, and this had to be told publicly, no matter what the result.

This attitude represented for us a great force. It meant that resistance does not depend upon success, that having spiritual roots it remains the same through the ups and downs of battle, independent of the results of our activity.

And the fact is, we did succeed. Our papers were read by more people; around each paper (Combat, Libération, Franc-Tireur, Coq Enchaîné, Le Père Duchesne and Le Populaire in the unoccupied zone; Libération, 1793, La Voix du Nord, La Quatrième République in the occupied zone) strong movements were built, the groups acting independently at first, then getting together through coordinating committees. They published in addition to their regular papers thousands of leaflets and began to organize public demonstrations like those of the First of May and the Fourteenth of July, when tens of thousands of people went out into the streets shouting, "Down with Laval" and "Vive de Gaulle."

Today our movements are growing strong. Two of the most important groups, Libération and Combat, have many thousands of members strongly organized and their papers are published every week with a circulation of 25,000 to 30,000 copies, which is quite important when one considers that every number is read by eighteen to twenty people.

Since the beginning of 1942 the prestige of Marshal Pétain has been gradually but steadily declining, for various reasons. First, with the return of the hope of victory more and more people began to think for themselves. What did they see? An incompetent administration unable to handle the food question or distribute properly the little that was left after the Germans' plunder; a foreign policy yielding more and more to the enemy, submitting French industrial life to Nazi rule and making French people suffer, work and die for Germany; the big trial at Riom, the only result of which was to enhance the prestige of the accused and demonstrate the real, big, personal responsibility of Pétain himself as well as the unpreparedness of our armies.

Finally, they saw the return of Laval, most hated and despised man in France, coming back to sell our manpower to Germany and introduce in "the Nono Zone" barbaric Nazi methods of dealing with the people.

Today Pétain's prestige is dead. Ninety per cent in the unoccupied zone follow General de Gaulle. They recognize him as their military and political leader and, for the time being, as the only legitimate representative of France.

This attitude is quite new; our resistance movements at the beginning hailed General de Gaulle as spiritual and military leader, but wanted to remain politically independent of what we called "the London people." Our opinions changed gradually, mainly for four reasons:

First, "the London people" have shown that they are just plain, free Frenchmen with free minds and free speech who defend on every occasion the permanent interests of our country even at the price of some discussion with our best friends; this independence has been the greatest cause of General de Gaulle's increasing prestige.

Second, in France there have been between the different groups some competition and conflict; there also have been attempts by military and political adventurers to put their hands on the movements in order to use them for their own purpose, sometimes by agreement with Vichy; the only way to avoid that appeared to be direct allegiance to General de Gaulle.

Third, psychologically also our attitude has changed. At the beginning we were full of sympathy for England and the United States, hoping that they would win the war and return to us on a platter our lost liberties. We soon realized, however, that if we wanted to rebuild something in France tomorrow and recover our lost honor, our country must re-enter the war in order to win back her liberty through her own efforts.

At the same time we realized that we had been becoming strong enough in our underground work to do something more than merely publish papers and organize mass demonstrations. We can become an army of the interior, ready to strike on the day a second front is opened; but for that we must be organized on a military basis, must receive from General de Gaulle's headquarters the necessary directives relative to the Allied Nations' strategic planning. It means that Free France and Captive France are unified in General de Gaulle's Fighting France movement.

Finally, we realized that when Germany collapses the situation in France will be tragic. The men of Vichy have been responsible for so many abuses, have been accumulating so much hate that, the day when Germany no longer is there to protect them, they will be murdered all over the country. The only way to avoid that is to have immediately a government strong enough to keep the people in order and give them assurance that the traitors will be prosecuted with due process of law.

Such a government cannot emerge from the former Parliament, which has lost face by surrender to Pétain; it cannot emerge from any former political leaders whose names have been associated with defeat and who have lost all political influence in a country which wants a new republic. It cannot emerge out of the resistance movements alone, which, if they were to form a government would immediately become divided into different factions and lose all their fighting power.

Here again there is no other possibility than a government with General de Gaulle at the head choosing its collaborators among the great economic and social powers of the country and representatives of the resistance movements. This can only be a temporary power lasting until the election of a National Assembly which with complete independence will choose the Constitution of the Fourth Republic.

In the meantime General de Gaulle remains for all of us the legitimate representative of France, the present incarnation of our lost liberties.

The New French Revolution

by Harold Callender

PARIS

A WAITER IN THE most conventional of tail coats gracefully poured
wine into a glass. It was Château Latour 1938. One of the dis-
coveries of the liberation period is that this was a fair wine year.
Napery and silver were as choice as they had been under that roof
in the time of the Third Republic or Second Empire. The waiter's
movements were framed against the rich browns and blues of
Aubusson tapestry hanging on the wall behind. By a slight dis-
placement, one's eye fell upon a smooth green lawn and sym-
metrically placed trees seen through a huge plate-glass window
of an eighteenth-century mansion. One might have imagined that
nothing much changed in France, or that "plus ça change plus c'est
la même chose." (The more it changes, the more it is the same
thing.)

But a girl opposite was telling, while the level of the Mèdoc rose
in glass after glass, how her father had been captured and tortured to death by Germans because he was a Resistance leader.
As the waiter discreetly offered excellent Armagnac, a young man
on my right described how he escaped madness when in solitary

From the *New York Times Magazine*, October 29, 1944, copyright ©
1944 by The New York Times Company.

confinement by pacing diagonally from corner to corner of his cell while he composed a series of sonnets without pencil or paper. He was one of the many intellectuals who joined up with the workers to form the Resistance movement, and came out of it a changed man.

The setting in which we conversed seemed to carry one's mind back to the eighteenth century. But the stories my French friends told harked back to the worst periods of the Middle Ages, or even of barbarism. Yet these youths who had fought and suffered had faces turned to the future in a more hopeful mood than that of French intellectuals since the year 1870, at least.

The mentality of France today cannot be understood unless one begins to examine it by studying the Resistance movement—all of it—including university men who forsook their studies to slink up on Germans in the darkness or plant dynamite beneath trains, factory workers who skillfully bootlegged machine-guns, youths who fled to the Maquis and lived a gangster existence. Like the great French Revolution, this one had its encyclopaedists and its tough guys. It could have dispensed with neither.

In the intimacy of darkness and common peril the two groups became acquainted and got on together. The intellectuals grew tough, while the toughs were at least somewhat affected by what may be called the ideology of Resistance. Especially in France must men have an idea to justify fighting and dying. Out of privation, struggle, destruction and death there has arisen something greater than liberation or victory—something which in the minds of these tried and tested youths lends additional significance to those words.

The French often say that those who have not been under the heel of the Germans cannot conceive of what it was like. Many fail, at any rate, fully to understand that what the French were fighting was not only German power. It was the Vichy regime, which to them stood for something even worse—French acquiescence and participation in the German oppression of Frenchmen. The people of the Resistance were fighting against this national shame, as they call it. Also they were fighting against the humiliation of defeat in 1940. Thus they fought to regain for France her self-respect and pride as a nation. They have washed out the stain of defeat with their blood, and every Frenchman holds his head higher in consequence.

But behind the defeat which let the Germans into France, and behind Vichy which played their game, was something else—the defective political and social system which the Encyclopaedists of Resistance hold to have been ultimately responsible for France's downfall and for the suffering which it entailed.

It was inevitable, therefore, that in the cells and torture chambers where the Gestapo and its French agents put captured patriots, in the secret cellars where the faithful met and plotted as Christians met in the catacombs, in caves and camps of the Maquis, there germinated and grew what I have called an ideology of Resistance—a social philosophy which sought to take account of the causes of France's ordeal and to insure against their recurrence. Consequently, for these men liberation is not merely the negative achievement of getting rid of the Germans. It has more positive, and indeed revolutionary, implications. Liberation is to be a new chapter in French history, introducing, perhaps, a new French social structure, or at least one greatly changed and economically democratized.

Since coming to Paris a few days after the departure of the Germans, this correspondent has met many Resistance veterans from the President of the National Resistance Council to the boys who have matured in the underground struggle. Some of these are Catholics, others are without religion. Some are conservatives, others are Communists. But on this point all agree—that democratic capitalism as France knew it in the years before her downfall must never be restored.

Emerson wrote that in the New England of his time nearly everybody carried a design for Utopia in his vest pocket. One is reminded of this remark by what one sees in France today. Nearly every Resistance organization has a program for restoring to the French people control over their economic life and consequently over the physical sources of their national strength.

These programs have been neatly embraced, necessarily in generalized terms, in a plan adopted by the National Council of Resistance on March 15 last. A direct reflection of them is seen in the Government's action in taking over control of the coal mines and in Gen. Charles de Gaulle's speech at Lille, urging a planned economy under the supervision of the State.

The direction in which France is moving seems clearly marked. But her precise path remains to be determined. Between various groups there are differences of what the French call nuance. But often a French nuance assumes the proportions of the Grand Canyon.

Far more noteworthy than an agreement upon the need of social changes is the new sense of virility and confidence that animates the French, or, at least, these youths emerging from darkness and the Battle of Resistance. The feeling of weakness and frustration so conspicuous among intellectuals and university youths in the Nineteen Thirties, and the paralyzing pessimism over the future of France and democracy which caused so many bright youngsters to turn Fascist, seem to have been washed out, as the humiliation of defeat was washed out, by the ordeal and struggle from which the French have emerged.

The French, as represented by this élite that has gone through the fires of struggle, have acquired a new sense of their country, a new devotion to it, a new confidence in its destiny. It is as if the trace of degeneracy which had stained the French society of the Third Republic had been removed by a surgical operation.

Many now contend, as François Mauriac puts it, that "the former ruling classes now accept willy-nilly the Socialist experiment," which France seems destined to undertake as a new test of democracy.

It is probably difficult for Americans to appreciate the French aversion to their pre-war capitalism. Let it be noted that this French capitalism was very different from its American counterpart in that it did not bring to the working class anything like our standard of well-being, nor did it provide the State with anything like our industrial equipment for peace and war. Above all, it failed to unite France socially or to see her through a war; some say that it led her to defeat.

In this new French mood, suggestive in many ways of the utopian spirit of the seventeenth and eighteenth centuries, when human perfectibility seemed a natural assumption, one finds an older France. A passion for legality and order exists side by side with potent revolutionary impulses. The individualism of the past seems to have accommodated itself more or less to the hope or acceptance of socialism in the future. A proud nationalism to which the wartime traces of a new and also of an old struggle has contributed does not exclude a sense of the limitation of even France's renewed national strength or recognition of the need of powerful allies in building a less illusory peace.

Giving full weight to whatever qualifications may be imposed by judicious cynicism, there is a new spirit abroad in France. There is a new élite coming to the fore which is far younger than the elderly statesmen dominant in the Third Republic, and if less experienced, this élite is also less resigned to the evils and inequalities of the past. It is fired by faith in the future of the country which they have saved from defeat and humiliation.

To many Americans, as to this writer, France will seem little changed. Décor is still here, as in that room with the Aubussons and the Château Latour and the sedate lawn. But as familiar wine trickles into familiar glasses in a familiar Old World setting, I shall never quite forget those who sat there with me or the new France which is their vision and their aim.

In What Direction Will France Go?

by D. W. Brogan

"THE LAST TIME I saw Paris" before the catastrophe was a lovely late spring evening of 1939. I went with an old French friend of mine up to the terrace in front of the Sacré Coeur and we looked down on the great spectacle, guessing with melancholy resignation how much of it would survive the coming war. All of it, or almost all of it, has survived, and this is the first thing that strikes a visitor who has spent most of the war in London.

But apart from the old, tempting and dangerous error of confusing Paris with France, even first appearances are very soon seen to be deceptive. Those first appearances are of course very striking.

Paris, the Paris of the Grands Boulevards, of the Rue Royale, is more like New York than London is. London, which normally looks all right to me, suddenly seemed to my memory shabby in the Paris of 1945, as it had seemed shabby in the New York of 1944. I came quickly to understand the odd impression that Paris must make on the visiting British or American soldier—an impression of ease, beauty, extravagance, almost immunity.

No more than New York does Paris give to the casual visitor the

From the *New York Times Magazine,* August 26, 1945, copyright © 1945 by The New York Times Company.

impression of being the chief city of a state that has been deeply involved in war. Still less does it give the impression of being the capital of a state whose political and economic future is the subject of bitter disputes and of conflicts of faith and skepticism.

Yet the moment you begin to move among French people the first impression peels off. There you find the nerves, the hopes and fears, the fatigue, the results of privations and still more the results of fears.

"We forget all the time," said a very competent French observer and actor. "We forget that the war and the liberation solved no old problems. It solved the new ones—we escaped being enslaved by the Germans. But all the old problems remained, made worse and more difficult by the occupation, by Vichy and by the material cost of liberation."

There is a deep truth in this and there is another truth to be noted. Liberation acquired during the German occupation a magical quality. It was like a party in the prophetic imagination of a child, like marriage and living happily ever afterward in an old-fashioned novel.

Just as no party or no marriage quite lives up to the publicity, liberation was bound to be a disappointment. People still recall with a touching nostalgia the magical days of August, 1944, the miracle of the rising of Paris, of the arrival of Leclerc's division, of the sudden transformation scene that made the captives captors. I have talked with several of the leading actors in this drama—romantic beyond the dreams of Hollywood—and in their voices and in the voices of many others there has been something of the inflection: "Bliss was it in that dawn to be alive."

I can remember in London at that moment how a friend of mine, active in the Resistance, got a message from a friend in Paris who had the chance to take part in the crowning of all their efforts, a message couched perhaps unconsciously in the spirit of Henri IV's message to Biron: "How I pity you for not having been in it."

There was, and is, bound to be a reaction to a hangover. The liberation was a triumph, a memory that will fortify millions of French hearts, but it was not, as some naively thought, a solution for more than the expulsion of the Germans from Paris. And the evil that the Germans did lives after them, even though there is no good to be interred with their bones.

At the very center of the French problem there is this disillusionment of the Resistance movement with what it has been able to achieve and with France herself. That disillusionment is creditable. noble, natural—dangerous. We should never forget that it was the Germans who decided to run France through Vichy; all that Pétain and Laval had freedom to choose was to play ball with the Germans; the rules of the game were decided by the Germans. That policy may have been from the German point of view a mistake in the long run; we won't know the answer to that for a long time.

It was the decision of some hundreds of thousands of individuals which first of all upset the German dream of profiting by a generally accepted government and then forced the Germans to abandon their tactics of "correctness" and show the French the real nature of the Third Reich.

The men and women who made that decision made it under conditions of terror of which nobody in America or England has any real conception, conditions in which so many fates were much worse than death, conditions in which entry into the underground called for rare and difficult combinations of virtue and character.

A man or a woman, a married couple, for instance, who made such a decision, burned their boats in a fashion that gave and gives them the force of conviction and something of the rigorous intolerance of men and women "converted" in the evangelical sense.

And these men and women are at the moment claimants to be a new governing class. Still more are they the apostles of a program for a France "dure et pure." The remedies they want their country to swallow are drastic and unpleasant and the patient shows some reluctance to take the dose. Humanly speaking, the impatience of the Resistance and the hesitation of the country are easily and not discreditably explicable, but they certainly add to the sense of unease.

There is nothing new in the organizing of a revolutionary government by a minority of eager, arrogant, bold, righteous and even self-righteous people. Some of the Resistance complaints about the apathy of many millions of French people are easily paralleled in the recorded opinions of Sam and John Adams. But the problems facing the leaders of the American Revolution were simple compared with those facing the present and any future rulers of France.

At the basis of the French disquiet, at the basis of the anxiety of the Resistance, is the realization that the future of France as a great power, as a modern society, is at stake. Victory in 1918 was bought so dearly that even before 1939 disillusionment with mere victory was widespread.

But whatever illusions were still held in 1939 about the slow but adequate adaptation of France to the needs of the modern world, they cannot be held now. France, still further impoverished by this new ordeal, can only recover by doing much more than recover, by breaking down in one way or another that paralysis of production that was so serious a symptom between the two wars.

The degree to which France was living on her assets, on the national patrimony, has been dramatically revealed now that so much of the patrimony has been stolen by the Germans. Twenty years ago André Siegfried told us that the modern world had to choose between Gandhi and Henry Ford; what most of many French friends tell me is that the choice must be Ford, that the religion of production must be engrafted on the French religion of thrift and individual skill and artistry.

But—and here is the dilemma—is it to be production in the manner of Henry Ford—that is, in the American fashion—or is it to be production in the Russian fashion? For, although it is in fact American production that is the visible miracle dazzling French eyes (and to some extent German production as seen by the prisoners), it is Russian production that provides the myth.

With all the will, the skill and the unity in the world, French recovery can only be slow without a shot in the arm, a blood transfusion from a richer society. And there is only one such society now, the United States, with possibly in a few years' time the auxiliary help of Britain.

But the vocal sections of French opinion which are most convinced of the necessity of a general transformation of French life on the economic plane are in general suspicious of, or openly hostile, to American "capitalism." It is not only the fear of economic exploitation that animates all debtors today, but something more doctrinaire and ideological. There is available a recipe for organization—"planning." The word is magical in France today. And Russia is the home of planning.

Of course, the campaign for Russian methods is not totally spontaneous. It is fostered by the French Communist party, totally devoted to Russian interests by passions—and its own interests. Moreover, the plugging of Russia frees French Communists from the necessity of defending their own role between 1939 and 1941. They cannot applaud General de Gaulle when he recalls the French declaration of war in 1939; they cannot celebrate the official birthday of the Resistance—the appeal from London on June 18, 1940.

It is wiser to insist on Stalingrad and on their own sufferings and achievements in the Resistance, after the invasion of Russia had made their ambiguous attitude toward the "imperialist war" obsolete. Their martyrs cover a good deal and the memory of Gabriel Péri's death stills speculation as to the activities of surviving leaders. But Russia is the trump card.

This is worth noting, since the Communists are now the most numerous, the best disciplined and the most active party in France. To look at the delegates at their congress of 1945 (the first since 1937; party democracy is intermittent in the "people's party") was to get an impression of a true mass party with deep roots— something very different from the English or American Communist parties. Here are real, vigorous and not very scrupulous candidates for the job of governing France.

But despite their widespread system of locals, despite the traditional provincial costumes of some female delegates, despite the exploitation of the grievances of fishermen and farm laborers, the French Communist party is the party of the cities and of the industrial workers in the great mass-production plants, in the mines and on the railroads.

However, if it were only that, it could not become by any normal democratic process a government, for the classes on which it draws for the bulk of its membership are still decidedly the minority classes in France. France was and is the European country in which the small business man—so small that he is hardly a business man at all—is a dominant factor in the economic life of the country.

It is not only a question of the peasant proprietor; there is also the small craftsman, the small shopkeeper, the small trader. According to Colin Clark's calculations, 33 per cent of French persons engaged in production were in family businesses or were "working proprietors." (Comparative figures for the United States were 25 per cent; Belgium, 20 per cent; Germany, 29 per cent, and Britain, 10 per cent.) France, that is to say, is largely inhabited and run by what, before they were liquidated, were called in Russia "Nepmen" and "Kulaks."

The country where Marxian concentration has reached its maximum is Britain, so the revolution ought to be imminent there. But despite the Labor victory, it isn't. Is it in France? Only if there is an economic *and* political breakdown at the same time. It must be remembered that in the Communist party itself are lots of Nepmen and Kulaks—either persons of the most unusual disinterestedness or, as is more probable, not very clearsighted people who "mean the other fellow." But a party doesn't need to have a clear-sighted rank and file to win.

The clear-sightedness is provided outside by the numerous allies or near allies of the Communists who face this dilemma. On the one hand, how can France be governed, be restored, without the collaboration of the leaders of the industrial workers, so important a body at any time, so decisively important a body today, with the needs of a reconstruction of industry paramount?

On the other hand, how can France be governed with the participation of a party with no political scruples, with a savage discipline that makes of its members in any government chartered spies for the party, and above all a party which in foreign affairs cannot have any policy that runs counter to the real or presumed wishes of the Russian Government?

The Communist members of a Cabinet cannot be really bound by any loyalty to their colleagues, the Communist leaders in the trade unions are no more bound, and had the Socialists accepted the Communist offer of union on the political front, they would have been swallowed—or if they resisted, would have become "social fascists" overnight as they have been before.

"France," said a very intelligent Socialist friend of mine, "is ungovernable"; and, were logic dominant in French life or in life generally, one would be inclined to agree. For it is easy to show that you cannot govern without the Communists and that you cannot govern with them. But as Mr. Dooley said of the divorce question: "In the Archey Road when a man and woman can't go on living together—they go on living together." And France may well be in this case the Archey Road rather than the home of logical consistency.

The constitutional controversy that now adds to French perplexities is in a sense the development of this fundamental question: Does France need and is she likely to get a revolution? She needs in a sense a revolution, but does she need a Revolution with a capital R? That question lies behind apparently academic disputes about the virtues of a single-chamber government, about a return to the old Constitution, about the rights and duties of a single Constituent Assembly.

The Communists, the Socialists and the Resistance groups, including the Catholic Democrats, are for a single Constituent Assembly to frame a new Constitution, but they are not agreed on what kind of Constitution is to be framed. The Communists have been playing their Jacobin card, complete with a parody of Citizenness Guillotine. It is possible they are overplaying the Jacobin card; that procession on July 14 recalling the good old days of 1793 is not going to be to the taste of millions of tired, worried, bewildered people in the small towns and in the countryside. A new "grande peur" might work against the Communists and against all the Left parties and destroy the hopes of a peaceful revolution or what General de Gaulle called a "renovation."

Some conservatives (many of them calling themselves, in the baffling French way, "radicals") already think so. Others more far-sighted think that since it is only by American help that the necessary lift upward and onward can be got, the delights of raising France by her own bootstraps will soon pall. And from a point of view in which economic prudence is all that matters, this last view is correct. But it is inadequate.

For, to go back to the beginning, the moral scars of the defeat and the occupation are as serious as the terrible destruction of Le Havre or Marseille. The shock given to the system of values by the invasion, by collaboration, by the failure of so much of the French élite to live up to its pretensions, remains.

The material resilience of the French people is one of the world's wonders. There are advantages, as well as disadvantages, in having a highly decentralized economic life that no one can really plan. A lot of people in France are probably minding their own business to their own profit at this moment—not necessarily to the nation's gain, but very often so.

But there is a danger that the French and their outside well-wishers (in Britain we have good selfish reasons for wishing the French well) may take too much comfort from that thought. For a great deal of French economic life cannot, in fact, be restarted in that automatic way. What was already in 1939 the very serious lack of adequate investment—as apart from savings—remains a problem reflected in the meager capital equipment of French industry and indeed of French agriculture. Complacency, routine—these will be very expensive intellectual faults.

So, too, will be taking the political question too complacently. A return to the old order would be a shattering blow to the hopes of the younger and more energetic Frenchmen and Frenchwomen, hopes that the old routine would not be allowed to reassert itself.

One of the great troubles of France at the present moment comes from the lack of an adequate basis for the authority of the state. For different reasons it was one of the great troubles of the Third Republic. The "Republic" is a general and generous idea that inspires hundreds of thousands of a true élite. The Third Republic has none of that magic in its recent record.

The memory of the great days of construction of the First Republic will be more appealing if the Communists do not revive the superstition that the First Republic was the Terror, and nothing else. But no government in France has ever survived or, if it has survived, done much without strong support from the people, without a dose of that passionate faith that fights in the French mind with ironical resignation. Only a new birth of freedom, ordered freedom, but not a mere revival of old forms, can give the future Government of France that sense of mission and of a people's mandate without which no shot in the arm from the outside, however well meant, can do permanent good.

I think it very unlikely that a genuinely democratic government in France could go in for total planning. But a genuinely democratic government would have sources of energy and faith at its disposal that mere technical proficiency cannot command. "Le peuple souverain s'avance" is the effective political text of the moment. And in what direction do they advance?

That, I—like all the world—can only guess at. But I do not think it will be a simple, dutiful pilgrimage to Moscow or a repentant return to Detroit. France cannot again know the greatness of size which was hers a hundred years ago. But she can use the good produced by that evil thing, the German occupation, to attack not only the gross evils bred by the occupation but older pre-German habits of postponement of decisions which must be taken if France is to survive as a great nation in any contemporary sense.

Part **3**

THE FOURTH
REPUBLIC

Tragic "Circus"— France's Parliament

by Jacques Fauvet

PARIS

ON THE BANKS of the Seine stands a vast building in the Greek style, a kind of Parthenon, blackened by the smoke of Paris. Passing in front of this monument, nine Frenchmen out of ten exclaim: "That's the circus."

The "circus" is the Palais Bourbon. Built in 1728, since 1815 it has sheltered the Chamber of Deputies, renamed in 1945 the National Assembly. It faces the Pont de la Concorde, a magnificent site, but a famous paradox. In spite of its name, this bridge has already witnessed three revolutions and numerous riots, the latest of which dates from only 1934.

In little more than two and a quarter centuries, the palace has seen the march past of four Republics, five kings, two Empires and —from 1940 to 1945—a French State. France's political history is a museum of defunct regimes, and there is every reason to believe that there are more to come.

Yet French Deputies do not deserve to be compared to clowns. In general, they are serious and, sometimes, courageous. One of them has remained famous. "Now," he cried, "you are about to see how a Deputy can die for 25 francs a day." That was in 1851, on the barricades, on a day of insurrection.

Today the Deputies are better paid. But their chamber still resembles a theatre. It is a semicircle with the stage—i. e., the rostrum—in the center, and, at the bottom of the tiers of seats, the Government, whose fate it is to be devoured. For if the Assembly recalls a circus, it is one in the Roman manner, in the days when wild animals were slaughtered there. Today it has become a place where Governments are put to death.

The French Parliament is composed of two chambers. The first is the National Assembly, numbering 595 Deputies. It is elected every five years by universal suffrage through proportional representation.

The number of Deputies from each of the six or seven existing parties is, in theory, in proportion to the number of votes the party obtains. But there has existed for the last six years the possibility of arranging *apparentements,* or local "marriages" of parties, which give several allied parties *all* the seats of a constituency if they have a majority of the votes. It was this system which made possible the reduction of Communist representation by one-third in the 1951 election.

The second chamber is the Council of the Republic, whose 320 members are called Senators. It is elected by delegates of the municipal councils of France and the overseas Territorial Assemblies. The electorial system is by majority, except in the seven most densely populated departments where it is proportional. The Senators can modify a law with the agreement of the Deputies, they can delay its passage, but they cannot veto it. Actually the Senators are important only once in every seven years—when they go into joint session with the Deputies to elect the President of the Republic.

It is, therefore, essentially the Deputies who make the laws, and they make a lot of them—more than 500 each year. A law is needed for everything in France. To create a marshal, as well as to increase the number of stallions in the national stud; to organize education, as well as to regulate the pressure in draft-beer apparatus. But before being passed in session, a bill must be examined in committee. There are fourteen of these, and they constitute fourteen little assemblies within the main one. When a bill emerges from this legislative mill, it bears little resemblance to its original form. It is mutilated, sometimes even destroyed. A law is no longer a law. It is 300 amendments, ten decrees, three administrative regulations. Even then, it is not necessarily put into operation. There was recently a case of a Deputy bringing in a bill to enforce a law already passed.

The Deputies also set up and overthrow Governments, and they overthrow them frequently. There have been more than 120 Governments since the Third Republic came into being in 1875. Their average length was six months. But the Deputies have no sense of guilt. In the first place, they know that the fall of a Government and a change of ministers are of little consequence. In actual fact, France is administered by high functionaries who, for their part, are permanent.

Secondly, the Deputies reckon that it is they in whom the power is really invested and who govern the country. Theirs is the Assembly system, inherited from the Convention, the Revolutionary Assembly of 1792, and completely different from the Cabinet systems of England or Germany. The Government does not rule; it gives effect to the decisions of Parliament; thus it can be dismissed like an unsatisfactory servant. In Léon Blum's opinion: "The Chamber governs just as much as the so-called Government." Maybe this conception is false, yet it has stood up against every political reverse, every defeat in war.

When a Government wants to escape from the tyranny of the Deputies, it often asks for "special powers" or "full powers." Sometimes it gets them for a definite period or a limited objective, though it does not always make use of them. It soon falls back under the almost daily supervision, suspicion and finicking, of the Deputies.

The Deputies, in fact, have the right to interpellate the Government at all times; it is enough that fifty of them demand a debate for it to be held, and for it to end in a vote of either confidence or censure of the Government.

The French Deputies do not like to recess; they prefer being able to keep an eye on the Government. So throughout the year, they remain in session for months on end, for many days each month and for long hours every day and night. This timetable—tiring enough for Deputies and ministers—is exhausting for the Premier.

Edgar Faure presided over his first Cabinet in 1952. "What makes Assembly rule intolerable to the head of a Government," he confided to someone shortly afterward, "is that the never-ending bout of catch-as-catch-can between him and almost 600 deputies is one-sided. The deputy organizes his life to suit himself; he can vote by proxy, dine and sleep when he likes. The President of the Cabinet is denied this relief." Governments often perish through physical exhaustion.

A minister is obliged to attend the Assembly's sessions whenever a question affecting his department is under discussion. The Premier, on the other hand, is obliged to be present at every debate of importance because, besides being the head of the Government, he is also the chief of the majority. This means he must always keep a lookout that the three, four or five parties on whom his majority depends are in agreement; he must conciliate the points of view—often at variance, sometimes even contradictory—of these parties, and must struggle, not so much against the opposition as against the individual or collective dissensions of his majority.

On their side, the Deputies are not obliged to be present even to vote. Their leaders can cast their ballots for them, except when the birth or death of a Government is at issue. Then they can be seen flocking in from every corner of France—of the world even, since there are fifty-two representatives from overseas, forty-one of them colored. When a Government is in difficulty, it may send a plane to Africa to fetch them, and they then vote for bills the greater part of which have nothing to do with their territory, but which can decide the fate of the Government. It is the African representatives who in this way arbitrate the quarrels of the parliamentarians of the mother country.

There are thirteen groups in the Assembly elected in 1956, but only two of them exercise discipline over their members: the Socialists and the Communists. The former number about 100 and the latter 150. These are two task forces which weigh heavily in Assembly battles. The other groups are less important and more divided. It is an unequal combat.

The Communist party has been excluded from Cabinets since 1947. It would, therefore, count for little, did not its members continually hold the fate of the Government in their hands. To be sure, there remain some 450 non-Communist Deputies who could, if they would, agree among themselves to form a majority and support the Government; but a sizable number of them are always ready to vote with the Communists against the men in office.

In fact, there are not one but two permanent oppositions. One is on the extreme Left, the other on the extreme Right. The first is made up of the Communists (since 1947) and, from time to time, the Socialists (from 1951 to 1955). The second consists of the Gaullists (from 1951 to 1953) or of the Poujadists (since 1956) and sometimes of the conservatives. When one opposition joins its votes to those of another the Government is in a minority, but as the two oppositions disagree on everything they can combine their efforts only to overthrow a Government, not to name a successor. So in comes a new team comparable to the previous one. Governments change; ministers linger on. There is only one man who has refused to play this game, where politicians turn each other out and then succeed themselves, and he is Pierre Mendès-France. He has been very popular in the country, but is very unpopular in Parliament.

These divisions in the Assembly are an exact image of the divisions in the country. Because there are so many and none of them predominates, a majority in the Assembly is impossible. It is true that there was none before the war either, when Deputies were elected by majority votes rather than by proportional representation. Governments were just as ephemeral. Those which lasted the longest were not the best, exactly as is the case today; for a Government that acts is turned out forthwith. That is why ministries do their utmost to carry out their programs in the early days of their existence: They know that Parliament soon becomes the master and ministers its slaves—then, before long, its victims.

Actually, French instability has a deeper and extremely paradoxical cause. Politics in France suffers, not because there is no majority, but because there are too many. There is a different majority for each important question.

For example, there is the educational problem: state aid to Roman Catholic schools. The Socialists are against such aid. They say: "Public funds for public schools; private funds for private schools." On the other hand, the Popular Republicans (M. R. P.) are in favor of it. They argue: "Educational liberty is an illusion if it does not have the material means for self-expression." It is an old quarrel and always bitter. So, although the Socialists and Popular Republicans are in agreement on other issues, they cannot govern together for any length of time.

A certain department in the Midi had two Deputies; more often than not they voted the same way, and they always traveled together when they left Paris. But when their train arrived in the south, each left his carriage by a different door. It would not do for their electors to see them together; they would not have understood. The two men were friends in the capital, but were obliged to appear to be enemies in their constituency.

The M. R. P., which has an understanding with the conservatives to defend the Roman Catholic schools (schools majority), is, on the contrary, in agreement with the Socialists against the conservative Right in defense of the workers (social majority). And the M. R. P., conservatives and Socialists are united in defending the parliamentary regime against the Communists and the Poujadists today, or the Gaullists yesterday (political majority). In short, there are as many possible ministerial combinations as there are parliamentary majorities—or problems. When the problem changes, the Government must change.

It is a very ancient evil, as old as the Republic, perhaps even as old as France. After the war, the Constitution and the electoral law were modified, but the situation only grew worse. Instability persists and the executive power was weakened.

There is only one way of assuring the stability of the executive power: a provision that the Assembly be automatically dissolved whenever it overthrew a Government. As things stand, in order that the Government may dissolve the Assembly, two Governments within a period of eighteen months must be defeated by an absolute majority of the Deputies. That has happened only once—in 1955. Edgar Faure then dissolved the Assembly. The one subsequently elected, the present one, has proved even more ungovernable.

Dissolution has as bad a reputation as Bonapartism. Republicans have never forgiven Marshal MacMahon for dissolving the *Chambre* in 1877, nor Marshal Pétain for dismissing Parliament in 1940, nor General de Gaulle for having demanded a dissolution in 1947. There is no likelihood of the Left Wing or Center parties agreeing to an automatic dissolution in the case of a defeat of the Government. At the most, they will agree that the right to dissolve the Assembly should be again entrusted to the President of the Republic, as it was under the Constitution of 1875. This is what Felix Gaillard proposes. But the French pass a part of their time making constitutions, another in modifying them and another in not applying them.

The evil goes deeper; it arises from divisions of a religious, historic and social order. It can be cured only by a radical change in the mentality of the élite and in the structure of the French economic system.

Like all peoples of a civilization essentially Mediterranean, the French are individualists and intellectuals; they have a passion for discussion and theorizing. They multiply their divisions *ad infinitum* and dislike discipline. More attentive to ideas than to facts, they are always quite ignorant of economic realities, and refractory to technical progress.

They are beginning to change. Science is replacing letters more and more in the universities; industry and even agriculture are being modernized with increasing rapidity. But today the incongruities between certain regions and a modern one in others are still adding new divisions and consequently new weaknesses.

In this respect, the National Assembly is truly a reflection of France. It is made up of idealists, even when they sit on the right, and conservatives, even when they sit on the left. This is not a matter of parties, but of temperaments.

General de Gaulle likes to quote a saying of Goethe: "At the beginning was the Word? No, at the beginning was the Deed." In France, things are just the reverse. The word takes precedence over action, the heart over reason; ideas come before facts.

Nearly half of the French Deputies practice some intellectual profession; 150 are lawyers or teachers. They love to talk; they talk well. A French audience likes to listen, even to conflicting opinions, provided that they are well expressed. A politician may be efficient, honest, industrious, but if he is not primarily an orator he will not succeed. Furthermore, his first subjects of discussion must be morality, history or philosophy, rather than politics.

It has been said of the Frenchman that he carries his heart on the left and his wallet on the right. He is as jealous of his revolutionary ideals as of his economic conservatism. As elsewhere, then, people are capable of defending their interests, but there is a great difference between methods on the two sides of the Atlantic.

In America lobbying is official and done in public. In France it is forbidden and therefore clandestine. It is camouflaged in the form of information offices and research organizations. They nourish the electoral funds of the Center and Right Wing parties. But the French employers and big businesses are not overly generous. Even the richest parties still remain very poor compared with those of other countries.

Any question that may arise about money, in fact, has something dubious about it. In ten years there have been only two such matters brought to the attention of the Assembly. A Deputy of a moderate party admitted to receiving money for his election campaign; he was not allowed to run again. Shortly afterward, a minister was accused of having distributed funds of an employers' organization before becoming a member of the Assembly; he was obliged to resign from the Government. In both these cases the Communists brought the charges. But now their adversaries maintain that the Communist party receives financial assistance from the U. S. S. R. Yet what is not permitted to an individual is forgiven in the case of a political party.

The average Frenchman is wholeheartedly for his Deputy and against Parliament, just as he is for his curé and against the Church. The French are always suspicious of power; they are afraid the Government is harming their interests and encroaching on their liberties. They count on their Deputies to defend both. The elector constantly keeps an eye on his Deputy, while the Deputy supervises the ministers. The Assembly is a vast observation ward.

Yet had not the French experienced so many different regimes, lived through so much history, suffered such frequent civil or foreign wars, they would not feel so detached from Parliament, they would not smilingly throw in one's teeth the word "Deputy" when they run short of jokes or insults. Nor would they brand the Palais Bourbon as "the circus."

Picture of an Average French Family

by Tania Long

PARIS

DÉSIRÉ LEFEBVRE, a postman, is typical of the civil servants of France who, with white-collar workers in general, have been hardest hit by the inflationary spiral which the Government is trying desperately to control. On the Government's success in this huge task may well depend its future.

Before the war M. Lefebvre could count on at least a little leisure and entertainment, but now even with tips and employment after regular working hours there is hardly enough income to provide the barest necessities of life. He and his family subsist —it cannot be called living—on "le minimum vital," which is officialdom's phrase for the lowest wage sufficient to maintain life at the lowest level.

It is the wives of men like him that one overhears in queues and on buses and in the Metro complaining that they "don't know how they're going to manage" until the end of the month. It is a comment which once uttered is invariably picked up by other women. Heads nod in agreement and the conversation goes on until it ends in a sigh.

From the *New York Times Magazine,* March 14, 1948, copyright © 1948 by The New York Times Company.

"Ah, oui, c'est bien la misère."

For Mme. Lefebvre, as for millions of Frenchwomen similarly situated, the end of the month when resources are depleted and there is no reserve is a time of struggle and despair. Budgets they have prepared so carefully are unbalanced by rising prices, unexpected expenses and illnesses. This is apt to be a period when, if a family is to be kept alive until the next payday, it will have to be on potatoes, carrots and thin vegetable soup.

That is what "le minimum vital" means—enough to keep one alive from one payday to the next but not enough to replenish a dwindling wardrobe, to provide a glass of wine, an evening at the movies or toys for the children. A year ago it was estimated that 7,000 francs monthly would provide that minimum. Now it is 10,500 francs and French labor says the sum must be raised again.

Lefebvre earns just that minimum. He says it isn't quite enough to keep body and soul together for himself, his wife and three children. How then does he manage? The answer is by going without everything that isn't absolutely necessary and counting on tips to bridge the gap between income and expenses. Others in his wage group solve the problem by putting the wife to work, finding a job for the oldest child, working themselves in spare time and even dabbling in the black market.

Lefebvre is as average a Parisian of the working class as can be found and his recent history is typical of that of millions of other Frenchmen of his class.

Short, swarthy, agile and quick-witted, he was by profession a chimneysweep. He made a good living in this manner until 1939 saw him called to the colors. Taken prisoner in the Vosges early in 1940 by the Germans, he spent the next five years in a series of prison camps, slave-labor camps and concentration camps from which he managed to escape fourteen times, only to be recaptured on each occasion. Together with thousands of others he was liberated by Allied armies in May, 1945.

When he returned to Paris he began to work at his old profession. But he had been so weakened physically by his years as a prisoner and slave laborer that he found himself unable for long to carry with him on his job the heavy equipment required to sweep the huge chimneys of factories and large business establishments in which he had specialized. In June, 1946, therefore, he joined the postal service and he has been delivering letters and packages by pushcart ever since.

M. Lefebvre works eight hours a day, six days a week. He pays 1.5 per cent of his wage of 10,500 francs a month for social security and 6 per cent toward a pension fund, so that he receives 9,713 francs net. Because he has three children he receives a Government grant of 4,250 francs additional and since his wife is unable to go to work and he is the only breadwinner in the family, he receives another 4,250 francs. When he is paid at the end of the month he therefore can count on an income of 18,213 francs.

The Lefebvre family lives in a shoddy old tenement house in the Menilmontant district of Paris. The building has no central heat, no hot water and the plumbing facilities are of the most primitive. The kitchen sink serves equally as washstand and laundry. There is, of course, no bathroom. The only toilet in the house is a communal affair in the basement and this is shared by seven other families who live in the tenement. With some money the Lefebvres had accumulated—part of it saved by his wife during the war when she worked in a factory and the rest received as a Government grant when M. Lefebvre returned from Germany— they were able to install electricity and gas but many of their neighbors in the building are still doing without.

Lefebvre had just come in from work when I arrived and he and his buxom wife Louisette were sitting at the table in the living room, one of the two small rooms which make up their apartment. In the back room the 6-month-old baby Jocelyne slept peacefully in a cot while the younger of two sons, Maurice, aged 2, played with his blocks on the bare floor. The older boy, Georges, 10, was still at school.

When I asked about the basic monthly expenses, Mme. Lefebvre quickly got pencil and paper, gathered some old bills and sat down to figure. In a few seconds she showed me the minimum expenses for a month. The total came to 19,355 francs—1,142 francs over the regular income.

Mme. Lefebvre then explained that her husband received tips for delivering packages and registered mail.

"Without these tips," she said, "I don't know what we'd do. On some days they're better than on others, of course, but if he can average 60 francs a day, that gives us another 1,800 francs a month added to his salary and grants. And that's the margin which carries us over—just."

She demonstrated by quick addition and subtraction that there were some 658 francs left from her husband's earnings and tips after minimum expenses were paid.

"And what can you do with 600 francs?" she asked, shrugging her shoulders. "A smock for little Maurice, a simple cotton smock cost us 475 francs the other day. You can see how if we've any unexpected expenses, however small, we just cannot manage to get by."

Maurice, she went on to explain, had never owned a coat, for the simple reason that to buy him one would take over 2,000 francs. As a result the child rarely goes outdoors in cold weather and when he has to go, his mother wraps him in an old wool shawl, a relic of pre-war days.

The day-to-day existence of the Lefebvre family like that of others in the same category is one of unrelieved drabness. With no money to spare for even modest pleasures what happiness they get out of life comes from within their family circle.

Even so, when speaking of their life the postman and his wife seem surprisingly cheerful. Their conversation is full of Gallic humor and wit, they still laugh easily and with gusto and even when Mme. Lefebvre refers to "la misère," it's more by way of stating a fact than in complaint. The Lefebvres grumble, of course, shrugging their shoulders and pointing up their remarks with their hands.

"We always were great ones for grumbling, we French," says M. Lefebvre.

It is when they speak of the future that one realizes that the cheerfulness of the postman and his wife is merely a surface manifestation of French character and good manners. The daily grind of existence could be borne easily enough, as the Lefebvres told me, if there were some promise of easier days ahead, if they could look forward to a date, even in the distant future, when they could say to themselves: "Now we can relax, bad times are over, so let's enjoy life."

As the postman put it, "There we are, my wife and I, going on toward middle age, with three children to bring up and worse off today than when we started together twelve years ago. It's not so much for Louisette and myself that I care—we had a few years of normal, carefree living—it's the children I am worrying about. What will their world be like? Will there in fact be a world for them to live in?"

Uncertainty about the future and fear of another war color his thinking and poison his sleep. Although he doesn't speak of it often, he believes that if there is another war France, the first victim, will be annihilated.

What about the Marshall Plan, one asks. Does he think that will help France's recovery and assist in maintaining peace?

"It will help France, of course," Lefebvre replies, "but whether it will assure the peace, who knows? God knows my country needs assistance and we are grateful to the Americans for it. And if it helps bring Europe closer together it will be a wonderful thing.

"The question I'd like to know the answer to is whether the Marshall Plan will help in bringing the whole world closer or whether it will accentuate a quarrel already existing between East and West."

It would be giving a false picture, however, to say that worries in the realm of international politics are uppermost in the Lefebvres' minds. Such worries are there but they are generally buried beneath worries about the business of keeping alive.

A recent survey of the purchasing power of French money today as compared with 1938 illustrated remarkably well the difficulties of families such as the Lefebvres. In the year before the war the worker earning 48 francs for an eight-hour day could buy with that sum the following goods: a pound of bread, a half pound of meat, a litre of wine, a pound of beans, five eggs, a box of cheese, four pounds of potatoes, a pack of cigarettes, a quarter pound of chocolate, a half pound of butter, a quarter pound of coffee, a litre of milk, a half pound of rice and a box of sardines.

Today the worker earning the minimum wage of 420 francs for an eight-hour day can buy less than half of these items: a half pound of bread, a half pound of meat, a litre of wine, a pound of beans, five eggs, a box of cheese and four pounds of potatoes. In order to buy the remaining items—actually most of them are not available except on the black market—the French wage earner would have to have 700 francs at his disposal instead of 420.

Most of what Lefebvre earns goes to feed the family for, as his wife said, "The chief thing is to keep healthy." Because of the high price of food, she has to spend an average of 500 francs a day, which is nearly fifteen times more than the same food would have cost before the war.

The Lefebvres rise to a breakfast consisting of bread, usually dry, sometimes but rarely spread with butter, and two cups of ersatz coffee known as "café national." The children have milk.

Mother and children have their main meal in the middle of the day and this usually consists of meat stew or of a steak of horse meat accompanied by vegetables and followed by a little fruit. The postman has his dinner when he returns from work; he goes on his eight hours of rounds with nothing to eat between his breakfast and his dinner. Toward 7 in the evening the family gathers again for a light supper of bread and vegetable soup and perhaps a little cheese if the budget will allow it. Frequently there is no meat or fish during the last week of the month. Then Georges, who is growing, suffers most, Mme. Lefebvre says, for she and her husband have learned to tighten their belts and the two younger children have their milk. There isn't enough milk to go around so the Government sees to it that most of it goes to young children.

One of the greatest hardships for the postman is that he can no longer afford to buy wine for his table. The French are brought up to drink wine at both meals and in the old days before inflation even the poorest beggar could buy himself a glass to go with a crust of bread. But for people like the Lefebvres wine has become a luxury they no longer can afford, for even the cheapest brand costs around 50 francs a bottle.

While he was talking to me his wife finished drawing up a quick list of her daily expenditures for food.

"This is the very least I spend, you see," she said. "One hundred francs for milk, 48 francs for bread, 150 for a small piece of meat or fish, 150 for vegetables and about 50 for miscellaneous items such as noodles, ersatz coffee and so on. At that, we never have enough bread and when my ration tickets have run out I have to buy bread at black market prices, which nearly doubles the cost."

At the rate of 500 francs a day the Lefebvres' monthly expenditures for food average 15,000 francs—a huge slice out of a postman's wages. Their other regular monthly purchases are coal and wood for heating which average 3,500 francs, electricity 320 francs, gas 300 francs. Their rent of 235 francs monthly is still extremely low because it's a pre-war rate.

With only a few hundred francs left over, once the immediate necessities are paid for, at the end of the month the Lefebvres naturally are unable to give any thought to buying clothes or replacing household articles which wear out or get broken through the years. The mailman and his wife have bought themselves no clothes since before the war with the exception of one pair of heavy shoes which M. Lefebvre got for himself when he returned from Germany.

His wardrobe consists of one pair of thoroughly mended gray flannel trousers, two shirts, one sweater and a leather, fleece-lined jacket which his maternal aunt sent him for Christmas from her home in the provinces. Apart from that he owns nothing. The postman's képi which the Government has provided him with as a sort of token for the full dark-blue uniform he is supposed to have some day is, of course, national property.

Mme. Lefebvre's wardrobe is just about as depleted and she says that if things don't get any better in a year or two she'll have to cut down her curtains to make dresses. At present she has one eight-year-old black dress, a pale blue smock or house dress, a coat dating back ten years, one pair of black shoes—at home she usually wears felt slippers—and an old black hat which, on the day I visited her family, had just been lent to a neighbor who had gone into mourning and did not possess the black headgear required of her. A few articles of underclothes and a carefully preserved silk scarf complete the list of her personal possessions.

Mme. Lefebvre smiled wryly when I asked what the family did for entertainment. "I leave the house only to do my daily shopping," she said. "In the evening we stay home. My husband is too tired after his work to visit friends and we can't afford to have our friends here, so it's just as well. On Sundays we stay home all day with the children."

"We avoid temptation that way," broke in the postman. "Ah, those Sundays before the war. . . . When we'd go out and have our little apéritif at the corner bistro, then maybe take in a movie in the afternoon or walk in the Bois de Boulogne if it was a fine day. We lived well then, always had wine on the table and plenty of good rich food and, when we needed something, well, we'd just save up for it. . . . But what makes it so hard now is that we cannot do more for our children."

Lefebvre is a man of more than average intelligence. He has not, like so many of his colleagues and others who live on the margin of subsistence, turned to communism as the cure-all of France's ills. However, he is just as disillusioned about the present state of French politics as most Frenchmen.

"The French who vote Communist do so because they don't understand what it's all about," he says. "What we need in France is a real labor party, a party that will really work for labor, a party in which labor can have some faith. Right now nobody but the extremist has faith in any party, for the obvious reason that no party truly tries to represent its following but instead engages in a game of politics while the nation goes from bad to worse."

He shrugged his shoulders when I asked what hope there was of the right kind of party arising. "It's probably the fault of the people," he replied. "We can't seem to get together on anything and as a result we have these hundreds of small political parties, none of which accomplishes anything."

There are millions of Desiré Lefebvres in France. Their problem is common to all but the wealthiest classes. For the gap between wages and prices is one that afflicts nearly everyone in France in different degrees. The workman who is getting higher pay than he ever got before the war still cannot buy half of what he could on a pre-war salary nor can he live nearly so well. But for the Lefebvres it is no longer a question of giving up luxuries or even of improvising for necessities. They have struck rock bottom.

De Gaulle Waits,
the World Watches

by C. L. Sulzberger

PARIS

ONE OF THE biggest questions on the continent of Europe is whether Charles de Gaulle will again come to power in France. If he does it will mean the end of the Fourth Republic.

Out of office nearly three years, the tall, serious-faced, religious General is today as much a man of mystery and as much a topic of discussion as when, in the early war years, he rallied the French people from London and North Africa and then, from 1944 to 1946, headed the Provisional Government of France. The reason is that de Gaulle has recently stepped up his political activities. After refraining from extensive speaking tours for a considerable period this year, he has renewed his call for a general election, has made it plain he is ready to assume power, and has taken his cause to the people.

Last month he journeyed through southern and southeastern France explaining his ideas to a region which contains a large de Gaullist faction. It was evident that his is an immense popularity, based on spontaneous enthusiasm, carefully fostered and organized by a trained political apparatus. There were a number of clashes

From the *New York Times Magazine,* November 7, 1948, copyright © 1948 by The New York Times Company.

with the Communists, who tried to break up the meetings. But the chief effect was a series of de Gaullist anti-government demonstrations.

Upon the General's evident bid for control depends this country's course, perhaps for years to come. The future of Europe, the Marshall Plan and the Brussels Pact are directly affected. And Europe's entire political development might well follow the trend of events in France.

What of the man who possesses such a tremendous power potential? What is de Gaulle like today? What does he stand for and who are his advisers?

The General, who will be 58 on Nov. 22, is an austere puritan, a devout Catholic and a retiring family man. In this he reflects the background from which he comes—conservative, perhaps somewhat royalist, and very religious. He is scrupulously honest and no breath of personal scandal has ever been whispered about him— in contrast with so many other French politicians.

Sincere and studious, he has a psychological make-up which appears to prevent him from being close to many people. For the most part he does not call those who work intimately with him by their Christian names. He is a man who lives in reflective solitude for considerable periods of time. There are those who have visited his family circle in his country home at Colombey-les-Deux-Eglises who say that, sometimes for hours, the General sits wrapped in his own thoughts and silence reigns. He is certainly distant and haughty; that was the impression both Roosevelt and Churchill formed.

At Colombey he follows a simple, country-gentleman's routine. According to some of his friends, he reads several newspapers each morning. Generally, he spends much time reading, even when he is actively engaged in public affairs.

As for his convictions, he seems utterly sure in his own mind of the rectitude of his thoughts, his analyses and his conclusions. There is undoubtedly a streak of the mystic in him. He appears to have an unusual feeling of "oneness" with France and his own destiny.

Cool and distant as he may be in private conversations, he has a curiously magnetic personality. Persons who have visited him or attended small meetings where he was present have been struck by this, whether they agreed with his ideas or not. His mind is precise and, aided by a gift of particularly fine phraseology he expresses his thoughts with special clarity.

As a speaker de Gaulle has a Gallic gift for moving crowds. His style would almost certainly not electrify American or other foreign audiences, but it appears to grip the French mind. His gestures are not overdramatized and they even give an impression of awkwardness when they are examined, for example, in the cinema. But they appear to be instinctively timed to the mood of a French audience.

His method of address is a combination of logic, sincerity and wit tinged with occasional sarcasm—something of especial appeal to *l'esprit Gallois*. Whether it manages to sway opponents or those neutral toward him is a difficult question to answer. But it excites the admiration of his sympathizers and the fury of his enemies.

His strength right now lies in the close-knit ranks of the "Rassemblement du Peuple Français." Despite the continuance of the Central Coalition Ministry, which may yet survive, the two most powerful political forces in France today are the RPF and the Communists. Together, grinding the center between their millstones, these two fundamentally revolutionary parties are managing to pursue a "politique du pire" (a "politics of making things worse") which forces the Government into a succession of pitfalls and toward a situation from which both the RPF and the Communists hope to profit.

The present organizational structure of the General's RPF is based on a select group of advisers, who are tantamount to a "shadow cabinet," and a "National Council," which has a structural resemblance to the "National Committee" formed early in the war. His "cabinet" is composed of eleven men, three of whom, comprising the Executive Committee, form the most important group around de Gaulle in terms of present influence. These are:

Jacques Soustelle, who is general secretary of the RPF and serves as political and administrative officer of that body.

André Malraux, the writer, who is in charge of coordinating the press, information and propaganda, and who also has a large influence on the general's sociological program.

Gaston Palewski, who is responsible for liaison and foreign-affairs reports.

Working with the eleven-man committee is a subsidiary body called the "Intergroup for True Democracy" and made up of former supporters of the Troisième Force. This is headed by Paul Giaccobi, a deputy from Corsica.

The RPF now claims a membership of approximately two million. It has one official journal—Le Rassemblement—which appears weekly in Paris, with special regional editions containing local reports. The organization is financed by annual membership dues of 200 francs and by voluntary contributions. It claims that it does not have its own police or parliamentary force, but it is safe to assert that, despite these denials, some protective body does exist.

What actually is the political theory and application which de Gaulle wants to put into effect in place of the Fourth Republic?

De Gaulle's supporters and the General himself explain it briefly in this way. They wish to establish a constitutional system similar to that of the United States, in which the three governmental functions—executive, legislative and judicial—are balanced, instead of a system of legislative control under which Parliament can continually bring about the overthrow of ministries.

The RPF insists on its respect for democratic theories and stresses that men and women of all the French religions, races and colors may be members. De Gaullists say that sociologically they wish to establish sounder relationships between the citizen and the government and more just nonpolitical relationships between labor and capital.

De Gaulle himself told this writer last year:

"The aim of the RPF is to group the French people in such a way as to permit a system in which policies can be decided and responsibilities assumed in the interests of France, independent of the aspirations of any single political party.

"The aim of the RPF is the reconstruction of France to its full productive capacity and power. It is necessary to restore productive capacity, and in order to do so we must provide for full free enterprise. . . . It is necessary to increase the volume of French production. Simultaneously it is necessary to find a solution to the problems relating to the working of capital and labor."

De Gaulle's critics and those who fear him can be roughly grouped in two large blocs. First of all there are the Communists. Curiously enough, much as they hate him, their obdurate refusal to cooperate in any way in alleviating the task of the Center Government is rendering de Gaulle's chances continually better. The Communists fear de Gaulle because there is not the slightest doubt that he will try to reduce and eventually eliminate their influence.

The other group comprises leftists and moderates who fear that de Gaulle—a second time in power—might head France along autocratic paths. They say he evinces too much faith in himself and too little in parliamentary democracy.

They fear the vagueness of his announced policy, his economic inexperience, some of his social ideas and the personality of many of his advisers.

De Gaulle himself has spoken on the subject both of dictatorship and democracy. At Bayeux on June 16, 1946, he analyzed dictatorship as "a great adventure" whose dynamism at first contrasts favorably with the anarchy it succeeds, but which then, in order to satisfy the public, leads it toward the path of disaster.

Nevertheless, those who fear his return are alarmed by several symptoms. First of all, they fear that despite public pledges a de Gaullist Government would not only terminate the Fourth Republic as now constituted, but might end the system of political parties and formal opposition. This, they maintain, would negate democracy no matter how well ordered.

There are many who, despite their own anti-Communist convictions, believe that a move by de Gaulle to outlaw the Communist party might pave the way to civil war and would certainly strengthen communism as it has been strengthened in other countries such as Italy and Greece where it was outlawed for years.

Finally, his opponents are frequently skeptical about flat assertions by de Gaullists that they have no paramilitary secret organizations supporting them. Old revolutionaries and resistance leaders like Malraux or Remy are certainly practiced at creating such bodies.

De Gaulle's enemies assert that Colonel "Passy," at one time the General's intelligence chief in London and often alleged to be a former Cagoulard [pre-war Fascist group], is playing a vital clandestine role in the RPF. The implication is that he has a lot to do with a secret "defense force." (RPF denies vigorously that "Passy" has anything to do with it.)

Some labor leaders frankly voice fears that the trade-union movement would be so drastically altered as to be vitiated if a de Gaulle government were able to install its "associations" of workers and capitalists. They assert that this idea—one of the planks in the RPF movement—has remarkable similarity to the corporativism of Mussolini.

Whether these suspicions and fears are well grounded or not is impossible to know. The French political atmosphere is replete with charges and countercharges.

But this is the kind of argument which involves all France these days and frequently ends up with harsh and bitter words. It enables the most vehement supporters of de Gaulle to engage in fisticuffs and even more vigorous battles with his enemies and it makes it easier for organized groups from both the RPF and communism to promote occasional scraps such as those which occurred toward the end of the General's recent speaking tour in southern France.

How would de Gaulle come to power? And what are his chances?

First of all, he clearly counts on a final collapse of what he has denounced as the unstable party system as it has existed in the Third and Fourth Republics.

He counts on the advent of a situation where a fed-up public will demand stability as represented by himself and his movement. Whether he could secure power through an election or a plebiscite —if that moment on which he bases his hopes arrives—cannot be said. It is illogical to expect a parliament which contains many members who would not be re-elected to dissolve itself.

If legal means were not available it is not impossible that the General might agree to unconstitutional methods to accomplish what he considers his mission of saving France. De Gaulle certainly has the authoritarian type of mind which is often associated with a military education and career. However, his term as head of the French state showed not the slightest sign that he sought to install an autocratic regime.

Can one count on this still? An absolute prediction cannot be risked. Should de Gaulle take over the reins again he might lean toward a dictatorial form of administration..

It is obvious that de Gaulle's chances are far better today than they were six months ago. But this does not mean either that the Fourth Republic has had its last fling or that the General's RPF will of a surety take control here.

It is no secret that neither Britain nor the United States would enthusiastically welcome such a development despite continual Communist charges that de Gaulle is an American stooge.

The General's strong Gallic pride, his diplomatic obduracy and his mystical faith in his ideas made him a difficult man for Anglo-American diplomatists to deal with during the war and just afterward. They are worried about possible autocratic tendencies should he again step to the helm.

But the decision will be made by France and Frenchmen regardless of foreign desires. And the situation this autumn contains many of those basic symptoms which are frequently preliminary to a political revolution.

Economic misery and inflation have not been eliminated. Workers and pensioners are not receiving enough real purchasing power. The regime of successive weak Governments has not been able to master basic issues yet. And de Gaulle's RPF is, in terms of political philosophy, a revolutionary organization clearly prepared to seek advantage from this situation and assume responsibility.

The only true test of the ability of the de Gaullists to govern democratically and successfully without infringing upon the civil rights of Frenchmen would be the actuality of a de Gaulle government. France will very likely have to decide whether it wishes to apply this test during the course of the next six months.

French Premier
with a Deadline

by Harold Callender

PARIS

LONG AGO George Bernard Shaw said his oculist had discovered
with much amazement that Shaw had absolutely normal vision,
which hardly anybody had. Shaw remarked that it was then clear
to him why he saw the world about him so much more accurately
than most other people saw it.

Pierre Mendès-France, the new Premier of France, has not the
intellectual vanity that Mr. Shaw professed to have. But he has a
remarkable confidence in his analyses and judgments and sometimes has not hesitated to express it.

Four years ago, M. Mendès-France said to the National
Assembly:

"To win the war in Indochina, we shall need half a million
men; you will never get them because you will never draw upon
conscript troops."

Two years later he said France's position for negotiating a peace
there was worse than it had been the previous year and probably

would be worse still when another year had passed. These fore-casts proved correct.

A year ago, after outlining a program for expanding French production, he told the Assembly he had placed before it facts that would be accepted sooner or later, the only question being whether that acceptance would be delayed until France suffered further from a stagnant economy. Ten days ago, he urged upon the Assembly the same facts and the same program he had proposed a year earlier, as confident as ever that he knew what France should do.

M. Mendès-France's intellectual vision has been proved by the test of time and events—and not alone in the field of economics and finance. Probably this clarity owes much to his self-criticism, his distrust of his own ideas until he has examined and analyzed them and subjected them to the comments of others. He is a man of studious and methodical habits, and his cautiously critical approach to the problems of his time causes him to make up his mind about them only very slowly.

A practiced lawyer, he can if he must make a speech extemporaneously, and some of his best speeches have been made in this way. But he writes laboriously and slowly since what he puts down is subject to reflection and self-criticism as he goes along. One of his friends said he sometimes spent hours over a paragraph. He spent more than three days drafting his thirteen-page speech asking the Assembly to make him Premier, but he spent about ninety minutes preparing an equally long speech answering his critics.

M. Mendès-France is an intellectual and as such is painfully aware of the inevitable disparity between thought and action, especially in politics. He seems to believe it is easier to serve his country as Mayor of the small town of Louviers than as a member of the National Assembly. He once remarked that as Mayor he could see real results of his labors—better roads, schools, gas and electric installations—but that as a Deputy about all he could take credit for was a law about rabbits, which, when passed, had quite ceased to resemble what he had proposed.

The French National Assembly is not the best place to acquire faith in the translation of ideas into facts. France has perhaps an over-supply of intellectuals, but in France, as in the United States, politics tends to be guided largely by the need to win the votes of the more numerous non-intellectuals.

Yet M. Mendès-France has not despaired of influencing policy through careful analysis of national needs, through the force of accumulated facts, through appeal to the intelligence of Frenchmen rather than to their sectional or professional interests or to their traditional doctrines.

He retains a hope that the disparity between the vision of the enlightened intellectual and the acts of political leaders may be diminished. Now he is going to put this hope to the test by trying a political experiment of bold proportions—that of revising France's policies toward her overseas territories and of freeing her national economy from the shackles that restrict production and trade.

M. Mendès-France has been called "a new man" in France partly because, although he has held Cabinet posts, he has not held the top ones and has never before been Premier, but mainly because his unexpected choice as Premier seemed to presage a change in the sluggish politics of the country and a Goverment that would at least try harder than its immediate predecessors to solve some major national problems.

Some observers have imagined him to be pessimistic because it has been his role to draw attention to unpleasant facts that others preferred to ignore, to sound the alarm for disasters that might impend. But he fought for his country when victory seemed hopeless, and he has fought for policies that seemed to have little chance of acceptance. He clings to the hope that France may improve her system of government and modernize her economy so as to play a greater role in world affairs.

His friends point out that no pessimist would try to learn to ski at the age of 43, as M. Mendès-France did. His sons, aged 18 and 19, consider his skiing a joke and he admits it is not brilliant. But he professes to understand perfectly the theory of skiing and persists in trying to apply it. Every winter he tries again, although he has repeatedly broken a leg or an ankle in the process.

In his adopted town of Louviers, west of Paris, where he practices law and meets constituents, M. Mendès-France seldom sits in cafes to gossip with the people.

He gives few dinner parties. But in the Department of Eure, which he represents in the Assembly, he apparently has won the confidence of farm workers, merchants and others, who continue to elect him.

M. Mendès-France is short and stocky, with almost black hair and a face that animates as he talks. He reads much, notably in history and economics, and sometimes plays the piano. In Paris he and his wife, who spent four years in the United States during World War II and speaks excellent English, live in a very modest apartment on the fourth floor of a fairly new building not far from the Bois de Boulogne.

Beginning his career as a lawyer and Deputy at Louviers, M. Mendès-France specialized in economics and finance. At the age of 19 he wrote a thesis on the stabilization of the franc by Poincaré. When World War II began he was in the French Air Force serving in Syria and later, from Britain, he was on bombing missions over France.

His first important venture in post-war politics was his proposal to General de Gaulle's Provisional Government to put an end to inflation by blocking bank accounts and issuing a new currency, as was done in Belgium. This plan was rejected and M. Mendès-France resigned as Minister for National Economy. The inflation continued and became a major post-war problem.

M. Mendès-France represented France at the Bretton Woods conference which established the International Monetary Fund and the International Bank for Reconstruction and Development. He became executive director and later a member of the board of governors of the fund. At Bretton Woods, he became acquainted with the British economist Lord Keynes, many of whose ideas he then shared.

Within the last year, he has been chairman of the Finance Committee of the National Assembly and he directed the huge work of a committee of specialists analyzing and severely criticizing the French economy. The evils of a protected system with little competition were depicted with complete frankness in an elaborate report often cited by the studious but little read by the public.

M. Mendès-France's speech as candidate for Premier a year ago was essentially a lecture on economics. He insisted that "to govern is to choose," and that France must decide how to use her resources and how to adapt her aspirations to her means. He questioned whether France could pursue the war in Indochina and at the same time build up her strength in Europe, and he contended she must choose which she would do.

He thus approached international problems from the point of view of France's military and economic capacity.

He urged increasing her economic power by expanding production. To this end he proposed a better use of resources, greater competition in place of cartels and the elimination of unproductive or high-cost industries. He wanted to expand, above all, exports and building, the latter chiefly to produce the houses that France has been slow to build.

At the same time, he urged greater progress toward self-government in Tunisia and Morocco, as he did again in his speech ten days ago outlining his program as Premier.

M. Mendès-France has been cited by conservatives as a bogy man who might come into power with Communist support and withdraw from Indochina. By others he has been considered the only man who might organize a Left bloc without the Communists. By his friends and many of the younger generation he is regarded as a man who might rejuvenate the Fourth Republic by breaking down the rigid party lines that divide and paralyze it.

Sometimes he has been accused of "neutralism," but in his speech of June 3, 1953, he said the neutralists were wrong in imagining that, if another world war came France could stay out of it.

But he argued that France must limit her objectives and not indulge in the "illusion of grandeur." The first article of foreign policy should be the build-up of the internal economy, he contended.

In his speech June 9, last, he insisted that France's vulnerability to Communist propaganda should be taken as a basic problem of

Western strategy. This vulnerability he attributed mainly to France's backward economy. Here again is the economic approach to foreign policy which dominates M. Mendès-France's thinking as he surveys France's position in the world in relation to her internal weaknesses, both economic and political.

The French Empire: "Time Runs Out"

by D. W. Brogan

IT IS unnecessary to underline the importance for a great imperial power of a military and political defeat such as that which France suffered in Indochina. The defeat, it is true, is not only a defeat for France; it is a defeat for France's allies, for all the nations threatened by the Communist powers. But it is for France a time for an agonizing reappraisal of the role and the future of the French Empire, or, as it is now called, the French Union. That the reappraisal is taking place is indicated by recent moves in Paris. One is Premier Mendès-France's plan to establish an all-Tunisian Government and to grant that strife-torn protectorate full internal autonomy under conditions that would protect the rights of French settlers. And the continuing tension in Morocco calls for fresh decisions.

It may and it will be said in America that this decline of the French Empire is a good thing. But in the American attitude on the question of imperialism there is often to be noted a belief that imperialism, *all* imperialism, is intrinsically evil. Yet the world is a bigger and more complicated place than an old-fashioned Fourth of July oration would suggest. In any case, the French Empire is

From the *New York Times Magazine,* August 15, 1954, copyright © 1954 by The New York Times Company.

still there and there is no guarantee nor, in my opinion, any probability that its disappearance would either promote the strength of the West or even the material well-being of the liberated inhabitants. It is, that is to say, to the interest of the United States and of Great Britain that the problems, the grave and very present problems of the French Empire, be solved in a manner that does not involve the dissolution of one of the main bastions of order in a world so badly in need of them.

An epigrammatic Cambridge professor said more than two generations ago that the "British Empire was created in a fit of absence of mind." He was at best half-right. It could more truly be said that the French Empire was created in a permanent fit of absence of mind by the majority of French voters and French ministers. It was created by a comparatively small body of soldiers, sailors, administrators, missionaries and business men, supported rather than led by a handful of politicians who saw in the empire the means of redressing the balance of power in Europe or (so their enemies alleged) of distracting the hopes of the French people from the dream of the recovery of Alsace and Lorraine to the more practical dream of finding compensation on the Niger and on the Red River.

The French Empire, like so many great French achievements, was not the direct, planned achievement of the French state. So that, today, when more and more attention is being paid in France to imperial problems, it is being paid in a country that, in the mass, is not accustomed to thinking about them.

This is not a peculiarly French phenomenon. Few Americans, today, can even vaguely remember the imperial oratory of Senators like Albert J. Beveridge. In British politics the living and difficult problems of imperial policy are discussed, too often, in terms that recall the bitter fights between the imperialists and their opponents who were scornfully called "little Englanders."

But the French situation is more complicated and probably more dangerous. It is not only that the country of the "Declaration of the Rights of Man and the Citizen" has never found it easy to invent a formula that could fit in the imperial fact to the republican theory. It is that the French Empire was largely created by people whose adherence to the principles of 1789 was tepid, at best. For example, one reason and a politically important reason for the French intervention in and then conquest of Indochina was that Annam was one of the greatest fields of French missionary endeavor.

We all know the psychological importance of the missionary connection between the United States and China. But France (proportionately to its population and resources the greatest missionary country in the world) had an equal interest in Indochina. The same interest was, in part, behind the occupation of Madagascar and of a great part of Africa. Trade, prestige, military power were all elements in the creation of the French Empire. But missionary zeal was at least as important, and one of the disasters of the present "settlement" in Indochina is the abandonment to the Communists of so many flourishing Catholic communities in Tonkin.

It is not accidental that, even today, some of the most lively discussions of the problems of the empire take place in Catholic circles, that Indochina, for example, has been regarded as a fief of the Catholic Democrats, the M. R. P., that the first and, possibly, fatal decisions when French authority was restored there, were made by the sailor-monk, Admiral Thierry d'Argenlieu of the Carmelite order.

It was not only a question of missionaries. Some of the most brilliant makers of the Empire were men like Lyautey, men of royalist families who found in a career in Indochina or Morocco a field of action denied to them in republican France. It was not merely a gesture when the Socialist party expelled Alexandre Varenne for accepting the post of Governor-General of Indochina. The empire was a "Right-Wing affair"; in the eyes of many, a Right-Wing racket. But apart from denunciations of imperialism in general and of abuses like the Congo concessions in particular, the amount of knowledge or thought that the Left-Wing parties were prepared to devote to the empire was small. And one of the tragedies of the defeat of the Government of Léon Blum after 1936 was that the necessary adjustments in Syria and in North Africa that were planned for were lost in the confusion of the years before the Second World War.

The Second World War suddenly gave to the empire a new

importance. For with the whole of France occupied, the empire *was* France. From equatorial Brazzaville and then from Algiers came the rallying cries that reinforced the voice of de Gaulle from London. The greater part of de Lattre de Tassigny's army of "the Rhine and Danube" came from the empire. The successes of the war that restored French faith in French arms, the feats of Leclerc, Koenig, Juin had their roots in the empire. For the first time, the empire became not a thing of specialists and special interests. It became an emotional reality to the mass of the French people.

Unfortunately, this emotional appeal was not backed up by a realistic assessment of the position of the empire. The new imperial institutions, loosely compared to the dominion status of the British Empire (itself busily becoming a Commonwealth), were, in part at least, based on a view of a France "one and indivisible," as they said in the Year One of the French Revolution.

Not many people were willing to notice the implications of the British withdrawal from India. Once that was done, the French position in Indochina was undermined. If the British, whose rule was so much older, whose prestige was so much greater, decided to go, it was impossible that the French should stay on anything like the old terms. Many French resent the British withdrawal in India and Egypt as a betrayal. Be that as it may, it is a fact.

But however odd it may seem to Americans, the problem of Indochina, the ulcer that has drained France for seven years, was, in French eyes, not the real imperial problem. Far more serious were the problems of Africa. For Africa is not very remote from France. Algiers and Marseille are a day's steaming apart.

Since 1830, immense amounts of men and money have been poured into Algiers, then Tunisia, then Morocco. During the late war and after, Morocco attracted even more people and more investment. There was created, across the Mediterranean from France, a new France. There were created the new European cities of Algiers and Tunis beside the old Arab pirate ports. There was created the great city of Casablanca where there had been, in 1906, a fishing village. There was imposed on the torpid or fanatical world of western Islam, the "Maghreb," a Western economy.

Some of the problems of Casablanca are those which New Yorkers are or ought to be familiar with in the Puerto Rican slums of Harlem. But, of course, they are magnified by the fact that the French are intruders, that North Africa did not ask for this sudden projection into the modern world. Its dogmatic slumbers might have continued, but for French energy and French capital.

Then the Maghreb could not hope to escape the stirrings of the Islamic world, especially of the Arab world. French authority has disappeared from Syria. British authority has disappeared from Egypt and from the Sudan. After centuries of torpor, the Islamic world is awakening. The results of that awakening, from the point of view of order, military security and modern techniques, may not be, are not, impressive in Java or in Egypt. But the movement is there. And that has presented the French with a special problem, for they alone among the Western powers have a great personal investment in the Islamic world.

It was one thing to find ways of evacuating the British troops from the Suez Canal. It is another thing to find ways for peaceful co-existence between the Arab-speaking Moroccans or the Tunisians on one side and the French "colons" on the other. It is difficult to make the fiction that Algiers is "just three French departments" fit in with the reality that its problems cannot be separated from those of Morocco or Tunisia. Indeed, it is painfully obvious how close are the connections, for some of the Deputies and Senators for Algeria in the National Assembly in Paris act as the spokesmen for their spiritual (and often their blood) kin, the "colons" of Morocco and Tunisia. More than once the chances of a settlement in Tunisia or Morocco have been sacrificed to the need for the votes of these spokesmen for the "colons."

Outrageous as it may seem, there is a case for the "colons." When the "colons" say that they *made* modern North Africa, they are telling the truth. When they express skepticism that the "Arabs" would have done much with the country, they are at least plausible. When they point out that the unity of Morocco (like the unity of Indochina or, for that matter, of India) was the work of the foreign imperialists, they are more than plausible. Nevertheless, the "colons" must adjust themselves to a world in which their old, exclusive, superior position must be abandoned. And that is the opinion of a great part of the French people which thinks about imperial problems.

The problems of North Africa are difficult, but not yet desperate. The complete disappearance of French authority would probably produce a breakdown of order and communications in Tunisia and Algeria. It might well produce a bloody civil war in Morocco. But —and the text should be studied in Paris as well as in Rabat and Tunis—Burke was right, "Great empires and little minds go ill together." There have been no great minds in North Africa for quite a long time.

South of the Sahara, the situation is different. Here the French are dealing with a fluid and plastic society, just entering the modern world. Here their role as teachers is still accepted. But the rapid approach of the Gold Coast to dominion status in the Commonwealth is being noticed. Which will prove more appealing, the career of M. Senghor, who plays an important role in Paris, or that of Dr. Nkrumah, who is Prime Minister of the Gold Coast? Will the élite which the French wish to produce and do produce, be content to seek their ambitions in the politics of metropolitan France or would they rather be bosses in their own backyard? No one knows.

Both Britain and France, in different ways, have undertaken to stimulate and push forward the mechanics of modern democracy in West Africa. In the Congo the Belgians, with no visibly bad results, have not. The French solution has been, roughly, to promote the subjects of the French Empire to the rank of French citizens, making them, as far as may be, French in spirit as well as in legal form. The English, perhaps because they think that attaining the rank of Englishman is something that only Providence can provide for, have chosen to allow their subjects to develop in their own ways.

Time is running out. It is running out fastest in North Africa. Only a strong government in Paris can impose on the "colons" a due regard for the Moslem majority and, at the same time, guarantee that the great work of construction is not undone. Yet the élite whom the French have created will have to be given the place in their own country that their education entitles them to.

South of the Sahara, the problem is less urgent. But the "promotion" of the Africans must be speeded up. And as France is poor in capital, the jealous mercantilist spirit of French business must be taught that its interest lies in encouraging foreign investment, not only in Africa but in Madagascar and other French possessions.

Frankly, few people in Paris expect the settlement in Indochina to last long. There it is five past twelve. In North Africa, it is five to twelve. In the rest of the French Union, it is eleven o'clock. There is still everywhere an appreciation of French culture and French ideas that can be used. There is a pro-French party everywhere. There is, in France, an increasing undoctrinaire interest in the Empire and a genuine concern about it.

If the two forces—the generous desire to make the French Union a spiritual reality that animates so many Frenchmen, Catholic and *laic,* and the reluctance that animates so many citizens of "France Overseas" to lose their status as members of the Union— can be brought together, the Union can emerge from the crisis strengthened. If that is not done, the winners will be not the Nationalists of Rabat or Tunis or Dakar, but the Kremlin. And the losers will be all of us in the West. The next two or three years at most will decide one way or the other.

Part **4**

THE FIFTH REPUBLIC

"We Are All Victims in Algeria"

by Joseph Kraft

ALGERIA CAN be summed up in a mot: *"Ce n'est que le provisoire qui dure"*—"The temporary is what lasts."

Forty-three months, five Premiers and three U. N. debates have passed since hostilities began. Repression has been mixed with reform, and alarm has crowded upon excursion. In season and out, generals and proconsuls have signaled what one of them once called "the last quarter of an hour." Still, the war goes on, and nothing—not even the revolts of the generals—changes the basic features of that unshakable reality.

Horror—the horror of a war visited upon civil populations and with heavy overtones of social and racial conflict—is the most striking of those features. No day passes in Algeria without reports of violence, a bloody engagement in the Aurès Mountains, a grenade exploded in an Oran cafe, a throat cut in Constantine, an Arab tortured to death in Algiers. Gutted schools and leveled villages stand everywhere in mute testimony to the rival terror tactics of French and nationalist soldiers. A European, missing an arm or a leg, or with an ear sliced off, is no longer an object of curiosity in the cafes. Along the back-country roads broken men, and near blind, stumble their way home—Arabs released from the torture chambers, each with a white note fixed to his clothing to indicate he is harmless. "This," one Arab doctor says, "is our daily bread."

One way or another, it is everybody's bread. "We are all victims in Algeria," Père Scotto, a Dominican priest in a working class section of Algiers, once said. But the victims are no more members of a single community than fifty men are a centipede. At least four major groups—the French Army, the nationalist rebels, the European settlers, and the mass of Moslem natives—can be counted.

Within each group the majority is passive, while firebrands force the pace. Relations between the groups, in consequence, are badly distorted. Poorly connected with each other, where they are not wholly cut off, they go their separate ways at cross-purposes, only dimly aware of the vast aggregate of a country four times the size of France. Here are some quick sketches of the four main elements in the Algerian picture:

The Army

French military forces, probably 450,000 in number and certainly the largest army ever sent overseas by France, are spread across Algeria in a *quadrillage* operation aimed at dotting the whole country with strong points. Draftees and recalled veterans, by profession farmers from Normandy or upholsterers from Arras, the overwhelming bulk of the soldiers have no love for the settlers and little stomach for fighting the nationalists. Day after day they go through the weary rounds of garrison duty in provincial towns so deeply steeped in ennui as to make Madame Bovary's Rouen seem a Babylon. On dusty parade grounds and in the muddy courts of newly built posts, they may be seen endlessly rolling little wooden balls, one after another, in a game something like the Italian *boccia*. "It's the national sport," a press officer once said.

A not dissimilar mood prevails in the very highest circles of military authority and in some of the sector commands. In the afternoon of lackluster careers, wary of harming innocent civilians, and conscious of being dependent upon the politicians for promotion, the top French generals go through their paces with one eye cocked on Paris, and in an air bordering on futility. One sector commander, not long ago, took his leave in Paris with the idea of selling a series of articles on Algeria to the newspaper Le Monde. His plan was that French forces, instead of manning fixed posts, should course back and forth across the countryside on permanent patrol. But asked why he didn't use that system in his own sector, he said: "Too hot."

The dust of battle, in these circumstances, has been borne by a relatively small group of professionals—notably the paratroopers. Superbly trained, in almost constant action since World War II, equipped with the most modern American arms, the paras are among the best troops in the world. To them belongs the credit for the only indubitable French victory in Algeria—the cleaning out of the Casbah of Algiers, a rabbit warren of interconnecting homes.

Assumption of security duties in the cities, though, has brought the paras into close touch with the ultra elements among the settlers and the local administrators. It has confronted them too with the ugly dilemma—the dilemma of "talk or else"—facing most police forces. Repeatedly they will capture a nationalist who can give intelligence that might lead to the saving of French lives. Making no headway by routine questions and egged on by the die-hards, they not infrequently resort to torture, sometimes of wholly innocent people. Whenever the facts get out, cries of protest go up in Paris.

Moreover, despite their valor, the paras have not been a winning force. They did not win World War II, nor in Indochina, nor in Tunisia, nor in Morocco, nor at Suez in November, 1956. Algeria they see as a last stand. "Here," one colonel, a fiercely blue-eyed man who spoke grandly in the Shavian manner of war, God and destiny, once put it, "the politicians can't cheat us."

In these conditions—brutalized by security duties, conscious of their strength but bitterly frustrated by their failures, idolized by the settlers but chastened by Paris—the paras became a hotbed of political dissension. "What France needs," one of them once said, "is a regime *pur et dur* [hard and clean]. What we have is a regime *pourri* [rotten]. Minister X took a hundred million francs from the Sultan for giving him Morocco. Deputy Y is pro-Arab because his wife has a department store in Cairo. They are all *bradeurs* [a rare French word, now much in vogue, meaning a peddler who, after crying up his wares, sells cheap]."

The Rebels

Like the war itself, the Algerian nationalists, or National Liberation Army, are everywhere and nowhere.

Everywhere, because in any city a foreigner can meet Arabs, many of them working for the French administration, who can put him in touch with the nationalist forces. Probably no village in Algeria is without a nationalist political officer, dunning the locals for funds, setting women and children to spy on the French, storing up food for nationalist soldiers who may happen by, yet, withal, unknown to the French. Many of the political officers have dug in as local nabobs, running the towns and billeting their wives and children and, in one known case, an elderly mother.

Nowhere, because the rebel troops—not more than 30,000 in all —move by night in the back country and in tiny units.

A thirty-man section is the usual fighting force, though sometimes companies of a hundred take the field and once a battalion was mustered. Troop leaders maintain only tenuous liaison with the five regional nationalist headquarters in Algeria, and these in turn have but the loosest ties with the topmost political leaders— scattered through the world, in Tunis, Cairo, Damascus and even New York.

In consequence, there is a large degree of local autonomy. "If I think I can take a French post," one sergeant once told me, "well then, I'll try it." But inevitably, the temptation is to pick easier marks—defenseless settlers' farms, for instance, or Arab villagers suspected of helping the French.

The rebel troops are largely fresh-faced boys, many still in their teens, but well-trained in camps in Morocco and Tunisia. They wear uniforms not unlike American fatigues, and are equipped with small arms—including machine guns and a few mortars—taken from the French, or transported across the Moroccan and Tunisian borders from sources as distant as Cairo, Belgrade and London. Like almost everyone else in Algeria, the nationalist soldiers have settled to a routine. "We get food and we're out-doors," one medical orderly once said to me. "What more do you want?"

Of ultimate victory, the rebels seem to have no doubt. "We may not beat the French," one captain said, "but they can't beat us. Not in a hundred years. Sooner or later something's bound to happen in France. When it does, they'll give way."

Istiqlal—independence—is, of course, the word on every na-tionalist lip, and sometimes it seems the only one in their patriotic songs. "Independence for what?" though, is a question that on more than one occasion has reduced the soldiers to embarrassed silence. And they accorded to one sergeant who answered, "To get the French off our backs," the kind of respect Aristotle might have received had he popped up in the twelfth century to settle a nice point for a pack of schoolmen.

In the rebel camp, too, in the very midst of determination, there exists an incongruity and aimlessness, of a piece with the rolling of wooden balls. A lieutenant once borrowed my typewriter—to write an order, he said. At the top of the sheet, he wrote, in capital letters neatly centered, "National Liberation Army." Evi-dently there then occurred to him a French phrase used in typing schools to employ every letter key in a single sentence. What he wrote on the order was, in translation: "I imagine a Zouave, play-ing the xylophone while drinking whiskey."

The Europeans

Few people can have been so much maligned as the million so-called "French *colons*" in Algeria. *Colons* they are not, for that term implies rich landowner, whereas nine-tenths of the settlers live in cities and work as clerks, artisans and shopkeepers at wages averaging 20 per cent below the prevailing French standard. A typical European apartment in downtown Algiers includes two small, ill-lit rooms—one serving as kitchen and eating quarters; the other, with a triple-decker for the children and a double bed for the parents, as sleeping quarters.

Neither are the settlers exactly French. Half, at most, are of French descent, the rest coming from all over the Mediterranean with a specially heavy sprinkling of Spaniards and Italians. Living with much less formal manners in a softer climate, and in day-to-day touch with the Moslems at home, in schools, at work and almost all public places, the settlers have taken on non-European mores. There is truth as well as pride in the claim, "We are Algerians."

What they have not taken on is a politics of their own. A heavily outnumbered minority, the settlers always have looked at times of duress to whatever powers may be. During World War II, they embraced in rapid succession the Third Republic, Vichy, the Germans, the Americans, the Free French, the Fourth Republic. More recently, in the absence of a strong lead from Paris, opinion has slipped its moorings. "They change ideas," Mayor Jacques Chevallier of Algiers says of his fellow settlers, "like the smile on the Cheshire cat."

To be sure, there are men and institutions working among the settlers to calm tempers and maintain good relations with the Moslems. Mayor Chevallier, a builder on the scale of Robert Moses and the Levitts combined, is one. Another is the Roman Catholic Church. "It is the duty of every man to avoid violence, not only in acts but in words," Monsignor Duval, the Archbishop of Algiers, said in a recent pastoral letter. Working with young men and women of the purest religious feeling, Père Scotto has established social service missions in the worst of the Moslem slums. "I deeply wanted," one of his workers said, "to fill the gap [between Christians and Moslems] by the performance of common tasks." But he said that from the dock of a military tribunal where he was convicted on charges of aiding the enemy. And a European spectator at the trial, questioned about the name of the Archbishop, replied: "Mohammed."

The truth is that die-hard extremists have increasingly come to dominate European opinion in Algeria. A handful of rich wine-growers, dependent upon French subsidies for their income and likely to go to the wall if independence came, take the lead. The dirty work is done by clubs, professional and veterans' organizations and other private groups. A university students' association, located on the second floor of a bank building in Algiers, is perhaps typical.

The stairs leading up to the office were plastered with posters showing Europeans mutilated by the rebels and bearing captions saying: "Frenchmen, meditate on this." On a table by the door was a pile of medical pamphlets, thick with pictures of bloody corpses, and purporting to show that ritualistic murder was an innate racial trait of the Arabs. Inside, a group of teen-agers—the boys in shorts, the girls in cotton dresses—lounged at their ease. Several days before, in reprisal for the nationalists' bombing of a casino, the boys had led a raid against some Arab merchants, actually pitching two of them off a cliff into the sea. "I don't regret it," one of them said. "My sister might have been killed in that casino, or worse, maybe lost an arm. Anyhow, the Arabs insulted us."

Minutes later a company of paratroopers paraded past in the street below. All the students crowded to the window, cheering and waving. What did their visitor think of the paras, they wanted to know. They were good troops, he believed, but not very different from the Wehrmacht. "That's what we like about them," one of the girls said.

The Moslem Mass

The Moslems—a thickly mixed blend of Arabs and Berbers making up 85 per cent of the total population of nearly nine million— were victims long before the fighting began. A backward people sent reeling into the modern world by the impact of France, they have been keyed up to demands their poor country cannot possibly support. Their population, thanks to medical science, doubles every twenty-five years, only to find not enough houses, not enough schools, not enough jobs. They remain largely rural, but in desperate straits hundreds of thousands have crowded into the *bidonvilles* (tin-can cities) around the major Algerian towns, or moved to France as industrial workers.

On the Moslems, too, has fallen the great burden of the war. Total deaths number roughly 100,000, of which less than a thousand are French civilians, with perhaps 6,000 in French military ranks. The rebel forces have lost perhaps 20,000. All the rest, nearly three-quarters, are Moslem civilians.

Even so, it is no easy task to determine Moslem public opinion in the struggle. Go into the countryside with the rebels, and the villagers will turn out in enthusiastic welcome. Go in with the French, and the same thing will happen. Traveling with the French once, I came upon an Arab playing checkers with a French officer at a command post, high atop a mountain. Spontaneously, it seemed, he began talking about what would happen if the French were forced out. "Half my people would be wiped out in a year. Like that," he said, sweeping the counters from the board.

Amidst much uncertainty, however, there are two clear points. One is that the best educated and most successful Moslems lean decidedly toward the rebels. Not half a dozen eminent Arabs in Algeria, if that many, support the French cause. Among the rebels' supporters, literally thousands speak Parisian French. France's civilizing mission, in short, has done its work. Having risen from the dead mass of their people, the educated Moslems want to lead them. As the Moslem hero of an Algerian novel modestly puts the complaint: "I am a one-eyed man in the kingdom of the blind; but I am not king."

The other point is that the French reforms, big or small, seem to make almost no dent. One big one which would have given the Moslems a considerable voice in local government was laughed off. "We want meat, and they give us milk," one educated Moslem said. As to the small reforms, they convince nobody. In Batna, for instance, the French have changed the name of the native quarter from Black Town to New France. But no European can enter New France without an armed guard.

What emerges in sum is the spectacle of thousands of men— life-sized but no bigger—caught up in the sweep of a gigantic event. Preoccupied with their own problems and prejudices, almost void of practical political programs, the actors on the Algerian stage play out their roles by rote, mindless of the consequences in the total drama. Purposeless drifting, punctuated by bursts of furious violence—that, in essence, is the Algerian tragedy.

Tormented Officer in a "Dirty War"

by Henry Tanner

ALGIERS

THE FRENCH ARMY in Algeria is one of the most tormented, most self-searching and self-doubting bodies of men that ever fought a war. Now in its sixth year of combat, it numbers about 400,000 men. Of its 30,000 officers, an estimated two-thirds are professional soldiers. Paris editorialists who write about "the Army"—what it does and thinks, and whether it is loyal or likely to stage another *putsch*—are writing about this corps of highly trained, highly intelligent, articulate and troubled regular officers.

What is the French officer in Algeria like? Captain Claude-André de V. is a valid example. He is 41 years old. The men in his family have been soldiers since Napoleon.

Captain de V. is a member of the last class to graduate from Saint-Cyr, the French military academy, before the Germans overran the country in 1940. After his graduation he joined the Resistance as a civilian. He was captured a few months later and spent the rest of the war in the concentration camp of Buchenwald.

In 1945, almost immediately after his liberation, he volunteered for Indochina. When asked why he was so eager, after years in the concentration camp, to go from one hell to another, he answers evenly: "My country had trained me as a soldier. It was time I started to be one."

Captain de V. served a total of seven years in Indochina. Between tours he was trained as a paratrooper in France. After Indochina came Morocco, then Tunisia and finally Algeria. He was a young company commander in the first paratroop regiment that was sent into the Aurès Mountains of eastern Algeria shortly after the outbreak of the nationalist rebellion on Nov. 1, 1954. Recently he was sent back into the Aurès after having served in Kabylia, another crucial mountain region, and on the general staff in Algiers.

The central experience in Captain de V.'s life was Indochina. It formed him, he says, and adds wryly: " 'Sensitized' perhaps would be a better word."

To begin with, he remembers his last day in Indochina. On that day he had to face the 150 Vietnamese soldiers fighting in his company. He had personally selected and trained them. They were his men. Now he had to tell them that France was leaving Indochina, that he, their commander, was going home and that they would have to stay, probably to be tortured and killed.

"I betrayed them. I betrayed their faith in me," he cries, and in a startling, abrupt movement, as if bent under the enormous burden of that guilt, he leans forward and sobs, his face covered with both hands. After a moment, attempting a smile, he says: "You must think we are a sentimental army."

Today, too, the captain commands about 100 local soldiers. Nearly 130,000 Moslems have been enlisted into the French Army as auxiliaries and are carrying French arms. Thousands of others have been organized in "self-defense" units and are guarding their villages with antiquated rifles. Thousands are cooperating with the French police and the Army's intelligence officers. And thousands have committed themselves by running for political office or accepting administrative jobs.

The captain tells of one of his friends, a much-decorated career officer, who resigned his Army commission last year and emigrated to Canada—partly, the captain suspects, because he feared that if he stayed he would one day have to tell his Moslem soldiers, as he had told his Vietnamese, that he was letting them down. This feeling of guilt and shame is one of the reasons for the vehemence with which some of the French officers here have turned against successive Paris Governments whenever they feared, as they did before May 13, 1958, and again last January, that the Army would be drawn into another "ignominious" withdrawal.

This fear has been revived to a considerable degree by General de Gaulle's latest offer to the rebels to go to Paris to discuss a cease-fire in Algeria—an offer that was quickly accepted.

"We are no *ultras,* no reactionaries," cried a major who had demonstrated his sympathy with the extremist insurgents last January. "On the contrary, we are the true liberals, the true Christians. We love these people [the Algerian Moslems]. We have nothing in common with the *colons.* We will never be rich, here in Algeria or elsewhere. But we are afraid of what the intentions of Paris might be. Let Paris dispel our fears, and all will be well."

Many of these officers have been agitating for "integration," the slogan of the civilian *ultras,* because they feel that the door will be finally closed to "abandonment" only if Algeria becomes permanently a part of France. But many of them, in fact, care little about the future status of Algeria and would go along with any solution, including independence, if it were attained in such a way that the Army would emerge from this "dirty war" with "its honor intact." Army control of the referendum, in which Algerians will choose their future, is thus the Army's frequently heard minimum demand.

The presence of General de Gaulle at the helm of the French state has not changed the basic outlook of these officers. Fifteen out of seventeen commanding generals, including the Commander-in-chief in Algeria, were replaced in an unprecedented command shakeup following the January insurrection by European extremists. Confirmed Gaullists or apolitical officers now hold all the most important commands. General de Gaulle's hold on the Army thus is stronger than it ever was, but nobody is in a position to know whether it will prove strong enough for all contingencies.

Except for a steadily decreasing number of aging colonels and generals, the great majority of today's career officers has no special loyalty to de Gaulle. These younger officers will tell you that *"le grand Charles"* is a fine figure of an old soldier but that he belongs to another world and another generation and that he has never really grasped the methods of revolutionary warfare which the Army has been waging in Indochina and Algeria.

These officers respect de Gaulle for what he was twenty years ago. But they have deep misgivings about his present role. They do not give him any blank checks. Their attitudes toward him and his Government will be determined in each new situation that arises by the actions he takes and the results he produces.

Captain de V.'s command post is an isolated village in the mountains. Once a week a heavily armed convoy moves slowly up the winding Army-built road with food, mail and soldiers returning from leave. On rare occasions a helicopter lands to evacuate a wounded soldier or bring in a superior officer for a quick inspection.

In the village and the ten square miles of empty country around it the captain is king—or, as he puts it, "almost God Almighty." Since this is one of the worst fighting zones in Algeria, there have been no local elections in the village. The captain is Mayor, judge, head schoolmaster and many other dignitaries all in one. Two of his soldiers are the community's only teachers. His company doctor is the only doctor.

The captain, far from enjoying his power, is overwhelmed by it. "How can a man have such a hold on people and keep from misusing it?" he asks. "And how can an Army which plays this kind of role keep from getting mixed up in the country's politics?"

A few years ago the population of the captain's village was eight thousand. Now it is nearly 20,000, all of them Moslems. The Army has emptied the mountains around it, liquidated the isolated *mechtas* (hamlets) and forced the peasants to bring their families to the village. A new community of squat, windowless structures of pressed earth, odd wooden planks and sheets of corrugated iron, sackcloth and straw mats has risen on the edge of the old village with its old but solid stone houses. This new community is what the Army calls a *regroupement*.

The Army has "regrouped" about two million Moslems or about a fifth of the Moslem population of Algeria. "Regrouping" is an essential part of the methods of "revolutionary warfare" which the Army has devised to meet the nationalist rebels on their own ground.

The theory of "revolutionary warfare" stems from the writings of Mao Tse-tung. It was practiced by the Communists in Indochina, where the French adopted and adapted it for their own use as the only possible answer to rebel strategy. The theory holds that the rebels need the support of the civilian population "as a fish needs water." Without it, they would be without food, shelter, clothes and information about the Army's moves. By the same token, the theory holds, the civilians start to live only if they are protected against the rebels' political commissars, tax collectors, recruiting agents and plain terrorists.

Finally, the theory continues, it takes all-pervading "psychological action" by the Army to restore the health of the civilian population once the process of subversion by the rebels has begun.

Thus the Army has adopted three commandments: The civilian population must be "protected," "engaged" and "controlled." To this end, it has developed a complex machinery for getting a total hold on the civilians through *regroupements,* self-defense units, re-education camps for brain-washing, networks of informers, sports teams, needlework groups for women, hospitals, schools and a vast general propaganda program.

Captain de V. believes in the necessity of "revolutionary warfare" and "psychological action." Like almost all officers in Algeria, he is convinced that the French Army here is the last bastion of Western civilization.

French officers here are in turn angry and deeply hurt that France's allies do not see them as they see themselves, as the last crusaders against communism. Mindful of the failure of the United States to support France fully in the U. N. debate on Algeria, Captain de V. says, *"Eh, non,* we didn't bear you in our hearts when you let us down."

One of his junior officers put it differently. "Well, how are things in Little Rock this morning?" he likes to ask the American visitor. For the only thing these officers resent more than the allied "betrayal" is the charge, or implied charge, of racism.

Frequently they will say, with mock admiration: "You were smart, of course. You solved your problem when you killed off your Indians. We pampered our Moslems and now we have ten million of them on our hands."

The worshipers emerging from the early mass at Algiers Cathedral the other Sunday included a famous general, a bevy of colonels and captains wearing the red or green berets of the paratroopers and scores of less conspicuous officers and men. They filed past the Tommy-gun-carrying police sentries who guard the church and, like the rest of the congregation, lingered in the sun-lit Moorish square to shake hands with neighbors and bow to the priest.

The spectacle is the same every Sunday morning at almost every church. The French Army in Algeria is a praying army.

Gen. Jacques Massu, whose removal from command touched off the abortive extremist uprising last January, is a devout and ardent church-goer. Most of the regimental commanders of the Tenth Paratroop Division, Massu's old outfit, which has fought some of the most merciless campaigns of the war and which fraternized with the extremists during the uprising, are equally strict in the observance of their religious obligations.

The Army's interest in religion is one of the many things that have combined to turn this total and "dirty" war into a bitter conflict of conscience.

Officers like Captain de V. are well aware of this. The captain speaks with relative serenity of summary military justice, arbitrary arrest and even torture, because, he says, his "conscience is clear— as clear at least as that of any police captain in Chicago or Birmingham."

He is trying as faithfully as he can to keep the war "clean" in his sector. And he relates how some time ago he had to detach an officer to keep an eye on a unit of the D. O. P. *(Détachement Operationnel de Protection),* a kind of military police and intelligence agency, which entered his sector. Moslem civilians had complained to him that people were unaccountably missing and that others had been brutally mistreated.

"Those are the boys who pull the rough stuff," he says of the D. O. P. And he adds: "It's always the guy from outside, from another neck of the woods, who commits the crimes, never the one who stays in an area. It's true of the rebel side, too."

In spite of his efforts the captain has no illusions about some things happening under his command that he isn't proud of. This kind of war is a tremendous emotional strain for every man and officer, he says.

"You are combing the mountains day and night—for nothing.

It takes a company to hunt down one man, and maybe miss him. Then you see some shepherds and you ask them questions. They haven't seen or heard a thing, and they grin. And so there is that wall again. And how do you expect a man to keep his temper all the time? One night he is going to lash out at the wrong people."

The captain knows that since General de Gaulle's return to power both civilian and military authorities have been looking for means to end all practice of torture by the Army. He thinks they have made some headway, but not very much.

There has been a suggestion, rejected in the end, to relieve the Army of the "dirty work" and create a special agency for it. He scoffs at the hypocrisy of the idea. And he says he is afraid that certain types of reprisals—immediate execution of a terrorist caught throwing a bomb into a Sunday crowd, for instance, and exhibition of his body in the public square—are indispensable weapons at times in this war.

The captain knows about the letter sent some while ago to the French College of Bishops by a number of Catholic priests who were serving their terms as reserve officers in Algeria.

The priests wrote that the war was fought with "means which our conscience reproves" and that interrogations too often were made with what "we must classify as 'tortures.' " They warned that these practices might haunt young officers and men in their later lives either as moral corruption or as unbearable conflicts of conscience.

The captain is aware of such dangers. He has heard that at Maillot, the military hospital of Algiers, and in various hospitals of the mainland, an increasing number of young officers, veterans of Algeria, are being treated for nervous disorders.

Captain de V. and his like are able to talk dispassionately about this side of the war only if they do not feel they are being attacked. Let a Paris newspaper or an American politician or an African delegate to the United Nations talk about "French tortures" and they will explode.

"We are no angels, and things will happen in a war," they will say. "But if one of our guys is quick on the trigger or touches a woman or kills a man, he is abominated. He becomes an outcast even to his friends and buddies. Not so on the other side. They kill. They cut the throats of a family, their own Moslem families, down to the children and the baby in the crib and the family dog. And then they proclaim the killer a national hero and make speeches about him and issue communiqués about his achievements.

"That's the difference. And you invite them into your palaces in New York and Washington. That's what we don't understand."

No one is able to predict what "the Army" will do if Algeria ceases to be French. Some of the officers were close to the European extremists in the abortive January uprising. Yet, at the same time, some powerful commanders quietly gathered the men and the means to intervene in Algiers and to save the Republic not only from the civilian extremists but, if necessary, also from the extremists in their own ranks. Some officers would not hesitate to march on Paris if they thought they could take it; others, fearing chaos and civil war, would hesitate and, in the end, obey the Government.

Immediately after the insurrection, a representative officer said: "The Army has obeyed this time, after pondering its moral obligations for a day or two. It is glad it did. But if there are more broken promises and if the threat of a sell-out is raised again—well, I wouldn't take the Army for granted then."

As Chanzeaux Sees
the French Crisis

by Laurence Wylie

THE TOWN clerk and the constable were trying to explain the implications of the local vote in the last elections, and inevitably this led to a discussion of personalities. For all villagers the discussion of personalities is a major sport, but it is in bad taste for public officials to sit in the Town Hall and analyze the citizens' political behavior, so we dropped the subject. I tried a less personal opening.

"How will Chanzeaux vote in the referendum?"

The clerk did not have to ponder this question: "You know Chanzeaux. You know what we say about de Gaulle. You can answer that one yourself."

Given Chanzeaux and given de Gaulle, the answer did seem obvious, and if Chanzeaux felt the way it did, then many other rural communities of France would feel the same way. I had chosen to make a study of Chanzeaux precisely because it is a representative community in its region. Now that I had lived there with my family for ten months I knew that beneath traditional labels and slogans it had much in common with the village where we had lived in the opposite corner of France.

Chanzeaux is in the Maine-et-Loire Department, about a six-hour drive from Paris, in western France. Of its 1,200 inhabitants about 300 live in the *bourg,* the village in the center of the commune. The 900 others live in isolated farmhouses or in the ten hamlets scattered through the countryside. There is a little basket factory owned by Monsieur Nicolas, the Mayor, but most of the people make their living by farming.

In the northern end of the commune, where the land slopes down to the Layon River, there are rich vineyards that produce some of the sweet white wine sold in Paris bars to men who order *"un coup de blanc d'Anjou."* On the plateau, at the other end of the commune, the farmers raise cattle for both meat and milk, and their crops are all for fodder—hay, oats, fodder cabbage, fodder beets. On the rest of the land a wide variety of crops is grown—wheat, camomile, potatoes, tobacco, seed pansies. By the variety of its economy Chanzeaux mirrors the economy of rural France.

Chanzeaux's distinction is in its history. It was one of the counter-revolutionary centers from which the Vendée War spread in 1793. The Catholic, conservative tradition is still strong, but in the last fifty years there has been a silent revolution. Inflation, a growing taste for city life, the fragmentation of the land through inheritance have weakened the domination of the nobles and left the land and the power in the hands of the farmers themselves. They no longer bow low to *M'sieu' notr' maître'.* Instead, they pity the poor noble who slaves at his business in the city in order to make money to keep the old château from falling apart.

When one settles in a rural community one is tempted to judge the whole community by the people living in the *bourg.* This is inevitable because contact with the villagers is easy and natural, but it is difficult to meet the farmers. Only after months does one make friends with enough country people to know really what life on the farms is like. It is essential, however, not to judge the farmers by what one knows of the villagers. The two groups share many ideals and attitudes, but the economic problems they face today are quite different.

As an administrative and spiritual center the *bourg* has a real function, but economically it is becoming obsolete. Farmers have cars and motorbikes, and the little city of Chemillé is only seven miles away. Angers is not much farther. Instead of shopping in the village of Chanzeaux the farmers do their errands in the city when they go to sell their cattle or eggs or butter at the weekly market. Country women also buy from the grocery trucks that drive out of the cities and crisscross the countryside, stopping at every farmhouse. There is little business left for the merchants of Chanzeaux.

Most of the artisans work at crafts that are dying out. M. Cesbron, the wooden shoemaker, retired several years ago, but he cannot even sell the stock he has left. Rubber boots and factory-made plastic sabots have taken the place of wooden shoes. M. Martin, the tinsmith, does not have enough work because people use so many plastic buckets and pans. M. Ragneau, the cabinet-maker, used to make the furniture for the young ménages in the commune. Now the young people prefer to buy ready-made furniture in Angers.

Our landlord, M. Boussion, was the harness maker, and he still has as much business as he can handle. Most of the farm work is done by horses, although since the Marshall Plan brought the first tractor to the commune the number has increased to twenty-three. When I asked M. Boussion what he intended to do with our house when we left, he said he would like to live in it himself if only he could retire.

"What keeps you from retiring?"

"I've looked everywhere for someone to take over my work," he said. "There aren't any apprentices any more. What boy wants to become a harness maker today?"

"So what's the answer?"

"I'll keep going as long as I can and then shut up the shop. There's nothing else to do."

The only artisans with a future are those who have been able to roll with the technological blow. M. Mosset started his career as a blacksmith but gradually gave that up to repair bicycles—and now motorbikes. His older son has become the electrician for the commune, and the next son is learning electronics in the army.

The other people living in the village are mostly public officials —the clerk, the constable, the postmen, the teachers, the priest— and retired people. Needless to say, this part of the population has been hit extremely hard by inflation. M. Durand, for instance, once owned the village cafe and hotel. His business was prosperous, but in the late Nineteen Thirties his health began to fail. He was told that he had to drink less.

"I didn't mind cutting down on wine," says M. Durand, "but I knew this meant the end of my business. You can't run an inn if you aren't ready to drink with your customers when they ask you."

So he sold out. Today the value of the money he received is less than a twentieth of what it was in 1938, and he can scarcely make ends meet. Fortunately, he did not sell his little vineyard and fortunately he is still able to work it himself.

"But it's hard at my age," he says. "My vines are a kilometer away from the village, uphill, downhill. I had to trade in my bicycle and get a woman's bike so I wouldn't have to swing my leg over. I have to rest a lot, but I get the work done. I've got to."

"Don't you have a pension?"

"My retired worker's pension, but that's not enough. Too bad I wasn't wounded in the first war. I'd been called up for maneuvers a month before it started and went through the whole thing down to Armistice Day without a scratch. I thought I was lucky then, but if I'd gotten a little wound I'd be getting a pension for that."

As a whole, then, the villagers are economically a rather depressed group. On meeting them you would not realize this because they are cordial, almost gay people. M. Cesbron cannot sell his wooden shoes, and he is going blind from cataracts, but his conversation is sprightly. Mme. Cimon's grocery is losing money, but as she gossips with her occasional customers their conversation is not gloomy.

It is when the Government is mentioned that the bitterness emerges, because it is the Government the villagers blame for the taxes and inflation to which they attribute their ruin. When Pierre Poujade started his anti-tax revolt many of the Chanzeaux villagers thought he might bring a solution to their problems. Now they have lost faith in him, but they are still ready for a change.

Traditionally the farmers as a group complain more than the villagers, but today they have far less reason to complain, for they are relatively well-off. M. Robineau can serve as a good example of the average Chanzeaux farmer. I met him when he brought us a load of wood for our fireplace, but I did not know him well until we took a walk one night. He had invited me to go with him to the cattle market, and one day in early June he sent word that we would go the following Thursday.

I arrived at his house at 1:30 in the morning. We had breakfast, drove four steers out of the barn and started down the road. His two sons went with us, and a neighbor, who was driving a cow to market, joined us a mile down the road. With the five of us the task was simple. The neighbor walked ahead to make sure the road was clear. The boys walked on either side to keep the steers from going into the fields. Robineau and I walked behind to see that they did not turn back. It was a beautiful night. Chemillé was seven miles away. All Robineau and I had to do was follow the cattle and talk.

"I should have sold them last week," he said. "With this Algerian business they've never brought a better price."

"Well, for once you farmers can't complain."

Robineau said nothing for a few steps. Then he answered: "There's no denying it. We've never been so well off. We run the land and our business as we like. My land still belongs to a noble, but I haven't seen her for years, and her agent comes around only to collect the rent. She doesn't modernize the property, but then I pay less rent because of it."

"But all of you complain that taxes take away your profits."

"Of course, taxes are too high. It's the Algerian business. But still the Government gives us lots of breaks."

He went on to point out that farmers pay less in taxes than any other economic class. The Government banking agency supplies ample credit at reasonable rates. Tariffs have protected key products. Farmers receive coupons so that they may buy gas more cheaply for their tractors. All sorts of advisory services are available, so that farmers may increase their production. Cooperatives are not taxed like ordinary businesses, and the farmers of Chanzeaux buy most of their equipment at the best possible prices. Its cost has gone up, but they pay for it with the inflated money they receive for their products.

"But what do you farmers do with all this money you make?"

This is not a question you can usually ask a farmer—or anyone. But when two men are walking together in the middle of the night they talk more freely. Still, Robineau answered at such length, in such detail, so indirectly and technically that I had only a vague idea of what he was saying—which was perhaps what he wished. He reads the government bulletins and the financial pages of the newspapers carefully, and he has definite ideas about the relative advantages of investing in gold or gold louis or stocks or bonds or land. Gold and government bonds guaranteed against inflation seemed to interest him most. M. Robineau is certainly making money and putting it aside.

So is M. Caillau. He is a wine grower, and normally the wine growers are even more prosperous than the other farmers. Along with all the other vintners of France, however, Caillau is experiencing a temporary squeeze. For the last two years a spring freeze has decimated the harvest, and his financial reserves are low. Of course, there was some compensation in the fact that the price of wine rose steeply, but now to force the price down the Government has imported quantities of wine from Spain and Greece. What M. Caillau says about this measure is not fit to print. However, his 1958 wine will be plentiful and of good quality, it appears, so that he feels his worries are temporary.

The fact that the farmers of Chanzeaux are prosperous does not mean that they have no problems. They have serious problems. Their equipment is not sufficiently modernized. Living conditions on the farm are often inconvenient and unsanitary. There is a shortage of labor, and at the same time farmers complain that their children are forced to work in the city because there is no land for them to farm. Roads need improvement. Hedges should be torn out and fields enlarged. One of the most desperate problems is the fragmentation of property, which prevents efficient use of the land.

However, the farmers have lived with the problems a long time and do not feel their urgency. The prosperity of the farmers today makes them economically as satisfied a group of people as the villagers are dissatisfied.

Still, there is a preoccupation shared by all the people in the commune so acute that it dominates every other consideration. It increases the bitterness of the villagers, and it outweighs the contentment of the farmers. The people of Chanzeaux are utterly exasperated with sending their sons to Algeria to die or to risk dying for a cause which seemed hopeless until de Gaulle took over last spring.

On Candlemas some boys asked me to take a group picture of them. After mass the class of 1958—that is, the boys who were going to be drafted in 1958—passed the *baton* to the class of 1959. After the traditional ceremony the younger men went off to the wine cellar belonging to one of their fathers. The class of 1958 ordered two bottles of wine in the cafe, filled the ten glasses put before them and sat glumly around the big table. Gérard Audiau had already passed his physical and would leave as their twentieth birthdays arrived.

"Algeria . . . Hmmmm!" Jean Oger made a motion of a knife being twisted into his ribs.

"Stop it, Oger," Audiau said.

"What's the matter? Are you afraid?"

"Sure, aren't you?"

"Just as your ancestors must have been afraid when they climbed the church tower and fired on the Blues," I suggested.

"At least they had something to fight for," said Lelu. "They had religion. And what have we got? Oil! Money in the pocket of someone in Paris."

"Don't think I wouldn't die for religion," Oger said, "but I don't see what religion has to do with this business."

At this moment Louis Mosset came by the table, overheard the conversation and stopped. He is 23 and has already put in his two years in Algeria.

"You've got France to fight for, and if that's not enough you'll find a good reason when you get down there. Wait until your best friend is killed beside you. Then you'll catch on. You'll want to kill every damned Algerian you see." Mosset walked off to join his own group.

"Now there's a noble reason to fight—personal revenge," said Lelu sarcastically. "No, the only reason I can see is that if we give up we'll feel ashamed, the way we did after Indochina. . . . No, there must be a change anyway!"

There must be a change! That is what everyone said. They might disagree on what the change should be, but they knew there had to be a change. The atmosphere was like that of the summer of 1939 when everyone was saying, "There must be an end to it."

And, of course, things have changed. When the blow-up came and de Gaulle intervened, the people of Chanzeaux welcomed him with a tremendous feeling of relief. The vagueness of his intentions permitted wide interpretation, so the enthusiasm was unanimous. Or almost, since there are a dozen or so Communists in the commune. Everyone else felt that de Gaulle offered the only hope in a situation that had seemed hopeless.

For the *Fête-Dieu* (Corpus Christi) the community prepares a half-mile carpet of flower petals and colored sawdust arranged in a series of religious emblems and designs over which the priest carries *le bon Dieu* in the procession. M. Horeau, the blacksmith, was going to make de Gaulle's profile and the Lorraine Cross in flower petals in front of his house. After much discussion the neighbors persuaded him not to. The mixture of politics and religion seemed inappropriate. They consoled him, however, by making it clear that they shared his enthusiasm.

How will Chanzeaux vote in the September referendum? Obviously for de Gaulle. But the constitution itself? Are the people for it or against it? "A good farmer can make a living with a horse and a plow," says Robineau, "and a poor farmer can go broke with a tractor."

The people of Chanzeaux hope the new constitution will be a tractor run by a good farmer, but the man is more important than the machine. When men fail their mechanisms fail. The failure of the Fourth Republic is blamed more on the men who formed the Government than on the constitution of the Fourth Republic. If the Fifth Republic succeeds, it will be because of the men running it. No one knows who they will be, but the people of Chanzeaux believe they have nothing to lose in a change. For the present, at least, there is de Gaulle. Their vote in the referendum will be a vote of confidence for him.

In its attitude toward de Gaulle and the referendum, Chanzeaux is no exception among the thousands of rural communes in France. Normally these communities are turned against each other politically by the traditional conflicts that have arisen in the course of history, that are complicated by each new national crisis and that are perpetuated partly by the political parties themselves. Today, as at other points in French history, the people of the villages of France are united by an anguish so acute that the divisive influence of the old labels and slogans is no longer effective. The people of all rural France, except for those of the extreme Right and extreme Left, will vote for the same reason and in the same sense as the people of Chanzeaux.

Whether the new constitution will foster this sense of unity is another question. The tragedy of French politics—as with politics anywhere—is that the traditional labels and slogans keep old fears so stirred up that the deeper causes for unity are overlooked. We went to live in Chanzeaux so that we might be able to compare it with the village of Peyrane in the Vaucluse Department, about fifty miles north of Marseilles.

Peyrane has always been a community of the Left, as Chanzeaux is traditionally to the Right. The elected representatives of the districts in which these villages are situated are consistently at each other's throats in the Chamber of Deputies. One might assume that the people of the two villages are basically antagonistic to each other. This is not true. The people of Chanzeaux and those of Peyrane are not really very different. If their representatives could leave off fighting old battles, which have little real meaning for the people today, they might discover that the basic interests of the communities are very close.

In Chanzeaux M. Aligon votes Independent, and M. Robineau probably votes M. R. P. In Peyrane M. Pelloux votes Socialist and M. Tamisier, Socialist-Radical. Their deputies in Paris have, to cite an example, perpetuated the battle over the relationships of church schools to the state, so that this problem is no nearer settlement than when it arose 125 years ago. M. Robineau, Aligon, Pelloux and Tamisier could reach an agreement on this divisive issue in a morning's conference and then they could go to the cafe and enjoy a bottle of wine together.

Once the old slogans are put aside, these men have no quarrel with each other, they agree on what is right and what is wrong, what is fair and unfair in human behavior. They share a common dream about the sort of life they would like to lead. They have much the same attitude toward their families and their communities. They face the same economic problems and could easily agree on means to solve them. Above all, they are far more tolerant and reasonable in religious and political matters than their elected representatives.

De Gaulle believes that by reducing the influence of the political parties he may weaken the traditional distrust which they perpetuate. This will certainly help, but a mere political solution is not enough in itself to liberate the essential unity of the people so that it may become a constructive force. There are many other forces, especially in the opinion-forming institutions of the country that perpetuate traditional quarrels. If de Gaulle is to succeed, he must seek reconciliation at all levels.

The danger is, of course, that in his drive for unity de Gaulle may destroy the freedom of expression of these institutions and the individual citizens. The people of Chanzeaux and Peyrane are aware of this danger. M. Durand says, "If he becomes dictator, we're finished. Louis XIV, two Napoleons, Pétain! Dictators mean disaster." But again, the distress of the Algerian situation overrides every other fear. M. Durand will still vote for the new constitution —that is, for de Gaulle—and hope for the best.

French Dilemma:
How Strong a Man?

by Robert C. Doty

PARIS

FRENCHMEN ARE engaged today in a new phase of their 300-year-old struggle to strike political equilibrium between authority and weak but representative government. From the absolute control of the 17th-century monarchy down to the incoherence and impotence of the closing days of the Fourth Republic in 1958, the pendulum has swung at least half a dozen times without ever coming to rest on a durable solution.

At one extreme, it produced a series of strong men—Louis XIV, Napoleon I, Napoleon III, Clemenceau, Pétain, Charles de Gaulle —to whom, for a time, France turned over her destinies. There were others who aspired to the strong man role but never quite made it—Preisdent Patrice MacMahon in the eighteen-seventies and the tragicomic Gen. Georges Boulanger, a decade later.

These men brought France both moments of intoxicating glory and of black despair. In the cases of all but Clemenceau—because he worked within the republican framework—and de Gaulle— because his story is not finished—the periods of strong rule ended

From the *New York Times Magazine,* October 28, 1962, copyright © 1962 by The New York Times Company.

only with the death of the strong man or a great national disaster that brought him down.

At the other end of the swing, the pendulum has brought periods of government—the Great Revolution and the Terror, restoration kings and Second, Third and Fourth Republics—marked, at best, by instability and, at worst, by anarchy.

It is against this background of three centuries of unsuccessful experimentation that the current struggle between President de Gaulle and the traditional political forces of the country is now being played out. The issue on the surface is comparatively simple. The President wants to amend the Constitution so that his eventual successor will be elected by popular suffrage instead of by a limited college of some 80,000 "notables" who represent and are controlled by the party organization as specified in the Constitution.

De Gaulle seeks to do this by appealing directly to the voters in a referendum being held today, instead of risking having his project blocked in the Senate if he were to choose the method defined by the Constitution for amendment—submission to Parliament. The pros and cons of this proposal are being endlessly debated across all of France. The debate recalls the historical sources of France's alternate fear of and fascination with the strong man, and suggests an assessment of the extent to which de Gaulle conforms to the classic figure of the strong man and an estimate as to whether fear or fascination is uppermost in French minds today.

The strong man has always been more popular with the masses, from whom he draws his strength, than with the normal political cadres of the country—whether nobles, party leaders, economic interests or social and professional organizations—which he largely displaces. The strong man's opportunity comes always with the decline of the efficacy and prestige of these traditional forces of leadership.

But if strong men find their opportunity in failure, they themselves are condemned to perpetual success. So long as they are winning, they are almost invulnerable. But let them once slip—at Waterloo, at Sedan—and the personal prestige on which their power is exclusively built is destroyed irrevocably. The contract they made with the apolitical masses to conduct their public affairs in such a way as to relieve the masses of direct concern with them is dramatically broken. And the masses turn on them unmercifully.

This is a fragility that the cabinet governments of the party system do not share. Socialist Premier Guy Mollet survived the disaster of his Suez Canal expedition in 1956 by more than six months because responsibility for the unsuccessful policy was diffused in the Cabinet-Assembly system of government. And when he fell it was on a matter completely divorced from the Suez affair.

In the bright light that beats upon a strong man there is no place to hide. The major decisions, the rewards of success, the responsibility for failure—and the punishment for it—all are his and his alone.

De Gaulle, in his imperious contempt for lesser men and notably politicians, in his impatience with opposition, in his reliance on "direct democracy"—referendum and plebiscite—to the virtual exclusion of traditional intermediaries, conforms in many respects to the characteristics of previous French strong men. Debate today centers on the question of whether he can escape the historical forces that pushed his predecessors along the fatal course to full dictatorship.

The debate is complicated by the tendency of Frenchmen—at least those of the political cadres—to draw excessively on precedent. All the history France has lived through has strewn the ground with political clichés and personal stereotypes. When a Frenchman of the political élite is discussing current events he reaches almost instinctively for a historical parallel and is not really happy unless he finds one.

The tacit threat of military intervention that brought de Gaulle back to power in 1958 is automatically likened to a new 18 Brumaire, the date of Napoleon's first coup against the Parliament of the Directory a century and a half before. And, of course, in the current political struggle, the traditional parties are campaigning at least as much against Louis XIV, the two Emperors Napoleon and even General Boulanger as they are against President de Gaulle.

However convenient this type of political shorthand may be, it also has its disadvantages. The application of historical references to current events tends to evoke, often with specious logic, not only the old event itself but a whole set of automatic emotional reactions to its context.

Thus, the conditions—of public education, of communications, of economic and social structure—that made it possible for Napoleon III to impose himself no longer exist. The people to whom de Gaulle turns for support in periodic referendums are in every way better informed and more politically sophisticated than was the electorate a century ago.

And yet, when Senate President Gaston Monnerville brands de Gaulle's policy as "enlightened Bonapartism" he stirs Pavlovian reactions of hostility in French republican breasts.

Former Premier Pierre Mendès-France presses on the same nerve when he writes in his current survey of French affairs.

"If Louis Napoleon, a century ago, and de Gaulle in our day, crushed the Assembly, it is not by chance. It is because their system [of personal power] leads directly to it."

But shortly after Mendès-France wrote those words the "crushed" French Assembly rose up and defeated the Gaullist Government of Premier Georges Pompidou. The President responded, as is his constitutional right, by dissolving the Assembly and turning the issues over to the voters to arbitrate in new legislative elections. This would appear to be reasonably democratic procedure.

But here, too, historical precedents come into play to cloud the issues. In 1877 the monarchist President Patrice MacMahon dissolved the Chamber of Deputies to rid himself of what was deemed a too republican majority and seek election of a more royalist chamber. Because of the obviously partisan nature of this precedent, dissolution of Parliament fell into permanent disrepute although it remained among the rights of governments of both the Third and Fourth Republics. Successive Presidents and Premiers preferred to struggle with chambers in which no stable governing majority existed rather than to incur the odium of imitating MacMahon.

When, in 1955, Radical Premier Edgar Faure at last revived the dissolution procedure after his defeat in the National Assembly, he won disapproval for not "playing the game"; it still haunts him and his political career. Similarly, de Gaulle's use of the threat of dissolution and appeal to the voters to get his way with Parliament for the past four years is one of the principal sources of his unpopularity with the parties and their leaders.

But, as yet, it appears that the fear that de Gaulle is leading France toward outright dictatorship, under either himself or his eventual successor, is limited to the political circles of the country —the so-called *pays légal*—the "legal country." In the *pays réel*— the "real country"—soundings intimate that his popularity remains high. The researchers of so anti-Gaullist a journal as the weekly L'Express returned from studies in five representative sections of the country concluding, with resignation, that de Gaulle would again carry the day with the masses.

With these ordinary voters subtle evocations of the Napoleons, of the violation of the constitutional amendment procedure by de Gaulle, weighed little. The reporters for L'Express found that the most oft-repeated sentiments were that de Gaulle, after all, was *propre*—meaning, approximately clean and correct in his dealings —whereas the parties—*eh bien,* the parties were that old tangle of feuding ambitions that had landed France in the soup before.

This is really the heart of the matter. To the average voter there just is no satisfactory substitute for de Gaulle on the scene. Regardless of their personal merits—which in many cases are notable —the political leaders of the opposition still symbolize a return to the weaknesses and humiliations of the Fourth Republic. As most observers read public opinion, the voters are far more afraid of that possibility than of the risk that de Gaulle or a successor in the Presidency might turn France into a dictatorship.

So strong is this revulsion against the old regime that not a single responsible voice is raised to defend it. Even the men who used to operate its shaky controls now deny with indignation Gaullist charges that they wish to taste again "the delights and poisons" of the sovereign-Assembly system.

The party leaders, despite their temporary and fragile unanimity and the support of most of the intelligentsia and provincial political personnel, have an uphill fight in opposing de Gaulle.

In the first place, they have been able to unite effectively only against something, as they used to do in overthrowing governments of the Fourth Republic. But, thus far, they have been unable to get together on a positive program to oppose de Gaulle's.

Secondly, their arguments against the strong man and his current initiative are sophisticated and juridical. The President's arguments are simple and direct.

The parties would be in a far easier position if they dared openly oppose the very idea of a strong executive. But, embarassed by the record of the Assembly regime and aware of a current of opinion favorable to strength at the top, they must concentrate their fire on what, to the average voter, are relatively abstruse considerations.

They must say, for example: "We are for a strong government but against personal power"; "We approve the principle of popular suffrage and sovereignty but the way de Gaulle proposes to bring it into play is dangerous, unsound and unconstitutional."

There is every reason to believe that the professions of reform by the old-line leaders are sincere. They *do* believe in the necessity for a strong executive and they *do* believe the one de Gaulle outlines would be dangerously overbalanced in the direction of strong man rule. But it is hard to make the voters believe it.

It is child's play for Gaullist propaganda to convince the voters that what the parties really mean by their position is: "We want to get back to the good old days of revolving-door governments where every man could at least hope to be a minister"; and: "You, the voters, are just intelligent enough to elect the Deputies but cannot be trusted to choose wisely a President of the Republic."

At the same time, the President is shamelessly blackmailing the country by threatening to resign if he does not get the massive support of the voters in today's referendum. In contrast to the subtleties of the party position, he is able to say to the voters, with simple flattery, looking each in the eye from the television screen: "I ask you, very simply, to decide that, from now on, you will elect your President by universal suffrage."

What could be more appealing than to vote "yes" and thereby affirm one's own status as citizen-arbiter and, at the same time, keep the President from resigning and casting the future into uncertainty? For it is true—unfortunately, from the viewpoint of the parties—that de Gaulle's withdrawal from the scene would leave a

void that might be filled by chaos. Technically, Gaston Monnerville, President of the Senate and a leader of the opposition to the
President's plan, would become interim President of the Republic
until new elections could be held not later than 40 days after the
vacancy. Depending on the referendum results, these would be
held either by universal suffrage or with the limited college of
"notables."

In either case, a vacancy of power would provide a tempting
opportunity for some of the really sinister forces lurking just off-
stage—the Fascist-minded elements in the army, the remnants of
the Secret Army Organization of uprooted Europeans from Algeria and the classic extreme right that has always existed in
France. It would require fast, effective coalition action by the
traditional "republican" forces—faster and more effective action
than they have demonstrated in the past—to close the door to a
coup d'état.

Against the simple, deadly appeal of such argument, the political leaders struggle in anger and frustration. Furthermore, as individuals they are badly overmatched.

Paul Reynaud is a lucid, intelligent man who, at 84, has the
vigor of one 20 years younger. His arguments against the Gaullist
regime are cogent and well documented. But he is also the victim
of his own stereotype. He is the Premier who presided over the
downfall of France in 1940, a downfall prepared largely by those
who preceded him in power, but with which his public image is
irrevocably tarnished. A battle for public confidence between de
Gaulle and Reynaud is clearly no contest.

Guy Mollet is a high-minded Socialist, devoted democrat, in-
tensely "European" and "Atlantic" in his outlook. He, too, in-
veighs brilliantly against the perils of personal power. But for the
average citizen Mollet is still the Premier who was in office when
the Algerian rebellion took several turns for the worse, whose
Government sponsored the Suez disaster and left the state considerably worse off financially than it found it. Again, a mismatch
with de Gaulle.

So it is, too, with most of the other leaders of anti-Gaullism—
a Félix Gaillard, whose brilliance as a financial expert was incapable of checking the Fourth Republic's slide toward bank-

ruptcy; the coldly intellectual Mendès-France, whose career has been spent in denouncing the weaknesses of the old regime as vigorously as have the Gaullists but who, fairly or unfairly, must remain identified with it in the popular mind; a Maurice Faure, relatively untarred, personally, with the failures of the Fourth Republic, but president of a party—the Radical Socialists—that was the very epitome of all that was compromising and uninspiring about it.

In the simple—the oversimple—judgments of the average Frenchman, these men, collectively, represent failure, while de Gaulle represents success; they stand for the divisions of a multiplicity of doctrinaire parties, de Gaulle for unity and a regrouping of political forces into big formations capable of operating a Presidential system.

Not even the ghosts of the two Napoleons are likely to reverse that assessment now.

A New Revolution Transforms France

by Stephen R. Graubard

FRANCE IS IN the midst of a major revolution. The absence of violence conceals the extent of the change, but those who know the country best understand that this is not the France they knew immediately after Hitler's defeat or even the one which they recognized as recently as 1955. In political life, as in everything else, the pre-1939 world seems strangely remote. The historian, looking back at the French 1962 Parliamentary elections in which Charles de Gaulle's party won an absolute majority in the past fortnight, will be impressed by the calm which characterized the nation in what was supposed to be a critical time. He will be struck by the number of men and women who refused to become excited, who absented themselves from the polls and who did not believe they were living at a historic moment, privileged to choose between the forces of order and disorder, between freedom and autocracy. The specter of another Napoleon III obviously did not haunt very many.

Perhaps the election experience will be viewed as one more evidence of the fact that old-fashioned French party politics is dead, having no more relevance to today's political situation than is offered by 19th-century armaments in the military sphere or traditional diplomatic methods in the relations that exist between France and her neighbors. France has a new opinion of itself, as it does of Europe and the rest of the world. In its relations with Germany there is revealed a spirit which no Frenchman, now alive, recognizes as issuing from the past. A new generation is coming to the fore, and there is little to suggest that it is prepared to accept the values of those who were middle-aged in 1939. Economically and socially, France is experiencing a change as great as any she has ever known. The change is affecting all classes—in the way they think as much as in the way they live. This is a revolution in everything but name. All the traditional caricatures about France seem suddenly dated.

In the sphere of foreign policy the revolution is at once apparent. The French are no longer frightened of Germany. It is not that they trust Adenauer; they did not flock to see him as the Germans did to see de Gaulle on his triumphal tour last summer. Their feeling about Germany and Europe is indeed very complex. In the present world, France is simply not large enough to mean anything by herself; she can realize herself only in and through Europe.

In one way or another, this idea is expressed by almost all who talk in anything but the old clichés. France is excited by Europe; she is curious to know it; she is even prepared to help invent the myths which will make it real for those who cannot yet feel its presence.

The French businessman who tells you that he is prepared to accept France as a province of Europe does not imagine that he is making an extraordinary concession to some abstract metaphysical or historical entity. Europe is real for him—and not in the old pre-World War I sense, in which Europe existed as a group of independent and rival nations, and the Government urged him, for patriotic reasons, to buy Russians bonds as a way of checking the German menace.

Those who search for the symbol of today's revolution a century hence may choose to find it in the automobile. Before the Second World War, the French bourgeois lived in Paris or in the country, and ventured forth each summer to "rest" in the country with a parent, a sister or some other close relation. The worker spent his brief holiday in the village from which he had come, or at the shore. The peasant remained on the land; there was no one available to take over for him. Travel abroad, except for the rich or the well-educated, was uncommon.

The nation was quite satisfied to know itself; nothing more seemed to be necessary. With this provincialism went other habits which cut across class lines. The French did not think it necessary to learn modern foreign languages; anyone who chose to visit France was expected to know French and to use it. Foreign books were sometimes translated; there was no great sale for those which were not. The United States was a world away; one neither went there nor thought overly much about it. The supremacy of French civilization was taken for granted. Events at home commanded the interest of the country; for most Frenchmen, there were no others.

Trade with overseas French territories was extensive, and in many foreign markets the products of particular French craft industries knew no rivals. The French Empire gave the country an interest in Africa and Asia, and this circumstance made France, or at least Paris, a major world center. The object, however, was always to export the French language, and with it the distinctive culture based on its use.

While it would be a serious mistake to suggest that all this is now changed, there can be no question but that these qualities no longer define even approximately the French nation. A lawyer's son, aged 20, tells you that he has visited Italy and Spain many times; he spent July and August with a family in Sussex to perfect his English; last Christmas he skied in Austria; this coming Easter he plans to go to Greece. Next summer, if all works out well, he will be going to America on a charter flight. What does he hope to see? New York and Mexico.

Conversations like this are standard in Paris today. More surprising, perhaps, is the talk of a mason, a master of his craft, and not a young man, who lives outside Chartres. The summer is too busy a time for him or for any of his employes to be absent. However, by law, his workers are entitled to three weeks of paid vacation, and he now regularly gives them four. "After all, monsieur," he says, "the workers in the large factories are given a month during the summer. Why, then, should my own have less, particularly when they take their vacations in the autumn or winter? Those with young children are inconvenienced because of school but the others like to be away when the hotels are un-crowded and when prices are less high. In any case, all seasons are made for travel."

Why so much talk about travel and vacations? Are they of such consequence to the ordinary people of France? The answer, very simply, is yes. Europe is no longer an abstraction for a great part of the French people. They have seen it—Milan, with its sky-scrapers; Vienna, with its baroque monuments; Amsterdam, with its quiet canals. The automobile—four years ago, a simple 2-horsepower model for those of modest means; today, a rather more elaborate affair—has given a freedom inconceivable before the war to any but the rich. It carries ordinary people to distant and hitherto unknown places. "Europe is remarkable, monsieur; not a dying continent at all, but alive and healthy." These are the words of a worker whose father never traveled 300 miles from the place where he was born.

It would be a mistake, however, to imagine that French interest is wholly consumed by the discovery of the outside world. There is too much happening within France for such a topic to dominate.

France, for the first time since 1914, has a normal complement of young people. When it is realized that one of every two French-men between the ages of 20 and 32 in 1914 lost his life in the Great War, it is possible to understand why the mood of the nation was so cautious and grim in the twenties and thirties. One generation was lost and another was not born as a consequence of the fighting that raged along the Western Front from 1914 to 1918. This kind of slaughter did not happen again in 1939-45. The old fears about a declining population are gone.

France now has to concern itself about its youth. Schools in vastly increased number must be built. The technological advances of the last 10 years make it essential that a greater number of students be admitted to the *lycées* and universities. The old élites are no longer sufficient for the tasks which now require to be done.

Likewise, the situation of women is entirely altered. Marriage and life within the family are no longer an acceptable solution for tens of thousands of middle-class girls who crave a different sort of existence. Their wish is not to live as their mothers did. The "great days" were not in the past, not in the nineteen-twenties, and probably not even in *la belle époque* before 1914. There is very little romancing about the past among those who are young.

For the first time in this century France is giving serious attention to its housing shortage. The end of the Algerian war, and the return of hundreds of thousands of Europeans, has only exacerbated a situation which existed before; there is insufficient housing for all classes in almost all urban areas.

To meet the need, whole new suburbs are being built. In and around Paris, quarters which remained untouched for decades now begin to have a new appearance. The creation of these new dwellings makes possible a life for tens of thousands of low-income and middle-income families which would have seemed inconceivable a decade ago. If the unimaginative architecture leaves a good deal to be desired, there is still a sense of space and modern convenience which the old tenements never afforded. The unfilled demand remains enormous, and is a source of constant complaint, but at last something is showing above ground.

In these situations, what can old political party labels mean? What are the Socialists, for example, to fight for? Expanded social-security measures? France boasts a system which will stand comparison with any in the world. More economic planning? The French planning effort is as extensive and as intelligently executed as any undertaken in a democratic society. Higher wages? This is always a welcome proposal, but elections are rarely won on this plank alone. The fact of the matter is that the French worker is not today economically underprivileged. While many continue to earn insufficient wages, particularly in the public sector of the economy, the pressure even among state employes, while serious, is not overwhelming.

As for the middle class, it has rarely known a more prosperous time. Superb financial management has made the franc one of the most stable currencies in Europe and has contributed to increasing the gold reserves of the country. Profits are high and there is no evidence that traditional French "thrift" is leading people with money to defer spending until prices become more reasonable.

Everywhere, in Paris as well as in the provinces, there are evidences of renovation, building, spending and consuming. The middle class does not appear to be saving for a stormy tomorrow.

The class which has not yet shared in this prosperity is the one which shows greatest evidence of discontent. The peasant disturbances that began quite suddenly several years ago reflect the fact that this group does not feel that it has profited in the way that others have. Peasants own tractors, motorcycles, automobiles and other major industrial appliances, at least in the more prosperous regions; even there, however, they do not appear to be satisfied. In the poorer regions, the extent of agrarian poverty is immediately apparent.

Peasant manifestations constitute a new problem for France; all this came upon the country like a sudden storm. No one was prepared for it. While the Government boasts about its plans for reform, the farmers are impatient and show their feelings in various acts of overt resistance—blocking traffic on the roads, dumping quantities of agricultural produce which would otherwise sell at low prices, and raiding the properties of absentee landlords.

To date, none of the traditional political parties has known how to take advantage of this discontent, or how to channel it in such a way as to improve its own electoral position. In a country where there is no single workers' party, it is not likely that we will soon see a peasants' party.

Under these new circumstances, conventional party labels now mean little. The old political distinctions between Left and Right are becoming increasingly irrelevant, at least to the young. They no longer describe what exists, and a generation unfamiliar with the old slogans is no longer led to think in those terms.

The Communist party retains its hold on those who have voted for its candidates since the liberation, but one has no sense that new cadres are developing. The man who sells L'Humanité each Sunday at the street corner is growing old. What will lead a new generation to embrace Communism? A high regard for the Soviet Union? That is unlikely; too many Frenchmen have been there, or have read about it, and they are not impressed. Internal social discontent? There is not enough for a party to nourish itself at this source.

Around the Sorbonne, the leaflets that are distributed by students are generally religious in character. Roman Catholic groups are strong and active. Even the trade unions seem to reflect the growth of Catholic influence. The major strikes in public utilities last spring were led not by Communist-dominated unions, but by the Catholic labor movement. Among intellectuals, Catholic opinions thrive as they have not done in many a year. Being a good Republican no longer seems to mean that one must also be anti-clerical.

The empirical social sciences have a new importance in the country. The young are interested in the problems of industrial growth, economic planning, urban reform, education. These are very real issues for them; they have little use for those who treat these questions too abstractly. Decisions are waiting to be made in all these areas; this is not a time for idle speculation or endless talk. The work of American economists and sociologists is much admired in certain intellectual quarters in Paris.

Many who visit France today remark on its resemblance to the United States. Their impressions are hasty and mistaken. Automobiles, neon and self-service restaurants do not define a nation's character. While France's rapid industrial expansion is unquestionably leading her to adopt practices and forms which resemble those that exist here, a close scrutiny even of these will suggest important differences.

France is, and remains, a province of Europe. Its experience, on the deepest level, in both the First and Second World Wars is one which it shares with Germany and not with us. Its imperial adventure, again, was of a European sort, and not at all like what we did in Puerto Rico or in the Philippines. Peasants are not farmers; they do not resemble those who live on the land in Vermont or Iowa. Workers have not yet begun to confuse themselves with the middle class. All this may yet come, but it is not the situation of today.

France is changing but it is not at all clear that she is becoming like us. She seeks her new destiny in a new unity, which is European. We would do well to reflect on what this may mean in the next several years, for if it creates problems for us, as it will, it also opens up vast opportunities.

France knows that it is not an island unto itself. Events abroad may still prevent the realization of important plans already made. Also, the continuing political problem may at any time take a serious turn and cause difficulties which will not be easily resolved. Europe is far from being an accomplished fact.

The French remain sufficiently skeptical to estimate with some detachment their present achievement. They are neither overwhelmed by it, nor are they dissatisfied. One thing they know—the France of today is alive and changing. Few regret the past; few look back to it.

France Transformed:
Seven Years of de Gaulle

by Henri Peyre

WITH NEXT month's election, France will begin the eighth year of a presidency which is, for all practical purposes a constitutional monarchy. No other ruler in Western Europe or North America has wielded powers equal to Charles de Gaulle's in the past decade. The President's critics are numerous and vocal in his own country but when all is said, he has used his powers skillfully and moderately. At 75, de Gaulle leads a nation that has changed the agonizing crises of seven years ago for some complacency in prosperity.

De Gaulle apparently commands the allegiance of two-thirds of his countrymen. The opposition is hopelessly divided, powerless to offer a constructive program or suggest new ideas. The general is not loved and he has not tried to make himself loved. But for the present, millions of French men and women see no other choice. De Gaulle's announcement that he will seek re-election on Dec. 5 to another seven-year term was greeted with significant

From the *New York Times Magazine,* November 14, 1965, copyright © 1965 by The New York Times Company.

calm; the French are only vaguely worried about the inevitable problem of succession. They realize that France has changed more profoundly under his regime than since Bonaparte consolidated the results of the French Revolution and established a national framework which was to last a century. Except among a few politicians who find it hard to renounce their old views and who cling to the shadows and labels of old parties, there is little nostalgia for the pre-de Gaulle era.

When the general was called from retirement in 1958 by the frightened politicians, the regime was moribund, the treasury empty, the army officers threatening civil war over Algeria. France's prestige abroad was shaken. As a wit put it, the Fourth Republic had died almost as soon as it was installed in the late nineteen-forties—to make way for the Third. Between 1948 and 1958, France lived in the past, split by party squabbles, mouthing meaningless slogans. But while Cabinet ministers played musical chairs, the country worked to achieve record levels of productivity and regain its health after the scars of war and occupation.

France yearned for a better Government and deserved one. But only a violent trauma could bring about the overdue revolution.

Though de Gaulle's achievements have been enormous, they are not all admirable. He has sown seeds of discord and eventual turmoil. It is disturbing for a country to have no alternative to the Government in power, and almost no alternative policy.

Many people wish the haughty President would occasionally pay a warmer tribute to the economic, administrative and cultural achievements of the Fourth Republic. A majority of de Gaulle's countrymen also would consider it fair and fitting of him to recall, in his public utterances, the debt of liberated, prostrate France to the "Anglo-Saxon" armies and American generosity. Instead, de Gaulle advertises his contempt for the materialistic "Americanization" of the Western European masses.

Then, too, de Gaulle has been needlessly imperious in rebuffing his partners in the Common Market, members of the French Parliament and trade union leaders. Of him, as of wrathful Coriolanus in Shakespeare's drama, it could be said:

> *You speak o' the people,*
> *As if you were a god to punish, not*
> *A Man of their infirmity.*

But whatever the manner and the Machiavellian opportunism of a leader who antagonized a number of his early supporters (generals and admirals, statesmen like Georges Bidault and Jacques Soustelle), the first seven years of de Gaulle's rule have completely altered the foundations of France as well as its facade.

In the financial realm, confidence in a strong and stable regime quickly reversed a previous trend that had emptied the coffers of state. Saving deposits climbed, gold and dollars flowed back into the country, the total national income grew. When de Gaulle advocated converting France's large holdings of dollars into gold, the move was misrepresented in the United States as a hostile act by an ungrateful country. In fact, other European countries—West Germany, in particular—bought gold from the American treasury before France did and bought more than France. West Germany, Holland, Belgium, Spain and Switzerland all have a larger percentage of their dollars converted into gold than France does.

France is again a rich country and the franc is among the stable currencies of the world. Such prosperity has not been experienced since Poincaré's monetary measures of 1926.

This year, against the protests of many industrialists and bankers, the Government stubbornly adopted a policy of mild deflation in order to stop a rise in prices and combat inflationary tendencies. As a result, prices rose less in France during 1965 than in any other Continental country. At the same time, total production increased by 5 per cent and reserves climbed to $5 billion, an increase of $500 million.

De Gaulle himself never claimed to be an expert in finance or economics. But he won the willing cooperation of brilliant civil servants and able men like Finance Minister Giscard D'Estaing. Today the French have finally shaken off the inferiority complex which made them believe they could not compete with the Germans or the British in industrial equipment and the export trade.

They have, contrary to what French industrialists long feared, done so well among the six nations of the Common Market that they have profited from the alliance more than any other power.

Neither the prolonged Algerian war nor the expenses entailed in building a French atomic bomb and the projected missiles and nuclear submarines have proved to be a drain on the economy. France has fewer superhighways and higher gasoline prices than any other industrial nation. But she still ranks third (after the U.S. and Canada) in the ratio of cars to population.

Frenchmen are eager for more enjoyment of comfort; *"le mieux être"* has replaced mere "well-being" as the goal outlined by the Government. And though it resembles American slogans ("You never had it so good") and those which lately assured Ludwig Erhard's re-election in Germany, de Gaulle does not seem to think the phrase contradicts *"grandeur."*

The changes resulting from seven years of stability and prosperity have, in turn, caused far-reaching social and psychological consequences.

Families are not afraid of the future; the baby boom continues in France while it has slackened in other countries, including the U.S., in the last two years. The population is likely to reach 50 million before the end of the decade, a rise of more than 25 per cent over 1938.

Even more significant than such an act of faith in the years to come is the change in working-class attitudes. Though French workers have traditionally felt alienated from the rest of society and ready to turn against it, they appear reconciled to the existing order and converted to the benefits of an affluent society. The Communist vote is still large in national and municipal elections, but party membership has shrunk to one-fourth or less of what it was in the immediate postwar years, when it reached almost 1,000,000.

A sizable number of Communist workers (and especially their wives) are expected to vote for de Gaulle in the coming presidential election. Behind the Communist decision to accept Socialist François Mitterand as the candidate of a "united" left against de Gaulle, there clearly lies the reluctance of the Communists to stand up and be counted—to find perhaps that half their usual voters prefer the aristocratic President whose foreign policy (and distrust of America) is more appealing than the program of the left.

The truth is, the French masses are fast becoming "depoliticized," as the phrase goes. Utopian socialism of the 19th century, the mystique of Communism, the once-fond belief that only leftist Governments could prevent war are dead and gone. A mere fraction of factory workers belong to labor unions, especially in the new industries of electronics, chemicals and oils. Strikes are relatively scarce and of short duration.

De Gaulle may not be an admirer of democracy, but he has increased the benefits enjoyed by the masses. He has adopted the goals of the now-weakened Socialists and fulfilled them with deeds. On Sept. 16, 1964, de Gaulle's Premier, Georges Pompidou, bluntly declared: "France has a Socialist economy and it has come to stay."

That indifference to politics, or to what used to constitute the typically Latin aspect of political life (heated debate, vituperation, reluctance to agree to disagree, differences of philosophy becoming passionate affairs of the heart) carries perils, too.

The French have become tranquilized, eager for social peace and for tangible benefits—social security, paid vacations, yearly raises, more consumer goods for more families. They enjoy these rewards under a paternalist ruler who talks to them benevolently on television and radio and during his tours of the provinces. Parliament counts for little in the new regime and voters seem unconcerned by the demotion, and at times, the snubbing, of their elected representatives.

Political life at the municipal level is, in compensation, more active. The people feel closer to the mayor of their city or town and expect from him, whether he is a Communist, Radical, Catholic or Gaullist, an efficient administration. They also feel close to the President, austere and inhuman as he sometimes seems, and are flattered by the system of referendums and plebiscites which bypass the Assembly and the Senate.

De Gaulle pours scorn on the old parties as powerless fossils and few would contradict him. The multiparty system is discredited. The two-party system apparently is unworkable in any country except Britain, the U.S., Canada and Scandinavia. The French left should have triumphed after 1945, when much of the right had been discredited by its failure to resist the German occupation. But, as in the past, though the left's emotional appeal to the French people is great, it proved unable to govern. The masses are resigned to their new presidential regime.

The wide powers granted to the President by the new constitution were tailor-cut to suit de Gaulle's wishes in 1958. Unlike the President of the United States, he even has the right to dissolve Parliament. He selects his own Cabinet outside the National Assembly, as in the U.S., and public opinion has apparently accepted such an innovation—startling in France—without demur.

No Supreme Court exists to help offset presidential prerogatives. Since France is not a federal republic and states' rights have no equivalent, the strong presidential regime has no counterweight in a deeply rooted local government. In the hands of a less popular ruler, or a reckless one, such immense powers could be dangerous.

A number of intellectuals have voiced their fears. But the people as a whole, during the last legislative election in 1962, gave de Gaulle the majority that he wanted—the largest in France for 130 years. They clearly approved, for the time being, an efficient Government led by almost anonymous technocrats.

Criticism is rife, to be sure. The press has been left free. Caricaturists, *chansonniers,* satirists mock de Gaulle freely. Opponents such as Bidault and Soustelle publish violent books against him. Television and radio, both Government-controlled, grant only limited time to the opposition, but relatively few people are indignant.

The bitterest opponents of the President include those who accuse him of having betrayed compatriots who dreamed of keeping Algeria French. Others say he has demoralized the army, spent too much on atomic weapons and not enough on education, jeopardized French agriculture and trade by threatening to break up the Common Market.

Yet on these scores, too, de Gaulle's achievements are imposing.

He alone could have freed Algeria, left the Sahara oil wells to the new Government and given nearly 20 African colonies their independence. Of course, some form of economic and financial neocolonialism has replaced the French Empire, but nowhere is de Gaulle more popular than in those African territories and no country, not even Britain, has managed to remain on such good terms with its former colonies.

The army is disgruntled, but it is being rebuilt along new concepts. It is clear de Gaulle's pursuit of an independent nuclear force and his brutal attitude toward NATO and U.S. domination of its European allies has been inspired, in part, by the need to restore the French Army's confidence. At the same time, he sought to encourage French science through autonomous nuclear research.

The lack of adequate educational facilities, due to the lack of foresight of the Fourth Republic, is acute. So is the shortage of adequate housing. Just the same, the budget for education, including funds for cultural relations and teachers' retirement pensions, in 1964 amounted to 20 per cent of the total French budget, double the 1958 figure and considerably higher than the defense budget.

On de Gaulle's foreign policy, there is no evidence the French as a whole strongly disapprove of his refusal to promote a European federation in which supernationality would overshadow the all-important "national fact." A number of idealists and intellectuals regret the President's nationalism. But I am convinced that de Gaulle's foreign policy, including the temporary exclusion of Britain from the Common Market and the assertion of French independence from NATO, would be approved by 80 per cent of Frenchmen—even by those who try to soothe their American friends by appearing to deplore the Gaullist style and ingratitude.

It would be a mistake for U.S. planners to expect a reversal of basic Gaullist foreign policy (at best, they could expect a gentler and less arrogant tone) if and when that strange Catholic general relinquishes power. Indeed, there is much to confirm the view that de Gaulle wants to make Europeans ("from the Atlantic to the Urals") think and act like Europeans, to become convinced that their fate cannot be decided without them. He may well be viewed by history as a European, rather than as a French, nationalist.

Gratitude has never swayed the people's votes very long, either in the Athens of Themistocles, the France of Clemenceau or the Britain of Churchill. The French are as fickle as any other nation, if not more so. They will probably give de Gaulle at least two-thirds of their votes on Dec. 5. But the question in their minds, and often on their lips, is: What next?

Gaullists have often cited 1970 as the crucial date for consolidating the changes in the social, economic and political structure of France initiated or confirmed by their chief. By 1970 France's independent foreign policy will have reached the point of no return. In another five years France intends to have her own H bomb, missiles and modest means of delivery. By then, the Common Market will either have been broken up or expanded to include Britain, opening new outlets for surplus French agricultural products.

By 1970, de Gaulle will be 80, two years short of completing his second presidential term. Will he live until then? "Be reassured, I shall die some day," he told journalists at the Elysée Palace a few months ago. But can he have ordered his eventual succession smoothly?

History would not justify optimism. One thinks at once of Alexander's feuding generals, of Charlemagne's empire disintegrating after him, of the sequel to Cromwell's rule. Some, like Pierre Mendès-France, conclude that no authoritarian personality like de Gaulle—who thinks of himself as a Promethean savior—has ever died without leaving behind the seeds of revolution.

France, however, seems very remote from a revolutionary mood. Neither Parliament nor political parties, nor labor unions, are likely to recapture much power. The state will remain strong and some sort of a presidential system is likely to remain the rule. Dissenting intellectuals have lost much of their influence in today's France. Literature and the arts do not flourish brilliantly in a regime where the chief of state writes the best prose of any French ruler in five centuries. Then, too, the general is surrounded by former professors: Pompidou, Joxe, Peyrefitte, Jenneney, Paye and others.

A power vacuum seems inevitable after such a portentous figure steps down or disappears. Who will try to fill it? It seems clear at present that Premier Pompidou—as different from his chief as Eden was from Churchill—suave, flexible, superbly intelligent, is de Gaulle's first choice as his successor.

A long biography of Pompidou, the son of a modest family who became an able *lycée* teacher, then a banker, then de Gaulle's confidant and Premier, was published last July, probably with de Gaulle's blessing. The President's, and perhaps the nation's, alternate choices would be Louis Joxe, another teacher-turned-diplomat and administrator or, more probably, Giscard d'Estaing, the brilliant and more aristocratic Finance Minister.

Those of us who live into the next decade may be surprised to see how little the economy and politics of post-Gaullist France will differ from the present. France *will* be different in manner and style. That may be the reason why the French strike us as much less anxious about the transition after de Gaulle than the friends of France abroad.

The hopes of some Americans to see a new French foreign policy are likely to be frustrated. Other European nations, less tartly to be sure, tend to agree with de Gaulle that the U.S. can no longer play the role of guardian for a healthy and arrogant European continent. They will clamor for a voice on the use of the U.S. nuclear arsenal, if they are to provide troops and bases in return. Also, they vaguely fear being relegated to a secondary role if the Russians and the Americans become reconciled to peaceful coexistence.

Gaullism, in that sense, is not limited to France and it will survive de Gaulle.

Raymond Aron once remarked, when France seemed hopelessly bogged down in the Algerian war, that a nation of skeptics (as France is supposed to be) has always proved the readiest to appeal to saviors or providential men. The French are in truth more Bonapartist than monarchist—or perhaps even republican.

Bonaparte swept away the litter of the past when he understood his role as the continuation of the Revolution. De Gaulle has also swept away much which deserved to die, and a few things which did not.

His successors are not likely to be endowed with similar charisma, to use the word which Max Weber, borrowing from St. Paul, made fashionable. But they may well, under another guise, pursue similar aims.

Two Who Bridge the Generation Gap

by Sanche de Gramont

PARIS

IT WAS July 21, half of France was on vacation, maintenance crews with steam rollers were spreading tar over paved streets of the Latin Quarter, several hundred of the riot policemen who fought the students in May had been shifted to their usual summer duty as lifeguards, and in the National Assembly a generation of fathers was holding a debate on the future of higher education and the unruly behavior of their sons.

In tones ranging from petulance to anger, deputies of the Gaullist majority (the Union for the Defense of the Republic) conducted their post-mortem on the spring events. Then David Rousset, a sort of overweight Danton with a congested, blotchy moon face, a thick, bristly mane of white hair and a booming bass voice, rose and began a lively exchange by saying: "Let's not get too indignant about students on barricades when we say nothing when peasants draw them up."

VIVIEN (U.D.R.) "They were *voyous.*" ["Young hooligans" or "louts."] *Laughter. Lively exclamations. Noises.*

ROUSSET: "They were serious young men, devoted to their

cause. This country will someday need these youths. We can and we must discuss with them." *Protests and clamor on the Gaullist benches.* "I am pleased, Monsieur Fanton, that we do not hold the same opinions."

FANTON (U.D.R.): "I, too, am pleased."

ROUSSET: "The decree on dissolution permits the Government to arrest young people for reconstituting dissolved movements, while what we should be doing is practicing a policy of appeasement. We cannot both initiate reforms and maintain repression. The vast majority of students, and not only revolutionary students, are bound to react." *Protests on U.D.R. benches.* "There is a deep solidarity among all students which one would be wrong to ignore."

This sort of exchange is common enough in French parliamentary practice and would hardly be worth mentioning were it not for two special circumstances. First, David Rousset is a Gaullist deputy. In the foregoing excerpt from the National Assembly record, he was arguing with members of his own party, which won an overwhelming majority in the June election but is split by the student revolt into rival Whig and Tory factions. Second, while David Rousset was speaking up for the students at the National Assembly, his 21-year-old son, Pierre, was awaiting trial in a cell at Santé Prison for his activities as a leader of the May riots.

Pierre is a founder of the Revolutionary Communist Youth, an anti-Stalinist party that broke with the French Communists in 1966 and was outlawed by them as heretical. It was one of the dozen or so "groupuscules" (tiny groups) in the Latin Quarter which gained some notoriety during May. Pierre Rousset spent so much time on the barricades that he feared at one point that the amount of tear gas he had absorbed had permanently damaged his eyesight.

The Ministry of the Interior, on the simplistic assumption that such groupuscules as the Revolutionary Communist Youth and Daniel Cohn-Bendit's Movement of the 22nd of March had planned and coordinated the spring uprising like some grand Napoleonic campaign, decided that by ordering the dissolution of the movements it would strike at the root of the evil. "Typical police thinking," says Pierre. "There has to be a guilty party. They think that by liquidating the organizations they will liquidate the problem."

Militants of these dissolved groups became active in other organizations, such as neighborhood action committees. And thus it was that on July 10, Pierre Rousset was present at a meeting of the 11th Arrondissement action committee in an auditorium on the Rue Charonne lent by a parish priest. About 40 persons attended this barricade alumni meeting. "I see some unfamiliar faces," a young lady said. "Since we don't all know one another, why doesn't each person identify himself before we begin the discussion?" Two of the unfamiliar faces promptly rose and identified themselves as those of police inspectors. Five of the 40, including Pierre Rousset, were held. An informer had given the inspectors his description: tall, husky, curly brown hair, tortoiseshell glasses.

It is one of the peculiarities of the Fifth Republic's judicial system that citizens can be detained for up to 10 days under suspicion of plotting against the safety of the state without going before a judge or having any charges brought against them. Pierre and the others were held for eight days in this manner, incommunicado, and were then charged with "attempting to reconstitute a dissolved movement." It is another peculiarity of the Fifth Republic's judicial system that bail is rarely granted, so Pierre and the others swelled the ranks of the Santé Prison inmates awaiting trial, who represent 70 per cent of the total prison population.

Pierre Rousset was puzzled by some of the Santé regulations. No singing or whistling (he had not been planning to sing or whistle); no lying down on your bed in the daytime; no hanging pictures or calendars on the walls, which must be kept bare. But soon he was moved to the section reserved for political prisoners. It had just been vacated by the last convicted members of the Secret Army Organization, including some of the terrorists who tried to assassinate General de Gaulle in 1962. They were amnestied by de Gaulle during the June election campaign as a gesture to win the support of the French right.

Political prisoners in French jails have reasonably comfortable regimes, which is only natural in a country where today's chief of state may become tomorrow's political prisoner, as Marshal Henri-

Philippe Pétain did. Pierre Rousset and his friends had their own courtyard, equipped with a badminton court. They had access to the prison canteen and to an unlimited supply of books and newspapers. They were allowed four one-hour visits a week. And there was always the hope that a change in the political climate would spring them.

It became clear to certain members of the de Gaulle Cabinet that keeping popular student leaders in jail on flimsy charges was not the best way to prepare for a quiet academic year. The new Minister of Education, Edgar Faure, came out strongly for the liberation of the students. Faure, a holdover from the Fourth Republic who has served in all the key Cabinet posts, including that of Premier, is emerging in his latest incarnation as a 1968 French version of Mr. Chips. He quotes Mao ("We must cure the illness without killing the patient"); he agrees with the students that their crisis is the crisis of modern man examining the foundations of his society, and he shocked the Gaullist right wing when he came out for political freedom in the university. He said he would never give in to "the pessimism of those who believe that if political freedom is allowed the most extreme viewpoint will prevail, whereas in fact extreme positions are the easiest to refute." Thanks partly to Faure's influence, Pierre Rousset and his friends were released "in provisional liberty" after six weeks in jail. There is a 50-50 chance that their case will never come to trial.

The 56-year-old Gaullist deputy and his 21-year-old revolutionary son: It would be tempting to make the French crisis fit into the neat category of generations. The sons rise up against their fathers, who have bequeathed them a botched civilization. The fathers see the image of their failure in the revolt of their sons. Subversion has not come from abroad but from within the family circle. The wisdom and institutions of one generation are held in contempt by its successor.

The story of Rousset *père* and Rousset *fils* does not, however, fit this comfortable stereotype. Instead of two generations in conflict, it shows the generation of sons taking over from the defeated generation of their fathers in a world where the problems have changed but the methods have not. Like his son, David Rousset was an extreme left-wing revolutionary student. Like his son, but for different reasons, he rejected orthodox Communism. As a philosophy student in the nineteen-thirties, he saw the hope of the Russian Revolution of 1917 grow into totalitarian Stalinist dictatorship. As an economics student in the sixties, Pierre Rousset broke with the French Communist party because he considered it counterrevolutionary, reformist and the stooge of the Soviet Union.

David Rousset grew up in a Europe in which the forces of the left were defeated in every major test. In Germany, with Hitler's rise to power. In Spain, where the Fascist powers ensured Franco's victory. In France in 1935 and 1936, when the parties of the left failed to exploit the revolutionary possibilities of popular discontent with governmental instability and the Depression, which led to a massive occupation of factories, settling instead for the reformist program of Léon Blum's short-lived Popular Front.

Like his son, David Rousset was a militant. He joined a Trotskyite group. Disgusted by the Popular Front's neutrality in the Spanish Civil War, he recruited volunteers and supplies for the International Brigades. He fought in a celebrated 1934 riot against right-wing groups trying to storm the Concorde Bridge and capture the National Assembly. The police opened fire; there were 17 dead and 2,329 wounded. David Rousset was beaten up more than once in clashes with right-wing groups. Thirty years later, in 1966, his son was distributing pamphlets in front of a *lycée* when he was attacked by a right-wing commando. He was cracked over the head with an iron bar and suffered a fractured skull. His assailant was identified but released after some of his political friends provided him with an alibi.

Thus, David Rousset's young manhood was marked by the failure of the left to provide a successful alternative to the rise of Fascism and by the failure of the Russian Revolution as an example for the non-Communist left. In this context, World War II seemed a penance being exacted from European liberals. After the disillusion of liberal hopes, the trauma of war. Rousset became a key member of a Resistance network which penetrated German Army groups stationed in the Breton port of Brest. He and his friends found anti-Nazi German soldiers who were willing to contribute to a German-language resistance newspaper secretly distributed to the occupation army. The network had created three cells of anti-Nazi soldiers by the time it was infiltrated by the Gestapo. Rousset was arrested and sent to Buchenwald in 1943.

When American troops liberated the camp in 1944, he recalls, "I had lost 80 pounds. I was concave instead of convex. I had also caught typhus, but I didn't tell anyone because I would have been quarantined, and I had to get out of there. I drove out in a truck with some Americans and I pointed out to them a fleeing Gestapo staff car. They let it go, saying, 'We won this war and we have to be good sports.' When I got back to Paris I saw a doctor. Fortunately I was not the cause of a typhus epidemic."

Rousset spent the next two years writing what has become the French classic on the camps, "The Concentrationary Universe." He had a disturbing insight: that the concentration camp, far from being a monstrous denial of civilization, was a possible model for a future civilization. The camps were such models of efficient bureaucracy that they formed a workable kind of society. They were not primitive but overrefined. Men did not die there as men but as part of an administrative system, according to a strictly defined bureaucratic mechanism. The concentration camps were the supreme example of planification.

This is what Rousset calls "the advent of a new barbarism." It was, he says, "the most profound kind of exploitation of man," far worse than the kind of exploitation Marx described as taking place in capitalist societies. Just as Stalinism had been the failure of a revolution, the new barbarism was the failure of an ideology. Nothing Marx wrote was relevant to this new and terrible form of human exploitation, the concentration camp. More than that, the camps also existed in the very country which claimed that it practiced Marxism-Leninism, the Soviet Union.

The other lesson David Rousset drew from his political experience of the thirties was that political parties were bankrupt. He had seen the liberal parties powerless before dictators. In France, the system led to the revolving-door governments of party hacks. So in 1948, with the existentialist philosopher Jean-Paul Sartre, he founded an antiparty movement called the Revolutionary Democratic Assembly, which proclaimed itself both anti-Communist and anticapitalist and stated its opposition to both the Soviet and the American blocs.

For a man destined to become a Gaullist deputy, Rousset had some harsh words for the general, who had just founded his own Assembly of the French People. He compared de Gaulle to Stalin, saying: "De Gaulle says to French society what Stalin says to the world proletariat: 'I am your savior and I mean to impose your salvation.'" With heavy sarcasm, he added: "De Gaulle is the man who possesses the revealed truth of the French bourgeoisie. He does not need to consult anyone, he does not need to examine himself, he knows ahead of time what is just and necessary."

But after a year and a half, Rousset broke with Sartre, who was moving closer to the French Communist party, and devoted himself to exposing the labor camps in the Soviet Union. He did not become a Gaullist until 1966, and says he was won over by the general's anticolonialism and by his foreign policy, which—like his own—refuses to choose between the Soviet and American blocs. Recruited by the Gaullists as a well-known left-wing intellectual and potential vote-getter, Rousset ran unsuccessfully for Parliament in the 1967 elections, but was elected in the Gaullist landslide this June in a northern industrial district.

Rousset sees the major failure of his generation in its inability to provide an ideology for the youths who are rebelling today. "Because of this," he says, "they still use the worn-out political vocabulary of Marxism-Leninism. They do not realize that the problems with which they must deal are not even broached in Marx or Lenin—the tremendous productive forces of the industrialized Western countries, for instance, which divided the world into underdeveloped and overdeveloped regions.

"Marx is no longer prophetic. He believed that one of the most important benefits of Communist society would be to give each man sufficient leisure time to fulfill and improve himself. Well, many of us have this leisure time today in our neocapitalist society, and we are discovering that it can be used to enslave man instead of emancipating him, thanks to sophisticated methods of persuasion.

"Today's young revolutionaries, those who are contesting the form of society they live in, have problems that the Russian revolutionaries of 1917 did not have. They are the first revolutionaries of the affluent society, in which goods and services are plentiful and want is no longer the principal problem. They are not revolting for bread, but from a surfeit of material goods. Everyone thought revolution in the second half of the 20th century would come from the Third World, from Africa and Latin America, but instead it is coming from the most industrialized states, from the youth and intellectuals in France and Czechoslovakia, and from the Negroes and the New Left in the United States.

"But since these new revolutionaries have not got their Lenin, they must formulate their ideology as they go along. They are still stumbling, they only partly understand their own action. Here in France they still believe in a tight party organization, but the May events proved the futility of that. No party can claim to have controlled or directed that great explosion. Events spread spontaneously, without any central directive. The May events marked the failure of the professional politicians who claim to speak for the people."

Student leaders agree with David Rousset that their organizations were taken by surprise. Jacques Sauvageot, secretary of the largest national student organization, says: "We were so poorly informed that it was not until I was jailed with Daniel Cohn-Bendit and we had a talk that I learned what had been going on at Nanterre."

Pierre Rousset adds: "We were astonished, although we recognized the spontaneity of the movement as proof of a latent crisis in French society. And we saw that some of the ideas we had been stressing all along had seeped to the masses.

"We believe that there is no possible alliance with the French Communist party, and the majority of the students sensed this. [Rousset says the French Communists gave the police membership lists of groups such as his that had broken away from them.] We believe that no revolution is possible without the collaboration of the working class, and the movement did spread to the workers. Finally, we stressed the international aspect of the struggle—it's the same struggle in Berlin, Rome or Berkeley."

If Pierre Rousset maintains his faith in Marxism-Leninism and in the party as the best possible political structure, it is perhaps because he has not suffered the same disappointments as his father. His is the first generation of French youths in this century which has not been involved in a war. Stalinism, Fascism, concentration camps—these are to him pages from history textbooks, while to his father they are spiritual and physical scars. His generation is undefeated because it has not yet really been tested.

It is also a generation which sees the world through a different set of problems. David Rousset grew up in a period of European conflict which led to World War II. Two conflicting ideologies, Fascism and Communism, fought within the framework of traditional 19th-century European nationalism.

Pierre Rousset grew up in a period of European peace in which the key problem was the emancipation of the colonial world. Too young to fight in Indochina or Algeria, he could analyze colonialism impersonally. He saw a French society in contradiction with itself, stressing the values of Western humanism, freedom, human rights, while denying those values to the colonial peoples it exploited.

He is unresponsive to the appeals of nationalism, for his generation has never had to feel that France was threatened. The deep strain of French chauvinism, which since 1870 has been essentially a compensatory mechanism for defeat, is absent from his mentality. He is incapable of feeling, as de Gaulle feels, that there is a certain idea of France and French grandeur to which everything else must be subjected.

On the contrary, he considers that the problems of his generation are not national, but applicable to Western civilization as a whole. To him, there are no national values to defend or national faults to condemn, but a certain number of diseases secreted by Western society. He feels he is part of an international more effective than the Comintern ever was, because the Comintern was imposed by a government which used it both to spread world revolution and to pursue the imperialist goals of Greater Russia, whereas the international he belongs to grew organically from small groups of students in different countries who found that they had identical goals. Just as Marx said that a French worker should feel more in common with a German worker than with a French bourgeois, Rousset feels greater kinship to Rudi Dutschke than to Edgar Faure.

Although he was surprised by the timing of the May events, he and other student militants had been preparing for such an occasion. "We were among the first to fight police in Vietnam demonstrations and we had some street combat experience," he says. "Then some of us, including myself, went to Berlin in February for a Vietnam demonstration. We had quite a fight with the Fascists there."

For a time, Rousset and his friends thought the movement in France would be able to topple the Gaullist regime. "We saw the signs of a vacuum of power," he says. "The ministers were incapable of making decisions. The policemen's union was grumbling. We knew that if de Gaulle called out the army the draftees would resist. But everything depended on the unions and the opposition parties, and the Communist party was the first to call for an election. Finally, the Communist party and the Communist-led unions saved the Gaullist regime; the call for a new election meant an end to the strikes and the demoralization of the revolutionary groups."

Pierre Rousset rules out another explosion of student rioting when the Sorbonne reopens. "We would be isolated," he said, "the workers would not go along. This will have to be a period of meditation and reorganization. We saw in May that outside the Latin Quarter we were powerless. We have to permeate the masses, create a national party. It's our duty to use the electoral system to advance our ideas, even if our ideas are anti-parliamentarian."

This is the dilemma of the student revolt. To pursue their action they are compelled to make use of the available instruments of the society they are condemning. In the same manner, the student author of a book on the May insurrection wrote in the preface: "The consumer society poisons everything it produces by turning it into merchandise. Everything is commercially exploited, even the barricades. My book does not escape that objection, but between the risk of doing nothing and the risk of doing something, I decided to publish." The writer also runs the risk of becoming a best-selling author and being completely swallowed up by the consumer society. Pierre Rousset, if he helps found a party and runs for office, runs the risk of being elected. Perhaps revolution is only for the young. Perhaps in a few years he will move closer to the Establishment, as his father did. Perhaps in some future regime he will be a Cabinet minister.

For the moment, he expresses his willingness to work within existing institutions in order eventually to scuttle them, and he remains loyal to his Marxist-Leninist ideology. "I see nothing else," he says. "The condition of the worker has not changed. He is still a merchandise on the labor market. Bourgeois thought is degenerate. French students have a Marxist formation and do not read Marcuse. Sartre has taught us nothing. Existentialism is dead. The sad thing is that there are no great new Marxist thinkers, because Stalin froze Marxist thought for a generation. We realize we are confronted with new problems to which we are applying dated categories of thought. Marxist thought must make a great leap forward."

Pierre Rousset believes the proven methods of political agitation and mass movements will change society. His father, although he is one of the Gaullists most sympathetic to the student movement, believes as a Gaullist deputy that revolution must come from the top, and that no one has a better chance of profoundly changing French society than the general himself.

David Rousset's faith is based partly on a private conversation he had with de Gaulle last April, 10 days before the start of the crisis. Rousset was summoned to the Elysée because he had long been writing about the need for social reform. After greeting him, de Gaulle sat down behind his desk and put on his glasses. Rousset felt relieved, for he had been warned that when de Gaulle wears his glasses it means he is interested in the conversation, but when he removes them it means that his mind has wandered to some private dimension.

At that time the student problem at Nanterre centered on whether the girl students should have the right to receive male students in their rooms. "First they wanted classes and teachers," grumbled the general, "now they want beds and mistresses.

"The French left," de Gaulle went on, "can't forgive me for carrying out the policies it was incapable of implementing itself.

They will only forgive me after my death when they will call me their precursor."

Then de Gaulle announced that he intended to devote his last years in office to the social transformation of France. In his most oracular tone, he said: "We must condemn capitalism, David Rousset, we must expressly condemn capitalist society. We must also condemn totalitarian Communism, for its solutions are unadapted and inadequate to our society. We must find a new way, a new solution."

De Gaulle went into an explanation of participation, in which workers, students and all citizens have a share in the highest responsibilities of the state. "If it's a matter of institutions," de Gaulle said, "I'm not worried, for when it comes to forming a concept or a policy, *la stratégie, c'est moi.* But the problem is that this society must be transformed at the same time it is being administered." De Gaulle indicated that some of his ministers would be reluctant to go along because a radical program of change makes day-to-day governing so difficult. "I need popular support for this," he confided. Since that April conversation, de Gaulle has received massive support in the June elections and most of the key ministers have been changed.

This leaves three principal possibilities for France: a revolution from the top masterminded by de Gaulle, a revolution from the bottom fomented by political agitators and student leaders like Pierre Rousset or no revolution at all, thanks to the inertia of the average citizen and to the resistance of those classes whose interest is to defend the social and economic status quo.

I have bets with David and Pierre Rousset that are really bets on the future of France. David Rousset has bet me that in two years de Gaulle will have succeeded in his "mutation from the summit."

Pierre Rousset has bet me that within the next calendar year he will be in jail again.

A "New European Man" Runs France

by Keith Botsford

PARIS

ONCE THE home of Mme. de Pompadour, now housing the President of the Republic, Georges Pompidou, the Elysée Palace in Paris is a building in refined 18th-century taste: elegant and symmetrical, chaste without and ornate within.

French politics has often seemed romantic, emotional and theatrical. France wept even as it executed its king; it manned revolutionary barricades which brought tyrants into power. While the Left has been sanctified in word and sporadically in deed, the Right has been more truly representative of the national craving for authority. Only the extremes have drawn the passionate attention of Frenchmen and in a country which makes much intellectual capital of Reason, only the rational Center seems to have had less than a fair chance.

All that is changing now. France has become richer, more European, less grandiose and more bourgeois, if you like. Its last king was Charles de Gaulle and he, as if realizing that after him the race of kings would die out, left two bequests to the nation: one was the new Constitution and strong presidency which he

From the *New York Times Magazine,* August 29, 1971, copyright © 1971 by The New York Times Company.

created with such effort, and the other was naming as his heir
the man who had been closest to him, in and out of politics, for
the last 26 years of his life, and the man who, in his opinion,
understood the new France best, Georges Pompidou.

Pompidou was not the man closest to de Gaulle in any romantic,
emotional sense, as were the general's companions in the war, but
he was the most *central,* the most indispensable for his sober
skills and that homely, elegant, brilliant mind and manner that so
perfectly mirrors the palace in which I recently talked to him.

For an audience with the President one walks in off the Rue
St. Honoré into the *Loge d'Honneur;* a policeman conducts one
across the gravel courtyard to the vast double doors of the palace
itself; a lackey in black swallowtails leads one up the ornate marble
stairs where one is met by the presidential usher; he, chain of
office discreetly settled on his waist, seats one in a large *salon* on
a formal, uncomfortable chair and between two allegorical Gobelin
tapestries representing October and March; then the President's
aide-de-camp, a colonel resplendent in air-force blue, his breast
invisible behind campaign ribbons, his shoulders under braid,
accompanies one through the antechamber into the presidential
office. It is solid gilt, walls and ceiling; the furniture is encrusted
in gold leaf; the presidential desk, which could have been Mme.
de Pompadour's, is covered with red leather and in perfect order.

So far, all is as it ever was. One was received in this manner
by Napoleon I and Napoleon III. Intervening revolutions, periods
of use as a printshop, then as a gaming house, have affected the
building little. Even with Charles de Gaulle residing there, finger-
ing the revolving globe and pondering on the world and France's
place in it, there can have been little discontinuity with the past.
But now?

Now de Gaulle's globe is gone. It went the first day Pompidou
moved in. Now behind the President's chair, on a little stand of
its own, stands a strikingly modern abstract expressionist drawing:
the economical, minimal culture of our times, one thinks, the
taste that money can afford. But then on a high chest of drawers
of exquisite marquetry, there sit photographs of Mr. and Mrs.
Pompidou, their son and grandchildren, all in the special bright
tan and disparate blue of sky that Kodachrome gives, and one

thinks, ah, he is one of us! The man, just turned 60, tall, bulky, striped in suit of sober blue, a blue tie randomly patterned and scrupulously knotted exactly bisecting his white shirt, steps forward to shake one's hand: this is the Pompidou whose discretion, modesty and financial cunning made him so acceptable to the politics and the money of the time that he could become both Premier of France and director-general of the Banque Rothschild and seem to alter his basic self not at all. Then when he sits down, lights up a filter cigarette and while talking leaves it dangling straight down from his lower lip, when one begins to listen to the deliberateness and pith of his conversation or watches him laugh, one recalls the stubborn, hard-working peasants of France from whom Pompidou descends.

So at one moment the *ancien régime* is still with us and Pompidou can say how he feels "completely at home" with "advanced" trends in the arts, with those painters whose works now hang in the palace, and then say, with a mixture of regret and lordliness, "No, I no longer visit painters now, I *receive* them." The next moment he will explain the presidency in terms of husbands and wives: "What is a quality in a private individual can be a defect in a man who has responsibilities. Lots of husbands are good husbands because they're a little weak. Well, there's nothing worse for a head of government or head of state than to be weak."

This blend of certainty and loftiness persists in many of Pompidou's declarations. When his party seeks to launch a "Year of Change," Pompidou can refuse the slogan, saying, "Social change is not yearly, but daily." Or, on quitting the premiership in 1968: "The business of a deputy is to meddle with things and talk, and what I want is to stay at a distance from things and shut up."

To spend any time in French intellectual milieus is to live in a world of loudspeakers and no receiving equipment: there is much talk and little listening and what counts is less what is said than the brilliance with which it is expressed. Pompidou's make-up is absolutely typical of these circles in which he and his wife—who is both very much an intellectual herself and a *mondaine,* a member of higher society—always have moved and still do; yet there is a difference. One feels that Pompidou could produce all that flash if he wanted to, but that he considers it both wasteful and foolish. He measures his words; he rations them. When they emerge, they are not brilliant words; they are simply clear, comprehensible and reasonable. And it is obvious that he has that rarest of gifts among Frenchmen: the ability to listen, to doubt, to question, to evaluate and hence to learn.

There are those in France who see in Pompidou Balzac's Rastignac or Stendhal's Julien Sorel, those heroes with the passionate desire to "make good," and to some extent this must at one time have been true of the man. But now Pompidou has *arrived* and in a real sense his is a "success story" of a kind that would not have been possible in prewar France. Not without some extraordinary deed: neither Rastignac nor Sorel could have risen as Pompidou has by sheer application, absolute self-confidence and so relatively minor an accident. And one might be tempted to think of Pompidou's "making it" as a freak, a sport of the times, were it not that we can clearly see other "New European Men," in the ascendancy: men as new as the united Europe of which Pompidou is such an ardent advocate, men as diverse and antithetical to their traditional national political and social patterns as England's Edward Heath and West Germany's Willy Brandt.

Pompidou's grandfather tilled the poor, hard soil of Auvergne with a hoe. His son, Léon, as a shoeless peasant boy, was, in the educational reforming zeal of the Third Republic, as sought-after for school as American blacks today are for business, faculties or government. In the ruthlessly competitive structure of French education, to be called is not enough; one must also succeed. Leon succeeded—becoming first an *instituteur,* then marrying one and ending his days as a professor of Spanish in a *lycée*—and his son succeeded even more brilliantly. "When I was 8 and I was asked what I wanted to be when I grew up, I answered without a moment's hesitation that I would be a *normalien,*" the President told me.

To understand what this meant—the flat declaration is still characteristic of Pompidou, who seems never to have doubted that he belongs by right among the elect—one has to understand that the Ecole Normale Supérieure, like Sciences Politiques, which Pompidou later attended, is one of the *Grandes Ecoles.* These are particularly French institutions and can continue to exist and flourish only because France remains, of all modern nations, the most absolutely centralized and hierarchical. It is as though Harvard and Yale, or Oxford and Cambridge, were recognizably and beyond dispute the *premier* educational establishments in their countries and that every young boy could aspire to go to them. To do so, he would take a national examination and be admitted— as well as, later, graduated—strictly on the basis of his rank in examination. Pompidou was admitted No. 1 written and No. 8 orally; he was graduated, naturally, at the head of his class. About which he said, again characteristically: "The result didn't surprise me. Of course, I was pleased."

Graduation gave Pompidou his *agrégation*—that is, his academic rank, but also much more. In France, this brings with it a position in society that is recognized and accepted not only by "top people," but also by the whole society; also, the graduates of the *Grandes Ecoles* form, at the apex of national life, not merely a network of connections, but also a society within a society that shares a common language, a common approach to problem-solving and a common system for dealing with the real world. In the most literal sense, Pompidou was a man not only groomed for success but perfectly conscious of the fact.

The only indeterminate in Pompidou's life as a young man in the early thirties was: In what field would success come?

Would it be politics? No, at first it was Greek, then literature; later it was administration, then banking. "No, politics was completely an accident," Pompidou said. But, *Monsieur le Président,* you never thought of an active role in politics? "When I was a young man," he answered, "I was interested in politics. I was not as extremely politicized as some, but still committed. I was of the Left, of course. What young man isn't? Or of the extreme Right? No one took that seriously. One of my classmates could yell out, 'Kill all Jews!' . . . That was the way it was to be a *Normalien.* In 1933 I was a card-carrying member of the Socialist party. I made a trip to Germany. I saw one of those massive Nazi demonstrations in Munich. . . . Its power, its violence, its mass, its order, its discipline, left an indelible mark on me. I was horrified and impressed. When I got back to France I tore up my party card. What could a political party in the Third Republic do to withstand such a force? Nothing. It was better to turn away from politics altogether."

Still in that mood, having married the young law student (who was also the charming, intelligent and lively daughter of a successful provincial doctor) he had met one day on the Boulevard Saint-Michel, he lived, as he put it, a "private life." He fought the war, as long as it was still being fought by France, as a lieutenant in an Alpine regiment. Then, when it was lost, he lived through four long years of German occupation without, he admits, much more than superficial difficulty; a teacher of literature in a Parisian *lycée,* at the Liberation he was preparing a critical edition of Racine's "Brittanicus." As for the romanticism of the Resistance, the heroes both real and self-proclaimed . . . "I hate all that business," he said with a quick wave of his hand and sharp displeasure in his bright eyes, "I hate medals, I hate decorations of all kinds."

Until 1944, then, French politics seemed to him either futile or sick (and therefore responsible for the debacle of 1940) or simply romantic. Charming but silly. Wasted energy. The institutions for viable politics just did not exist at the time; they were not to come into existence until de Gaulle created them.

In 1944, de Gaulle, who throughout the war has been bereft of money, support, staff and power, returns to Paris to create a Government out of nothing. He needs men around him, he needs bright young men. A fellow *Normalien,* René Brouillet, who had been the head of Bidault's personal staff when Bidault headed the National Council for the Resistance, heard from Pompidou—then 33 and beginning to realize that teaching would not satisfy his ambitions—that he was "looking for something to do, some job where he might make himself useful." Pompidou meets the hero he, like every Frenchman in his heart, has been looking for, his life is transformed.

To Pompidou at first fall such tasks as drafting letters, writing memoranda, analyzing and reducing to order immense, complex files, and the skills he learned were such as unobtrusiveness, brevity, accuracy, unbiased evaluation, clear summary, style, loyalty, discretion. After much work and long study, Pompidou learns to operate as de Gaulle operates; he can take some of the load off the general; and he cultivates his own special talents—especially those dealing with figures, economics being a subject that profoundly bores de Gaulle. Discretion and loyalty, which are for de Gaulle the greatest (they are the most Roman) virtues, come so naturally to Pompidou that in all the years of their association, there is no single exchange of words between the two men ever recorded by Pompidou or by any third party. He is twice as useful to de Gaulle precisely because he is self-effacing and easily overlooked: the bright stars in the political firmament think of Pompidou as a superior office boy. He is never irked by this, for the mistake is theirs: the secret of success is to get on with the job, whatever it is, and, as he has said, "to let life come to one."

But Pompidou is more than just "useful." He has a great capacity for friendship. The man who starts working for de Gaulle unburdened with a past, either glorious or awkward, who serves in a humble capacity out of conviction, goes on to become the *friend* who can be trusted with any task and who will always *understand*. In 1946, de Gaulle gives up power for the first time; nearly all his collaborators at the period thought the general was finished; they left him to look after their own political careers. Pompidou continued to serve his master. He is de Gaulle's political secretary during that first exile. By sorting out the raveled finances of the Foundation for Handicapped Children established in memory of their dead daughter, Anne, Pompidou earns the personal gratitude of the de Gaulles, and more important, the unswerving support of Mrs. de Gaulle. It is while working on behalf of the foundation (he is still its president), that Pompidou becomes friendly with René Fillon, who moves in the upper levels of high finance. Fillon covets a senatorial role, Pompidou is able to assist. . . . As one of Pompidou's closest associates put it to me: "Pompidou has always known how to make friends and how to keep friends. In all those years in which his chief profession has been government, I do not know a single friend or contact he has ever lost. Each step in his career has simply added new contacts and new friends."

Political skill of a high order. But after the 1951 elections, de Gaulle retires again to Colombey, and Pompidou, who has excelled at every stage of his career so far—the scholastic, the administrative, the personal—now makes a third decisive change. "I could not see an administrative career being a live, interesting career for me," Pompidou has said. "I like the law, but I don't find it gives sufficient scope for activity." This time the general's return to private life seems absolute and final. Pompidou's similar return would have been equally final for any other man: he enters the Rothschild Bank, thanks to René Fillon, and once again he begins to ascend with dizzying speed; in no time at all he is director-general.

In 1958, there is the attempted coup in Algiers; de Gaulle comes out of retirement and "borrows" Pompidou from his bank. After six months, as agreed, Pompidou returns to the Rothschilds: "Despite the interest of the work, I still felt a sort of doubt toward the servitude of public life. . . ." In April, 1962, he is Premier. It is another switch, but it is no longer so great a leap. It is like moving to another chair, but all the rest remains the same, the milieu, the friends—artists, intellectuals, politicians, financiers.

A new man of this sort is in some way bound to be both enslaved by his superiority and deeply conscious of it, and when Pompidou talks about his political peers, this sense of being a more complete, more self-sufficient man than they, comes out sharply. Perhaps because he is a classicist, he tends to think of character as being inextricably mixed with history, and yet few men who have grasped as much power as he have been less concerned with "destiny" or with their role in history. If there is any abstract vision with which Pompidou is closely attuned, that vision is the *New* Europe.

He has just come back from a weekend of wine and Lorelei on the Rhine and . . . I get the impression that the President thinks of the Germans as being preoccupied with thoughts of power. "Of course, they do not always do so consciously. I do not think that with Hitler it was conscious; but with Bismarck, yes it *was* conscious." And with Brandt?

His "summit" meeting with Edward Heath has been a personal triumph for both men; it has cleared the way for Britain's entry into the E.E.C. And yet, Pompidou recognizes that although he admires Heath, he finds him puzzling: "He is a complex man, not at all simple." Perhaps a kind of British eccentricity, that peculiar insularity, remains the main obstacle to the Europeanization of England: "Ah, yes, Mr. Heath, he has his yacht." However, what strikes Pompidou most is a feeling that he and Heath must have shared: that whatever one's ideas, real responsibility toward those ideas comes only with power. "Heath," he says, "has been a European for 20 years, but it is only since he has headed his Government that he has really and truly been *convinced.*"

Mr. Nixon might be, were he European, much the same sort of man. Of course, Pompidou says jokingly, though some Americans are very much Europeans, the majority cannot be: "They take everything much too seriously." He does not know Nixon well, but two things commend him to Pompidou. First, "I said when he was elected that here at last was the President who would finally extricate America from that disastrous war in Vietnam, and I was heavily criticized for doing so, but more than ever I believe that to be true." And, second, Nixon's penchant for private correspondence between heads of state that bypasses protocol and routine; Pompidou says the correspondence is "regular" and "very useful." (This correspondence apparently didn't forewarn the French President of Nixon's new dollar policy, and when the surprise announcement of it came, Pompidou, obviously displeased, interrupted his vacation to huddle with his currency advisers.)

Pompidou's enjoyment of his job is apparent. That is why most observers seem to feel that, barring an unforeseen political crisis (which many feel could stem from the unrest of the young, from the lack of outlet for aspirations and ideals, or ultimately from an economic stagnation that at this moment in France is, unlike in the United States and Great Britain, no more than a shadow on the horizon), or ill-health, Pompidou is almost certain to run for re-election in 1975: in a straight fight against the Communists and a Left-coalition led by François Mitterrand. It is a subject on which Pompidou refuses to speculate. Asked on a recent television interview if he liked being President, he answered: " 'Like' is the wrong word. I am possessed. . . . I mean 'possesed' in the literal sense. In the Dostoevskian sense. Don't forget that in Russian, the title of the novel ["The Possessed"] is 'The Demons.' "

The presidency, then, is Pompidou's demon. But where is the anxiety, the fear, the real "possession" that drives the character Stravrogin to ever greater excesses?

Sometimes it is the very professionalism of Pompidou, limitless neutrality and common sense, that seems likely to cause him the gravest problems. After all, behind the Elysée facade, is France, is Europe, in such rosy shape? Perhaps not.

He has enemies. The deputies, shorn of their real power under de Gaulle's Constitution, are restive; there are those who hold Pompidou's success against him, who see a sinister connection between high finance and political power, and those for whom he is the archbetrayer of Gaullism, and his rivals for 1975, and those who whisper about land-acquisitions through straw men. What can the rising generation of young men in France—whose economic freedom is threatened by the new giant international combines, who feel their identity threatened by the abstraction of a "New Europe" they see as little more than a "market" which benefits the financial potentates and the poor hardly at all, for whom political life in the Fifth Republic has become a politics of absurdity—what can they feel toward a man who says their problems "[don't] weigh on my mind?" That he is "concerned, of course, but their protest was perfectly natural" and that "they wouldn't grow up to much if they didn't protest?" Who dismisses them, in short, as just nice kids?

The least the young are going to feel is that Pompidou does not speak their language. And that sometimes he speaks the same old language that French Governments have always spoken, the language of repression. "Order is respect for law, and law the expression of the general will," Pompidou has said. "But that belongs to a society of the past. We face a different situation. There are individuals and groups who deny not just the law but the expression of the law, who turn their backs on the elections by which the general will makes itself felt. And then, more and more, there is in the modern world a kind of need for violence. . . . The old outlets, colonial wars, explorations, are gone. . . . There could be general subversion, an attempt to overthrow the Government. . . . Well, I'd repress subversion with patience, firmness and, if needed, harshness. And then there is this generalized, scattered, sudden violence. . . . One cannot foresee everything. Ultimately order may be respect for law, but above all it's respect for human beings, respect for others and self-respect. Which is why order isn't in the streets; it's inside the citizenry and it depends on them."

True, these are the words of moderation, of a patient man. But to many they are also the language of an administrator, a technocrat, a man who, for all his *bonhomie,* for all the smiles and friendliness he dispenses in his ceremonial functions, remains faceless. Such people may conclude, as did one of his former associates, that Pompidou is not at all a natural neutral, a moderate, a representative of the new European Center, the rational consensus. "That face," they say, "is merely the mask." "Do not forget," this man told me, "that men who have risen to high position in society, very largely because their society is organized in such a way that men *can* rise to the highest offices, have every reason to congratulate themselves: not only on their native skill and talent, but also on the nature of the society which made their ascension possible. They are bound to feel that society is, in fact, the best possible society, and they have every reason to defend its interests." The answer that one might make to this charge is that, if true of Pompidou, it may also be true of the majority of Frenchmen. Pompidou then emerges as the natural leader of the French silent majority.

Being President hadn't changed Pompidou in any essential way. He still read at lot, he still had a private life, he had not ceased being an intellectual. He still saw his intimate friends; the same writers and painters and connoisseurs of the good life he had known as the director of the Rothschild Bank, people like the novelist Françoise Sagan and the painter Bernard Buffet. They could come and dine with him; they could still talk freely. Of course, it was more difficult as President. Mrs. Pompidou was less restricted. On the whole, he had ample contact with the public; it was something he insisted upon. A President need not feel isolated.

He didn't think he was out of touch with the young. He had his son, who was now a doctor, and he saw quite a few of his son's friends: because he liked to see young people and because he thought talking with them "kept him in shape."

And, no: "There are some things that are less interesting than others, but, no, I am never bored."

Some of the ambiguity which people see in Pompidou is undoubtedly due to the nature of the French presidency itself. The "strong" presidency is still an innovation but in many respects it seems like a repetition of the old: there's the cutting of ribbons and the bussing of Olympic heroes, for the presidency is part ceremonial and part symbolic. The President *is,* after all, the nation. Certainly, de Gaulle was the living incarnation of that truth. But Pompidou?

Like so many "solutions" to the perennial problem of politics in France, the Fifth Republic was created as a reaction to its predecessors; the creation of a "strong" presidency was based upon the scorn de Gaulle, Pompidou and most Frenchmen felt for the "parliamentary game" of the Third and Fourth Republics.

The innovation, not unsurprisingly, has worked well so far: the nation relishes leadership, and voters a direct vote as to who leads them; the professional politicians recognize and covet the greatest power. But that greater power has never been precisely defined. In appearance, there are two parallel powers: the President and the Premier, Pompidou and Jacques Chaban-Delmas, deputy from Bordeaux and also mayor of that city. As for many years there was General de Gaulle and Georges Pompidou. Pompidou is head of state, Chaban-Delmas head of the Government. Pompidou is the apex of the nation, Chaban-Delmas the pinnacle of a legislature of deputies, of ministers, of other political powers.

The two men see each other constantly, nearly every day. Pompidou is very precise about that. Punctilious even, as he was when *he* was Prime Minister and many mistakenly thought that because de Gaulle was President, Pompidou was just his lackey.

Pompidou explained his relations with his Prime Minister: "Chaban-Delmas," he said, "that's the daily business of the state. I don't have to do that; that's what I have a Premier for. Take the budget. That's an important matter. Well, once a year, it costs me two or three hours' work. But Chaban-Delmas, for him it's 50, 100 hours' work." The President, then, deals less with the formulation of policy than with decision. "Yes," Pompidou answered, "ultimately power rests in this office, but it is a question of how and when one exercises it."

Was there, I asked, a *réserve spéciale,* as there had been under de Gaulle? The President exclusively concerned with matters of major moment, almost exclusively international, and everything else left in the hands of the Premier?

As head of state, obviously the President was especially interested in foreign affairs; it was he who had negotiated with Heath, who had just come back from meetings with Brandt; but it was not correct, any more than it was true with de Gaulle, that "the rest" was left to the Premier to handle. In the first place, everything is discussed mutually; in the second, while the President, like the kings of France, has the right of *evocation*—that is, the right to say that such-and-such a thing shall not be discussed but is His and His alone to decide—the business of government would become impossible if the President interfered, either too little or too much. "And those," he added, "who think the President has too much power are always the first to demand that I exercise my power when it suits their own requirements." He was thinking, he said, of a deputy who had asked him to use his Presidential power to prevent the mayor of a provincial town from prohibiting the showing of a particular film.

Pompidou's argument was that if a President was to be President of all the nation he must use his power sparingly, and mainly in those areas where it sprang naturally from the nature of the office.

As for his relations with the legislature and with "his" ministers, he had known "from before the war that power had to have another source besides Parliament," but also that "Parliament was necessary." A constitution had to check the penchant of any executive toward authoritarianism, "which exists just as any parliament has a penchant toward anarchy. When the executive rules alone, the people tire of it . . . an elected legislature is there to prevent that happening." He insists that despite rumors to the contrary, there is no "inner cabinet" or "executive staff" *à la White House,* parallel to the ministries.

But it is a curious system and the French themselves do not yet see it very clearly defined. For one Gaullist deputy on the left wing of his party, the division of powers actually seems to be as follows: each man responding to his own inner nature, Chaban-Delmas had been assigned the liberal, progressive, socially minded sector, and Pompidou the traditional and conservative. Another said: "It is just as it was under de Gaulle: the Premier takes care of France, the President busies himself with the rest of the world."

In his recent television interview, Pompidou seems to have cast himself in the role of the "heavy" vs. Chaban-Delmas as "the People's Friend." "By nature," he declared, "I am really a rather nice man. I like to please. And in the job I have . . . I seem to be forced to refuse all the time. . . . I find it harsh to quash demands that seem to me perfectly understandable and which seem, however, to be quite impossible to comply with. And yet I try, I try. . . . I remember a piece of advice General de Gaulle gave me: 'Be tough, Pompidou!' he said. I try, but I find it very hard."

Many I talked to seemed to find this explanation of Pompidou as President a piece of calculated disingenuousness. But then in Paris you can find men to theorize about anything: that the Republic will collapse because President and Premier are at war; that Chaban-Delmas is Pompidou's lackey; that he is his stalking horse for 1975; that Chaban-Delmas only tolerates Pompidou because he himself is running for the presidency; that. . . .

Pompidou is ambiguous; the system is ambiguous; France in 1971 is ambiguous. But the "New European Man" is the one subject on which Pompidou himself is totally unambiguous; it is the only shred of ideology to which he seems genuinely attached. Many see this "New European Man" as a creature of selfish interests; he is motivated only by profit and not by humane values; he operates as a great leveler, rubbing out national, regional, even individual distinctions; he wants to turn us all into one mold, to make us all into his own image. "No," Pompidou says passionately, "the New Europe cannot be all alike." He considers it his most important task, in France itself, to decentralize, to allow of variation.

No, he sees the New Europe in a different way. "I see it more as a restatement of the age-old quarrel between the Ancients and the Moderns," he says. "The Moderns claim pre-eminence over the Ancients. They have progressed further; they know more. But at what cost? What have they lost? Does the Modern really imply the tearing down of all tradition?"

The Europe Pompidou sees is, as he said on the Rhine, conservative, rural France wining with socialist, urban Germany, as if distinctions had vanished in a river mist. No, emphatically no, Pompidou does not want the Moderns to triumph by the destruction of the Ancients. "For me," he says, "European Man is the man who is constantly renewing himself, and when I think of the Europe we are building, what comes to my mind immediately is the Middle Ages. I think of the *cité,* that good place in which all men know each other, in which there is a real sense of community, of belonging. And I wonder," he adds with an ironic smile, cigarette—another, the third or fourth—still dangling straight down from his lower lip, "if I am not, after all, becoming a reactionary. . . ."

Then, as I am ushered out the great double doors of the palace by the chamberlain with his chain and start down the stairs, I see on either side of me the Republican Guard, brilliant in their cuirasses, bandoliers, helmets of shiny steel and horsehair plumes, curved swords held motionlessly upright by their chins, arranged in a hemicycle. . . . I am supposed to exit through that? I take two steps backward into the arms of the frock-coated chamberlain. *"Mais non, monsieur,"* he murmurs politely, "It is quite all right. . . ."

And it is all right. From the depths of a black Citröen emerges the Co-Prince of Andorra—cloaked, shriveled, his mouth full of gold teeth and a *bicorne* on the top of his narrow head—come (as he and his ancestors have done without fail since 1607) to pay his yearly feu duty of 960 francs to his suzerain, the Co-Prince of France. . . .

Suggested Reading

So many people have written good books on modern France that making choices among them is nearly as hard as finding a good cheap French restaurant in New York City. The following list is no *Guide Michelin;* it covers only a few main courses and skips over much tantalizing fare. Only books that have appeared in English are included.

The best study of France under the Republics is David Thomson, *Democracy in France Since 1870* (5th ed., New York and London, 1969). Gordon Wright, *France in Modern Times, 1760 to the Present* (Chicago, 1960), affords a longer and broader perspective on the French past. Stanley Hoffmann's contribution to Hoffmann, *et al., In Search of France* (Cambridge, Mass., 1963), is indispensable reading for anyone interested in France since 1930. Other contributors discuss aspects of the sweeping social and economic changes which have overtaken France in the twentieth century. These changes, along with certain intellectual trends, are also assessed in John Ardagh, *The New French Revolution* (New York, 1968). Ardagh concentrates on the period since the end of the Second World War.

One of the best studies of France in the 1930's remains Alexander Werth's eyewitness account, *The Twilight of France, 1933–1940* (New York, 1942). An unsurpassed essay on the debacle of 1940 is Marc Bloch, *Strange Defeat* (London, 1949). On

France during the war years see Robert Aron, *The Vichy Regime, 1940–1944* (New York, 1958), and the same author's *France Reborn: The History of the Liberation* (New York, 1964). The best source on the Gaullism of de Gaulle is, appropriately enough, Charles de Gaulle himself: *The Complete War Memoirs* (New York, 1964); *Memoirs of Hope: Renewal and Endeavor* (New York, 1971). As studies of the London-based Resistance and the Allied coalition, however, the *War Memoirs* need to be read with great care and compared with other accounts. An excellent short biography of de Gaulle—perhaps the best of any length—is Jean Lacouture, *De Gaulle* (New York, 1966).

The best analysis of the Fourth Republic in any language is Philip M. Williams, *Crisis and Compromise: Politics in the Fourth Republic* (3rd ed., London, 1964). On the French phase of the Indochinese war see Ellen Hammer, *The Struggle for Indochina* (Stanford, 1954). George A. Kelly, *Lost Soldiers: The French Army and Empire in Crisis, 1947–62* (Cambridge, Mass., 1965), examines the causes and consequences of the army's entry into politics. Philip Williams, in collaboration with Martin Harrison, has carried his investigation of postwar French politics into the Fifth Republic with *Politics and Society in de Gaulle's Republic* (London, 1971). Social change at the grass roots is best examined at the grass roots: Edgar Morin, *The Red and the Black: Report from a French Village* (New York, 1971), and Laurence Wylie, *Village in the Vaucluse* (rev. ed., New York, 1964), are local studies done with great sensitivity. A fairly straightforward account of the events of May is Patrick Seale and Maureen McConville, *Red Flag/Black Flag: French Revolution 1968* (New York, 1968). An excellent short analysis is David Goldey, "A Precarious Regime; The Events of May 1968," in Philip M. Williams, *French Politicians and Elections, 1951–1969* (Cambridge, England, 1970).

Two episodes whose significance transcends the frontiers of France have recently received excellent treatment at the hands of documentary film-makers: Marcel Ophuls, *The Sorrow and the Pity* (1971), on France under the German Occupation; Yves Courrière and Jacques Perrin, *The Algerian War* (1972).

Index

A Note on the Editor

John E. Talbott was born in Grinnell, Iowa, and studied at the University of Missouri and Stanford University. He is the author of *The Politics of Educational Reform in France, 1918–1940,* and is now at work on a study of France and the Algerian War. Mr. Talbott teaches history at the University of California, Santa Barbara.